FLYING WITH THE OWLS
CRIME SQUAD

PAUL ALLEN
AND
DOUGLAS NAYLOR

JOHN BLAKE

Published by John Blake Publishing Ltd,
3, Bramber Court, 2 Bramber Road,
London W14 9PB, England

www.blake.co.uk

First published in hardback in 2005

ISBN 1 84454 093 6

British Library Cataloguing-in-Publication Data:

A catalogue record for this book is available from the British Library.

Design by www.envydesign.co.uk

Printed in Great Britain by CPD, Wales

1 3 5 7 9 10 8 6 4 2

Papers used by John Blake Publishing are natural, recyclable products made from
wood grown in sustainable forests. The manufacturing processes conform to the
environmental regulations of the country of origin.

Every attempt has been made to contact the relevant copyright-holders, but some
were unobtainable. We would be grateful if the appropriate people could contact us.

In memory of Scribbler, Tin-Tin and the mystery that was Mr Me, Stevie Steve.

REST IN PEACE, LADS.

ACKNOWLEDGEMENTS

I have met so many people down the years who have had an influence on me, both good and bad, so please forgive me if have missed out your name here, or in the book. When I was writing, I tried to name as few people as possible – mainly due to the fact that I am poor at thinking up alternate names!

Thanks go out to the following people:

First and foremost: Carron who has been, and continues to be, a rock for me. Without her constant support none of this would have been possible. My family, who put up with my erratic behaviour down the years, and all those who took the time to contribute to this book; namely Dougie, Stevie, Steve B, Steve W, Andy, H, Jambo, Craig, Mark G and Anthony. Thanks also to Stuart, Sid, Tom, Hopey and Dougie's young 'un for supplying many of the pictures.

The lads from the Ball Inn at Intake, Old Blue Ball and Freemasons in Hillsborough, the Gate and Travellers, and of course the Birley.

The Stocksbridge Owls, the Donny Owls, the Mexborough Owls, the Kiveton Owls.

I really don't want to name each and every person who has made it special down the years. I would probably forget someone, so I just want to express personal thanks to a few people who were always there and from whom I learnt and shared a great deal. If you are not on this list, don't be offended: Craig G, Matt I, Andrew C, Darren and Spenny, Dirty Dick, Richard and Dave W, Steve O, Trevor and Chris, Phil, Mick E, Shaun W, The G Brothers, Andy and Mark L, Steve and Kev W, Big Ev, Dave F, Ash, Lee S and Mad Dog Lee, Scott H, Ian and Timmy, Jimmy and the new breed, Dingle and the Ecclesfield crowd – and last, but by no means least, Martin, the best lad we ever produced.

To the rest of the lads, who do not fall into one of the categories above, I treasure the memories, good and bad, and miss each and every one of you.

The final thank-you goes to all the patrons of those long-demolished establishments, the Rose Inn and, of course, the Limit. Gone, but never forgotten.

From Dougie ...

Saturdays kids living the dream, but what for? To end up in a dead-end job grafting on a 12-hour shift? Okay for half decent dollar, but not with the older generation dictating the odds. We take the first chance to break free and let our feelings out on Saturday afternoon, and don't need some nondescript out for the extra dollar, telling you to take to your seat or dragging you out of your £20 mortgage for the afternoon. Now call me what you want, but getting out of bed on a freezing Monday morning with dollar signs in your eyes, which are firmly fixed on the Saturday, shouldn't be a problem.

ACKNOWLEDGEMENTS

GARDENS BOYS

Graham (TOMMO): I take my complete hat off to this individual. I only scraped the surface in the odd story I lobbed at you, and never began to describe an away day with Tommo; totally fearless and a proper front man. I've no greater respect for anyone in the Wednesday world.

Nigel (IBBO): I grew up with all the gardens boys, but this lad was the hardest to beat. Through thick and thin we stood side to side, but on the odd occasion we tested each other.

Zuts: What can I say? Game as fuck, and a proper front-line man. Not a big lad, but what a heart, and a punch to go with it.

Johnny: I would stand toe to toe with any fucker with him. Game as they come.

Dave (SHIVERS): My best mate. We've drunk the Don dry together, and sang the odd tune.

Wrighty: Simply the best. A good lad, game, and loves a drink.

Garnet: Probably the coolest dude you've ever met, and still front line.

Budgie: The Scottish twat. Pound for pound there's no fella with as much bottle. You're the man.

Muddy: To describe this lad would take forever. A character if ever there was one. Ten stone wet through, and dropping bouncers like their going out of fashion

Puppy: Once again front line. Keep the faith.

Acky: Came to an off with us, and showed his true colours. Cheers ACKY.

Jamie: Always there. Came on the scene later in the show, but a very good lad.

Halty: Born and bred gardens. His influence came from the Gate boys.

Browny: Yet again front-line. A quiet lad, but when called to action never lets you down.

Wayney: Another good lad, but with his upbringing that's no surprise.

These are the lads I travelled with far and wide, and will love until I die.

CONTENTS

INTRODUCTION

The freezing rain falls in sheets from the grey Ontario sky as I sit down to write an introduction to this book. It has been more than eight years now since I left my home town of Sheffield, and at times it feels longer. On that day in April 1995 I left behind my family, friends, job and life as a member of a group of individuals who attach themselves to Sheffield Wednesday Football Club. This group, to whom I still feel an intense sense of loyalty, is known as the Owls Crime Squad, or OCS as I shall henceforth refer to them.

My association with the OCS began in earnest back in the 1985–86 season. In fact, the name OCS didn't actually appear until late in 1986 – it grew out of the old East Bank Republican Army, or EBRA, which was a name that the travelling Wednesday fans gave themselves during the 1970s, when Owls followers rampaged through the lower divisions of the football league. I had been involved in skirmishes before that season, but I had always felt I needed to be at least 18 before I could get involved seriously, and so I bided my time. I was actively involved with them for ten years, and those ten years saw many changes. The biggest was the rise of the rival Blades Business Crew (BBC), who followed Sheffield United.

For years the hooligan elements who followed Wednesday were the dominant force in Sheffield, but that began to change in the mid-1980s, and by the end of the decade few would have argued that the BBC were not the largest, most active 'firm' in the city. By the time I left Sheffield in 1995 it was looking like the OCS was a spent force by and large; we had been whittled down to a hardcore of probably fewer than forty regular participants. The success that the club had enjoyed on the field had left few with any reason to seek success off it. Recent seasons, however, have seen the OCS awake from its deep slumber and they are now turning out numbers that we could only dream about ten years ago. For the first time in years, they are seriously beginning to challenge the BBC again, although this surge in hooligan activity has gone hand in hand with a serious decline in the on-field product.

So why write a book? And why write it eight years after giving up an active role in the hooligan scene? After all, I now live more than three thousand miles away and have built a successful life for myself away from the violence. There are also many, many people who have probably seen much more than I. So why am I the one writing? Well, I am not the 'top boy' leading the troops into battle every week, but I have seen a fair bit, and am fairly well respected by those 'in the know' among the hooligan element at Hillsborough. I was also very much involved at a time when things were not going too well. What's more, many people have urged me to write a book about our firm, because they respect my opinion and honesty and they know that I will tell the story straight without trying to overdramatise it, or create heroes. Trust is an important element in this game that we play – or played, as the case may be – but I think the most honest answer to the question of why I am writing is because I have seen so much criticism of the OCS. A great deal of that criticism was justified, but there is also no doubt, in my mind, that the majority of it is wide of the mark. Two books have been written chronicling the BBC and their rise to power, but there are two sides to that story and only one side has been heard. The picture that has been painted of us does not look too good, and it has been taken as gospel by the world at large. I want to set the record straight about certain things, and tell our story from our side.

What's more, many other participants in both the OCS and EBRA wanted to have their voices heard, and that is why this book will not just be a recollection of my experiences from 1985–95, but will also feature stories about events from the 1970s through to the present day, written by participants in those events. All of us will tell the stories as we saw them. Those on the other side of the same fence may see them differently and there is nothing wrong with that. We have all strived to be completely honest and there are stories of defeat and despair alongside stories of triumph.

I do not intend to re-create entire seasons – with one exception – because to be honest much of the time little happens, and so I will only relate specific incidents which I believe can give a fair impression of events in general at the time. I will not re-create imaginary conversations either, and will only mention incidents that I can recall vividly. Let's face it, not many people can remember in detail a conversation they may have had twenty years ago. I will also not harp on about what people may or may not have been wearing – others may remember in detail what footwear 400-strong mobs were wearing, but I cannot. There will be no bad-mouthing of other teams or their firms in this book, and neither will I refer to Sheffield United as the 'pigs'. For any outsiders who did not read Steve Cowen's book, the term 'pigs' is a derogatory term that fans of the two Sheffield teams use for each other. I have always felt that term to be puerile and childish, and so I will refrain from using it, whenever possible.

The essence of this book is about the feeling that you get when you know that it is going to 'go off'; it is about that surge of adrenaline felt during that split-second pause when silence hangs heavy in the air, before the roar goes up and combat is joined. It is about pain and despair, and it is about laughter and elation. It is about ordinary lads with a compulsion for terrace culture and all its trappings. It is not in any way meant to alienate the majority of football supporters who have no part in the misdeeds, and it is certainly not intended to glorify acts of violence. Football hooligans, in my experience, are just as passionate as any other fan, but they may occasionally cross the boundaries of acceptable behaviour in their love of the game and their team.

To all the lads who have fought for Sheffield Wednesday down the years, whether as the EBRA, the OCS or just as Wednesday fans, this book is written by you and is dedicated to you.

The names have been changed to protect the innocent ... and the guilty!

1

A LONG TIME AGO IN A STADIUM FAR, FAR AWAY

On Saturday, 26 April 1975, Sheffield Wednesday played the final match of what was officially their worst season – points wise, at least – in history. The game was at Hull City, and predictably ended in a 1-0 defeat. The result was irrelevant really – indeed, the side had been relegated to English football's third tier, for the first time in their history, weeks earlier. It would be five long seasons before they climbed back. I had attended my first Wednesday match that season, and witnessed another 1-0 defeat, this time to Southampton; I stood on the Leppings Lane end that day along with 8,504 other hardy souls, in a 55,000-capacity stadium, watching a team in decline, devoid of talent and ideas.

Sunday, 4 May 2003 would see Sheffield Wednesday heading back to the third rung of the footballing ladder. This time the result was a 2-1 victory over Walsall at Hillsborough, and incredibly the team finished the season on a seven-game unbeaten run, including an away win at champions Portsmouth. A season that had promised an improvement on the struggles of the previous couple had turned into a nightmare from which there seemed to be no awakening, until it was too late. Terry Yorath had started the season as manager, and had brought in players of his own, but the team struggled badly to get out of the blocks, one of the few bright spots being a victory at Hillsborough against Sheffield United. Yorath did not make it to twenty games before he was gone, replaced by former Owls favourite Chris Turner, who had worked wonders at Third Division Hartlepool. Under Turner performances seemed to improve, but still the results did not come and relegation had seemed inevitable from early March. This time I was sitting 3,000 miles away, watching events unfold on a computer screen, and reflecting on how the club had been brought back to a plight similar to that of 28 years previously.

The season had marked the climax of a rapid decline in the club's fortunes. Only ten years earlier they had been talked of as genuine championship contenders, and could field a side bristling with international stars. Poor decisions on the playing side, and more importantly on the financial side, had brought the club I loved to its knees, and all I and other supporters could do was hope that we could tough out the financial storm that was hovering, and make a speedy return to the upper reaches of the league. The days of Wembley appearances and hefty transfer fees were becoming a rapidly fading memory.

To make matters worse, our bitter rivals from across the city, Sheffield United, had enjoyed a season rarely paralleled in their recent history, reaching the semi-finals of both Cup competitions, and the Division One play-offs. I had to smile, though, when I read some of the boasts of their supporters, especially the ones claiming that we had never enjoyed such a season. A major problem with our red-and-white brethren often seemed to be one of selective memory, but I was not one to take it personally. The

Wednesday fans had certainly rubbed the United fans' noses in it down the years, and I know deep in my heart that the wheel will turn full circle again in the not-too-distant future.

Off the field, the hooligan element at Hillsborough had begun to grow rapidly. The OCS had travelled extensively during the season, taking a firm of around two hundred into the centre of Leicester, undetected by the police, in March. Other excursions over the course of the season had seen violence flare on several occasions – indeed, a police constable had received stab wounds during fighting at a game with Derby County.

As the on- and off-field dramas played out over the course of the season I sat in my Southern Ontario home, merely a spectator, receiving updates on the team's performances via websites, and receiving updates on the 'firm's' performances via text and telephone. As I sit here today typing, my mind constantly goes back to events and situations from the past. Even though I am sitting thousands of miles away, my heart still beats for Sheffield Wednesday and everything it stands for. I feel goosebumps rising at memories of pain and anguish, coupled with other memories of pure elation. I look back to where it all started, and I start to try and piece it all together.

My story begins back in the dark, distant, depressing decade known as the 1970s – a time before mobile phones, PCs and the Internet; how on earth did the world cope? Well, cope it did, and it was coping quite well on the day of my first visit to Hillsborough: 31 March 1975. I went to that game, against Southampton, with a friend of my mother's and my older brother. I wasn't even a Wednesday fan at the time. In my infinite wisdom, I supported Leeds United and came from a family of Blades – which was strange really, as we lived barely a stone's throw from the Wednesday ground. My overriding memory of the game, aside from the Wednesday keeper Peter Fox's cap, was one of great sadness. A huge stadium, which should have been witness to scenes of triumph, was instead an empty, hollow, soulless place filled with despair, and reeking of decay.

My allegiance to Leeds United fell by the wayside shortly after. Maybe it was my experience at Hillsborough; maybe it was my disappointment at Leeds' failure against Bayern Munich in the 1975 European Cup final. Either way, it wouldn't be long before my next trip to Hillsborough. That trip came on a wet, rainy night in August and again it ended in despair. This time I witnessed a 2-0 home defeat in the League Cup to Fourth Division Darlington. Wednesday went on to narrowly escape a second successive relegation that season, surviving by the skin of their teeth with a last-day victory over Southend United at Hillsborough.

It would be a couple of years before I attended another Wednesday match – my mother lost touch with her friend and no one else in my family went to Hillsborough. My grandad was Wednesday through and through, but had long since ceased to attend. I did go to a few matches at Bramall Lane with family members on my dad's side, but I really didn't feel anything from those trips. The terraces of the Shoreham seemed cold and inhospitable, and the pies were mushy, tasteless and grey.

By 1978 my mother had remarried, this time to a Wednesday fan called Jim, from Shiregreen, and it was Jim who would take me to my first away match at Rotherham. It was this game that opened my eyes to another side of football – the phenomenon of football violence – and set me on a path that I followed for many years, and which is still of more than a passing interest to me.

During the 1970s football violence had evolved from attacks on trains to mass warfare on the terraces of football grounds the length and breadth of the United Kingdom. Huge gangs of rival supporters would fight pitched battles in a never-ending war for supremacy. The concept was simple: the away fans would descend en masse and attempt to get in and take over the home team's end, and the home teams fans would attempt to stop them. The violence escalated during the 1970s and the brawling thugs injured thousands of people. Town centres would close down on match days, and locals would barricade themselves inside their homes. The most notorious group at this time was the Red Army of Manchester United. The sheer size of their fan base meant that they left a trail of destruction in their wake wherever they went; even Hillsborough had not been spared, and a visit by the Red Army in December 1974 saw pitch invasions and mass brawls around the ground.

Even at a young age I was aware of Manchester United's reputation, and this led myself and two friends to offer to protect people's cars when the Red Menace came to Hillsborough in 1976, for an FA Cup semi-final with Derby. In contrast to other kids who tried this trick, we actually meant what we said, and spent all day on guard. Our endeavours netted us the grand sum of 5p each, which was almost immediately spent on sweets at a nearby paper shop. Who would have thought you could get forty jelly teddies for such a small amount of money?

The following season would again see Manchester United visit Hillsborough for an FA Cup semi, this time against a team with equally notorious fans. The opposition was, of course, my old favourites Leeds United. Again we tried the 'watch your car' enterprise – jelly teddy greed held us in its fearsome grip – but this time we came up empty handed. Our consensus was that people, on the whole, were tight-fisted bastards and deserved everything they got. Of course, none of the vandalism suffered by cars on Balmain Road that day had anything to do with us ...

It was against this backdrop that I began to develop an interest in the terrace culture that seemed to leave a trail of destruction wherever it went. Although Wednesday had developed a sizable hooligan contingent by this time – the aforementioned East Bank Republican Army – I had not seen much up close. This was mainly due to the fact that few Third Division teams brought any sizable support to Hillsborough, and those that did were quickly and quietly routed without too much fuss.

Stevie (now deceased), an old campaigner from the 1970s, recalls that the Wednesday mobs of the time were no pushovers.

The Seventies were a great time for football violence. Wednesday generally came out on top at most places, and at home we were almost invincible. The only mob I ever saw take the piss at Hillsborough were Manchester United, and with a mob of thousands they took the piss everywhere. Aston Villa reckoned they took the kop in their promotion season, and our relegation season, of 1974–75, but they didn't. What happened was that a few thousand of them got on very early, and before kick-off a few hundred of us got alongside them. All the game we kept on charging into them and pushing them further towards the left-hand side of the kop, so by the end of the game a few hundred of us had half our kop and the Villa fans were, I swear, shitting themselves.

We left at the end and waited outside the ground on Penistone Road. The Villa wouldn't come out. Probably four thousand of them and they daren't leave the ground until the OB had charged us away. I've never seen such a large mob shit themselves like that, either before or since.

The Seventies trips to most places were a case of a good piss-up and Wednesday taking the piss, but with a few exceptions. Trying to take the Fullwell at Sunderland in an FA Cup game was a disaster; a couple of hundred of us got on but we took a bit of a pasting before getting on to the relative safety of the pitch. Some places like Pompey, Birmingham and Middlesbrough were very dodgy and we never really got a result away from home at places like that, but at Hillsborough it was different, and we used to go on the Leppings Lane end for most teams.

My trip to Rotherham, in September of 1979, would finally bring the full enormity of the situation into focus, and I would be hooked. As with most disturbances, while my memories of the actual violence is very vivid the events leading up to it are a little fuzzy. I remember we had gone by bus. Rattling through the Don Valley to Rotherham – the area at the time was still a massive centre of special steel production, and mile after mile of dark factories held little interest for me. The next memory I have is of being at the ground, and what surprised me most was the complete absence of Rotherham fans. Everywhere I looked was a sea of blue and white. Into the ground we went; we sat in a side terrace of cheap plastic seats, entrance to which had cost us the considerable admission price of 90p. Once inside the ground I finally saw the Rotherham fans: they were penned into the right-hand side of their own kop, the Tivoli end, and the terrace opposite where I was sitting. The rest of the ground, including half of the Tivoli, was filled with Wednesday fans.

As kick-off time approached a feeling of malevolent tension filled the air – and with good reason. In each of the preceding three seasons this fixture had seen Wednesday fans running amok, and it is my belief that most of the crowd in attendance at Millmoor on that sunny Saturday afternoon would not have been surprised to

7

see a repeat performance. The behaviour of Sheffield United fans at the ground a week earlier had added another ingredient to the mix. Marauding Blades fans had caused a wall to collapse, injuring a number of spectators. In the culture of one-upmanship that prevailed, that incident would need to be bettered by the Wednesday boys.

I don't really recall much of what was happening on the pitch, as my thoughts and eyes were constantly being drawn back toward the situation at the Tivoli end of the ground. I swear that I saw Wednesday fans hammering on the wall in an attempt to knock it down. Maybe I did, and maybe I didn't, but I do remember thinking that it would be just a question of time before the Tivoli end became a battlefield. The time duly arrived, when long-serving Owls defender Jimmy Mullen put Wednesday ahead. It seemed to me that the entire end erupted. I looked to see that the right-side of the kop, the side that had held the Millers fans, was being invaded by blue and white. I could see fighting breaking out all over, and hundreds of people pushing to escape. The Rotherham fans tried to flee over to the terrace, many headed for the safety of the pitch as the police tried manfully to contain the situation. Large swathes of terracing opened up as the police sought to push the Wednesday fans out of the Rotherham section. I watched in a kind of stunned trepidation as St Johns ambulance workers helped people who had been injured in the melee. Within minutes, however, the police had restored order and were bringing Wednesday supporters round the pitch into the Railway end. My next, and probably most vivid, recollection was of one of the Wednesday lads who was being brought around the pitch, shouting to a friend of his sat behind me:

'Did you see us? Fucking brilliant,' was the lad's cry.

'I'm ashamed of you, Dave,' was the far from impressed reply.

Maybe that chap wasn't moved, but I certainly was. Finally I had seen it kick off, and I wanted more. Wednesday went on to win the match 2-1, with Terry Curran scoring a screaming free kick for the game winner. The rest of the game seemed largely trouble free. The Rotherham fans returned to the Tivoli, but this time in a far more sombre mood. My mind was a whirl, however. It was like that first whiff of beer to me: I hadn't actually tasted it, but I had been in its presence and I knew it tasted good.

I remember waiting at Ickles roundabout for a bus back to Sheffield after the match. It seemed that every bus went past full of Wednesday fans. Victorious, happy Wednesday fans who had seen their team win, and maybe had even taken part in the off-field activities of the day. Years later I would work at a steel plant near the Ickles, and stand at the same bus stop, and many would be the time that I would think over the events of that day years earlier, while waiting for the number 69 bus to carry me home.

The following week in school I was buzzing with tales of the scenes I had witnessed. Just the season before I had started attending games with another lad in my class, called Andy. He was jealous of what I had seen, and decided that from now on we would always stand on the 'Lep' and forego our usual spot on the giant Hillsborough kop. The Lep was the name we Wednesday fans gave to the Leppings Lane end of the Wednesday ground. It was supposed to be the away fans' part of the ground, but in those days few teams brought many followers and we were allowed to stand there. The Lep was also the part of the ground where the Wednesday hooligan element would congregate. Its reputation around Sheffield preceded it, so much so that my mother would say to me as I was leaving the house, 'Don't you be going on that Lep, it's where all the idiots go.'

Of course it's where the idiots go, and that's why I went there. I wanted to be in that world. Andy and I would go and stand in the bar at the back of the terrace, just to be around these big, tough hooligans. I really could not wait to be one of them. The only thing that bothered me was that these lads all looked so big. At that time I was quite a thin, pale-looking individual with way too much blond curly hair. I would have looked more at home in an episode of *Andy Pandy* than charging around fighting on the terraces.

For much of the rest of the season I went in the Lep. Every time an opposing team scored I would scan the terrace for signs of away followers. Rarely did I see any on the Lep, but occasionally I would see some in the stands, and they would be swiftly dealt with by any nearby Owls fans.

To be honest, the only time I saw any away fans up close that season was when Barnsley came for a visit. I had decided to take up residence in the West Stand for the first time that day. The West Stand was above the 'Lep', meaning that we would be seated directly behind the Barnsley contingent. Now, I really am at a loss for words to explain why I did not realise how many 'Dingles' (Barnsleyites) had made the short trip to Sheffield 6. I honestly did not become aware of them until the Wednesday team ran out and I heard booing; I was amazed, and peered over the edge of the stand to see about three or four thousand scruffy-looking Barnsley fans standing below me. The game itself was dire, with our infinitely uglier South Yorkshire neighbours avenging an opening day 3-0 defeat at Oakwell with a 2-0 victory over a lacklustre Wednesday team. The only incident of note came some time in the second half, when a couple of older Wednesday lads came down to the front to hurl insults at the Barnsley fans. The enraged Dingles starting making threats and one of the Wednesday lads said to his mate, 'There are four of us, we can have a go!'

I looked at Andy bewildered, wondering who the four he was referring to were. And then it dawned on me: he meant him and his mate, and me and Andy. Now, I may have been keen on getting into the hooligan scene, but I had no intention of going on a suicide mission against thousands of scowling Barnsley fans, and so slowly but surely we spent the rest of the match edging up toward the back of the stand, and we slipped away unnoticed about five minutes from the end.

The rest of the season I didn't really see anything noteworthy on the hooligan front, but trouble erupted at a number of away games that I was not witness to.

Jack was just starting out at the time, and recalls the trip to play Swindon at the County Ground in early 1980:

The year, I'm sure, was the promotion year of 1979–80. We were in the dire Third and not too sure what we would come up against; I was still at school but eager as fuck for Saturdays, and the trip to Swindon's County Ground.

The skinheads had made a revival, and I remember how me mam cried buckets when she saw my no. 1. Still, undeterred in my Levi's and white Fred Perry, I thought I looked the biz.

The events that happened next are 100 per cent fact.

After consuming copious amounts of long-life lager – even the warm stuff that someone said had been left next to the window and tasted like piss – we arrived in Swindon. The police were quick to spot us and not let us off our coach until we got to the ground, but before we were allowed off the OB came on our coach and told us all real horror stories of the Swindon mob. Now if this was supposed to scare us it did the opposite. The gentlemanly officer told us the rules and regulations at Swindon.

'Don't mind a bit of swearing or even a bit of banter, but spitting is a big no-no,' he said.

As he turned to leave our coach his dark blue tunic was getting whiter, greener, yellower and definitely wetter.

On entering the ground I saw a graffiti sign threatening BOTH SHEFFIELD CLUBS WILL DIE.

'We'll see about that, fucker,' said Micky.

'Come on, let's get on their kop.'

Not experts in blending in just yet, we got on the side terrace where a poxy wire fence separated us.

Some lads did manage it and gave it all before being dragged off by the OB and marched round the ground to the chants of 'Hooli-, Hooli-, Hooligans.'

Meanwhile we had made a hole in the fence and thirty of us were in with no game plan, which was very rare in those days. It was a matter of just waiting for some mad bastard to start – and it had to be Micky! He gave a shout of 'The Wednesday!', then all of us joined in the second time round. The Swindon lads were straight into us, but we held our own until the inevitable OB presence arrived and escorted us back to the side terrace. I couldn't help but notice Micky was quiet.

'What's up wi' thee?' I asked.

'My fucking gob's killing me,' he replied. 'And I can see the bastard that did it.'

We couldn't believe our luck – the OB hadn't noticed our hole in the fence and we were straight back in. Micky went straight for the lad who had lamped him and banged him. As

he fell he got round the back of him like a wrestler, put two
fingers either side of the inside of his mouth and pulled hard.
We fucked off back sharpish into the side terrace. Job done.

The visit of Sheffield United for the now infamous Boxing Day
Massacre in 1979 saw a massive police operation in force, and
an 11am kick-off. The game was played in front of a record
crowd of 49,309 and resulted in not one single arrest. I was on
the East Bank that day, and was feeling very much under the
weather, but a 4-0 trouncing of our city neighbours brightened
my mood considerably – until I threw up all over the bathroom
later that night. That game proved to be a catalyst for the
Owls, who went on to storm up the league and ultimately
achieve promotion.

The return match at Bramall Lane saw another crowd of over
45,000, but this time the match did not pass off so peacefully.
Wednesday fans had about half of the Shoreham kop, and
fighting broke out before the game. Unfortunately for me, I
missed much of the trouble. I had a ticket to go on the John
Street terrace, and did not get into the ground until just before
kick-off. The bulk of the trouble had subsided by that time, but
the sight of so many Wednesday fans on the Shoreham end was
a source of great pride to me. The game ended in a 1-1 draw,
which was good enough for a Wednesday side now in the thick
of the promotion hunt, but it signalled a death knell for United's
fading hopes. They would be relegated to the Fourth Division
just over a year later, on a day that ultimately passed into
Sheffield folklore as 'Thank Givens Day' after United player Don
Givens missed a last-minute penalty against Walsall. That defeat
meant the Blades had sunk lower than Wednesday ever had.

The rest of the 1979–80 season was one long party, and on the final day of the season more than 32,000 fans descended on Hillsborough to witness the joyful promotion party. The match itself was a tame goalless draw with Carlisle, but that result was immaterial. The Wednesday had finally escaped from the Third Division and the fans had something to shout about for the first time in a decade.

The 1980–81 season promised to be a real challenge for Wednesday, both on and off the pitch. For the first time ever I looked at the fixtures with more of an eye for potential flashpoints than for whether we might get the two points. Two of the most feared sets of fans in the country were now in the same division as us – West Ham United and Chelsea – not to mention the beer belly army from Geordieland.

Anyone who was not aware of the fearsome reputations carried by the two London clubs would have had to be living on the moon. Along with Millwall, they made up a capital punishment of unstoppable violence. I had read the newspapers and seen images of the kind of violence shelled out in spades by the Londoners. It was a different kind of violence to what I had witnessed so far. Wherever they went, a trail of stabbings, slashings and destruction followed. The East Bank Republican Army was going to get a real test of its mettle. For the past five years it had ruled the roost in the lower divisions, but now it would be time to kick it up a gear. The fixture list also threw up a cracker of an opening-day clash against the fanatical black-and-white legions from Newcastle.

Number one on the agenda, however, was a two-legged League Cup clash with Sheffield United. The first game was at Hillsborough, and the Owls ran out comfortable winners by 2-0. The second leg came a few days later, and at this match I would meet up for the first time with a character who remains a major face in the OCS to this day. This individual I shall call Laver. His older brother was a big hitter in the Wednesday mob, and his reputation preceded him. I got to meet Laver through a mutual friend of ours called Tony, and although he was two years my junior he was a big lad for his age.

I recall walking past the Masons on Hillsborough Corner that night and seeing Laver's brother with his cronies plotting up in the beer garden; we figured something was on the cards. Tony, young Laver and I stood in the Bramall Lane end that night. We could see a largish group of Wednesday in the Shoreham, although much smaller in number than had assembled for the match of the previous season. It was a dark evening and it was difficult to see what was going on at the other end of the ground, but I could sense something was afoot. A detailed account of the evening's events from a participant in the naughtiness will follow in a later chapter. The game ended in a 1-1 draw and we were through to the next round at the expense of our greatest, and bitterest, rivals.

The opening game of the season saw the Owls defeat Newcastle to get the season off to the proverbial flyer. To me the match was most memorable for the sheer passion of the Geordie supporters; they brought about five thousand fans, who never stopped singing and chanting the entire match. There was some trouble after the game, when the Newcastle supporters forced open the gate from the Lep, and some fighting spilled onto Leppings Lane.

For the early part of the season things seemed to run opposite to the promotion campaign. Games were easily won at home, but the team struggled on the road. The tone was set for the rest of a season that saw Wednesday win only three times away from S6, but lose only three at home. The season petered out toward the end with four straight defeats to finish, but I was in attendance at every home game that season, sometimes going alone if my usual partners were unable to attend.

The major talking point of the season off the field was without a doubt the events of 6 September 1980. On that day Wednesday made the short trip across the Pennines to play Oldham Athletic. Owls fans rioted after Oldham's Simon Stainrod feigned injury to get Wednesday favourite Terry Curran sent off. The match was held up for twenty minutes while the police battled to quell the disturbances and the words of a famous terrace song were subsequently altered to reflect the day's events:

Hark now hear the coppers squeal
Remember Oldham town
When chunks of concrete and bottles flew
To knock the bastards down!

I was not in attendance at Boundary Park, although to this day I wish I had been, and I was most upset to find that there was no television footage of the incidents. Of course, the Football Association did not take the scenes of chaos in Oldham lightly, and so it was that Wednesday were forced to close all standing areas at Hillsborough for four games, and Owls followers were banned from attending the next four away games too, although that failed to stop more than 3,000 making the short trip to Derby during that stretch. The Derby County programme for the game even had a piece welcoming the Wednesday fans.

One other incident from the season occurred against Chelsea in January. I had noticed that a lot of Chelsea supporters were gathering across from my house, at the Beehive pub. Undeterred, I was determined not to be put off and prepared myself for the match. I donned my scarf, which was blue and white just like those of the Chelsea boys, and readied myself to stroll by the pub on my way to the ground. These bloody cockneys wouldn't scare me, even when my mother pointed out their fearsome reputation. I was not worried – or so I told her.

With that I walked out the door and down the path toward the road. Now, I am not exactly sure what my line of thinking was, but for some strange reason I decided it best to zip my coat up, over my scarf, and jog all the way into Hillsborough – not the way I usually travelled to the ground. My family members had been watching me through the window, and my sudden change of heart was a subject of merriment to them for some time after, but I like to think of such incidents as character building.

There was a lot of trouble after the game, when the Chelsea hordes strolled down Parkside Road on to Penistone Road. Fighting broke out, and continued for the length of the road into town. I was with Laver and we were some way behind, but the sounds of violence could be heard in the distance. We tried to catch up and see what exactly was going on, but did not manage it.

The rest of the season was a mixture of highs and lows on the pitch. Wednesday consolidated very well in their first season back. I struggle to comment about events off the field. There would be the odd flare-up in the stands, but I had to come to realise that it was the away games that held the most fun and activity, and I had no one to go with at this time – a constant source of frustration to me.

The 1981–82 season was a case of 'what if?' for the club. This was the first season of three points for a win, and would see Wednesday missing promotion by just a single point. Ironically, if the old system of two points for a win had remained in place it would have been the Owls celebrating promotion at

Hillsborough on the last day of the season, instead of Norwich.

From my point of view, all was quiet on the hooligan front. There was trouble at the home game with Derby early in the season, when a small group of Owls, led by the legendary Fat Sid, infiltrated the Lep.

I was also on the Lep for the visit of QPR, where I finally got a small taste of action. It was the first time barriers had been erected on the Lep, and we were all in the middle section. The London club had brought about five hundred supporters, who were to the right of us. At half-time virtually the entire middle section, myself included, attempted to invade the QPR section, but we were beaten back by mounted police. They chased us back down the centre passage on to the terrace (the same passage that would allow ticketless Liverpool fans to enter the ground, and lead to 96 Liverpool fans being crushed to death seven years later). The buzz I felt from that tiny piece of action was tremendous, and I knew I wanted more, but sadly it was going to have to wait. Other than that I saw very little. I returned to Millmoor on the day that HMS *Sheffield* was sunk during the Falklands conflict, and although there was trouble in the Tivoli again it was not on the scale of three years previous. Trouble at Bolton, near the end of the season, made the front page of the *Sheffield Star*, but yet again I had not travelled all season, apart from Rotherham.

At the start of the 1982–83 season I was determined that I had to start getting away, not only to try and spot trouble, but also because I deemed it necessary if I was to be a true supporter. My older brother had, by this time, started following Sheffield United all over the country, and he was constantly ribbing me about my lack of travels. Even though I had not missed a competitive game of any kind at Hillsborough since January

1980, his constant jibes about my being a 'part-time supporter' had begun to hit home.

After narrowly missing out on promotion the year before, a great deal was expected of the 1982–83 season. Another push for promotion materialised and a spot in the FA Cup semi-final was gained and then lost in a poor showing against Brighton at Highbury. Once again I attended every game at Hillsborough, and increased my away trips to a record *three*. Those trips were to Barnsley, Rotherham and of course the semi. Other than that there was nothing that really stands out in my mind from the campaign. The only trouble that I recall seeing that season was in the first game, at home to Middlesbrough, and that was the 'Boro fans ripping down advertising hoardings.

Looking back, I think at the time I was starting to feel that being a hooligan was beyond my capabilities, and maybe I should sit back and just support my team vocally. The mass violence that had been the hallmark of the football mobs in the 1980s was now becoming a thing of the past, and the era of the 'Casuals' was dawning. The trouble had moved away from the grounds and into the town centres. I was not a part of it, and neither could I afford to buy the new fashions doing the rounds; my three paper rounds at the time only paid me the modest sum of £7.20. My dearest mother did buy me a lovely black Farah sweater around that time – but then proceeded to ruin it in the wash!

It was a very frustrating time for me, but at least I did have the football, and I lived for Saturday afternoon. By now, though, the lads I had been going to Hillsborough with for years were finding other things to do, and it didn't sit well with me. Why would someone just stop going? It was inconceivable to me, and I ended up going to quite a few games that season on my own, including the trips to Barnsley and Rotherham. Andy, who had I been going to the games with since 1978, got involved with car theft and we lost touch, even though we still went to the same school and lived on the same street; petty crime of that sort simply did not interest me. Before the season was out I had found other lads from school to go with, but it was like the end of an era and the beginning of another. I did not realise at the time how close to making the breakthrough into the Casual world I was, and how that would be the start of another era.

* * * * *

The summer of 1983 saw Big Jack Charlton leave Sheffield Wednesday. Jack had taken over in 1977 when the club was in dire straits, and had turned it around. Even today I credit him with being the man who put Wednesday back on the straight and narrow, until Messrs Richards and co. put us back on the road to nowhere in the early 1990s. I was in Majorca when I heard the news of Big Jack's resignation, and I remember sitting on the balcony of the Hotel in Palma Nova wondering who the next manager would be, and wondering if I would ever see Division One football. Oddly enough, I am sitting here now wondering the same thing.

The new manager was ex-Wednesday player Howard Wilkinson. Upon hearing the news my first reaction was 'Howard who?', which was probably the reaction of many in the football world. I honestly expected nothing from him, but he showed he had a fantastic footballing brain, if not the personality to match. Wednesday stormed out of the blocks with an 18-game unbeaten run, and they were never out of the top 2 positions. I also got to six away games that season, and not just local trips either. My travels would take me to Barnsley, Manchester City, Leeds, Newcastle, Huddersfield and Cardiff. I saw some trouble on my forays too, most notably at Leeds and Cardiff.

Probably the most sickening thing I have ever seen took place on my trip to Elland Road. I travelled to Leeds alone on the service train; a lad I was supposed to go with dropped out at the last moment, but I decided I would go anyway. The train was full of Wednesday fans, a mixture of lads and scarfers, but they were unlikely to cause too many problems. At Leeds station we were met by a large police presence, and escorted to the ground. The atmosphere was good natured and jovial, with the usual chants of support. Although I knew of Leeds' reputation I felt safe and unthreatened, even when we arrived at the ground to be met by a baying mob of Leeds fans. The game itself ended in a 1-1 draw, with the main talking point being a handled effort from Andy Ritchie, which rescued a point for the home side.

After the game, though, it was pure chaos. Fighting broke out everywhere, and I found myself walking back toward the station wondering just exactly who was who – I had ceased wearing a scarf back in the 1982–83 season. It felt very uncomfortable not to know what was going on. My concerns eased a little when I spotted a man and his son walking in the same direction as me. My chief fear was that I would miss my train home. They were clearly Wednesday fans because they both were wearing scarves. I didn't expect anything untoward to happen to these two, and so I followed a few feet behind them. We were walking through a grassed area – it may have been a park – when a group of about 15 Leeds fans appeared. There were lots of other Leeds fans walking in our direction, but I sensed these lads were trouble. They spotted the father and son, and started goading them – 'Fucking Wednesday wankers, where's your boys?' and similar idiotic remarks. Suddenly one of the lads punched the young kid, who was about 12 years old. Another hit his dad, and tried to wrest his scarf from him. When one of the gang tried to point out that what they were doing was wrong, the lad who hit the 12-year-old said – and this is the God's honest truth – 'We have to get some practice in for Chelsea next week.'

He then hit the young lad again, and the rest of the rough, tough Leeds boys laughed, before they headed off in search of more easy sport. I don't mind admitting that I was pretty scared at this point, but fortunately the station was not too far away and we made it back with no further problems.

In the years that have passed since that episode I have seen many unsavoury incidents, but this ranks as the lowest thing I have ever seen. To this day I have no respect for Leeds, and many in Sheffield, both red and blue, regard them as nothing more than seat-smashing bullies. A couple of years later I went to Bramall Lane to watch Sheffield United play Leeds. I sat in the new South Stand that day with United's boys, hoping for a chance to exact a little revenge. It really does come to something when I would turn out with our bitterest rivals in the hope of being able to turn some of the pain those shitheads caused back on them.

The Hillsborough meeting with Manchester City was the final home game of a successful season. The Wednesday mob had by now taken up residence in the uncovered seats of the South Stand at Hillsborough. I was sitting in the North Stand for this match, directly opposite the Wednesday boys. At various times during the game the City fans rushed the fence separating the two firms; on each occasion punches were exchanged over the fencing before the police moved in. After the game I exited from the stand on to Leppings Lane – right into the City mob. My timing could not have been worse, for seconds later the cry went up, 'The Wednesday!' I looked to see the Wednesday mob pouring out of the South Stand, and I was in the middle of the wrong team.

'Come on City, fucking stand!' said a well-dressed youth by my side, but I could see the City lads were a little unsure of what to do. I decided my best bet was to try and get away from the City fans, but it was too late. The roar went up and it seemed like the world was exploding. A huge lump of man ran up and kicked me; I didn't know if he was Wednesday or City, but I knew I had to get out of the way, and so I pushed my way out of the melee and headed up Leppings Lane. By now the South Yorkshire police had joined the fray, and were in full-on truncheon mode. I limped home, a little peeved at the lump on my leg, but feeling absolutely exhilarated by the events, even if I did get mixed in with the wrong crew. My mind was made up: I was going to Cardiff the following week even if I had to go alone.

That season I had gone to most matches with a schoolfriend called Pete. He was a nice lad, but a little soft, and not really the type to travel to away games in search of misbehaviour. I knew that he would not go, and so I booked on a coach run by Law Brothers on Leppings Lane. Cardiff, even back then, was known as a rough place, where the natives were not likely to invite you in for tea and cake. I expected it to be a battle, but I was quietly confident that Wednesday would be at Ninian Park in large numbers, hopefully to celebrate the winning of the Second Division championship. When our coach pulled into the coach park in the Welsh capital I saw something I had never witnessed before: a policeman wearing a turban. Now, that's not intended to sound racist – I had simply never seen an Asian officer before, and it surprised me. The game itself ended in victory for the Owls, but Chelsea had also won and pipped us on goal difference. All through the game the Cardiff fans kept up a barrage of coins, golf balls, bricks and bottles. The Wednesday support responded in a similar fashion. At the final whistle the joyful Owls support poured on to the pitch to celebrate the end of 14 years in the footballing wilderness; some Cardiff fans came on to the field and fights broke out, but the majority exited the stadium without too much fuss. I did not see anything afterwards, and so cannot comment on anything of an extracurricular nature.

I boarded my coach, and headed home a pretty happy camper. Now, it seemed that someone forgot to tell our coach driver that Cardiff is quite a way from Sheffield, and that maybe he should let us take a piss-break on the way back. The bloody idiot did not stop until Woodall Services, just outside the city. I remember reading the *Star* on the following Monday half expecting to see that fifty people had died from kidney failure after their bladders burst.

The 1984–85 season was a great time to be a Wednesday supporter. The return to the First Division saw a very successful campaign, one that almost ended in European qualification. There were victories at Anfield and Old Trafford, and a real sense of optimism emanated throughout the whole organisation. On the hooligan front I was not active in any real sense during the season. I did get involved in a vicious clash with West Ham supporters at Upton Park, of which more later, but by and large I was out to enjoy the football. The season opened at the height of the miners' strike, and incredibly the first game of the new season was at home to Nottingham Forest. Feelings were obviously running high – a coach full of Forest fans was attacked on Hillsborough Corner, and a number of the supporters on the coach were injured. Wednesday have traditionally drawn a lot of support from Doncaster and Rotherham, and both areas at that time were deep in the heart of the Yorkshire coalfield. Attacks on the 'scabs' from Nottingham were seen as legitimate in any form at the time.

Other highlights – or lowlights – of the hooligan season saw a drawn-out League Cup tie with Chelsea. In the first of three meetings to decide the tie, Wednesday gave a good account of themselves in London. Two coaches pulled up outside the Shed, and kicked off very successfully with the Chelsea hordes. That success proved to be short lived, however: a week later, the Chelsea mob came into the Wednesday seats, and chased the Wednesday firm on to the pitch. Fighting after the match also saw one Wednesday lad slashed across the face.

I was present at both those games, although not with the firm. Indeed, I only missed two games, home or away, all season. I was out of school now, and, although I was only working on a YTS programme at Lee Steel Strip, I had money to spend on football. I had also started attending games with a group of people that I had known at school but had never really socialised with. Most of the home matches saw me standing on the kop; I had foregone the Lep for the time being, and by and large my hooligan leanings seemed to be in decline. I was discovering new things such as drinking, nightclubbing, and, of course, the opposite sex. The other lads in the group were not interested in the harsher side of football, and looking back it seems that I was happy settling into a comfortable world of growing up and having fun, without the threat of a smack in the mouth.

The following season started in much the same vein, but by the end of it I would be firmly entrenched in the culture and troubles of the terrace.

The turning point came in September 1985, when I started working in the forging department of a Sheffield tool manufacturer. There I met a chappie who I will call Paul Dawes.

Paul was a Sheffield United supporter, but he had many Wednesday mates and had travelled to a lot of Wednesday games with his friends when United didn't have a game. He would turn out to be my gateway into the world that I had yearned for since childhood. (From what I hear these days, he is quite the large gateway – and hairless to boot, but that comes to us all over time, it would seem.) I started going to big games with him, mainly at Hillsborough, but I did go with him to the Lane on three occasions, and even travelled with the Blades to their game at Huddersfield in January 1986. Paul introduced me to quite a few of the Wednesday firm, who he knew and was friendly with, such as Clocky, Oz and Steve Bowen.

I had finally got my toe in the water, and was now ready to take the big plunge. I still drank with my old chums at night, and socialised with them away from football on a regular basis. Eventually I would move my allegiances so far away from my former match-day pals that we became nodding buddies only, and looking back on that it is something I do have tinges of regret about. At the start of the 1985–86 season, however, my passion for Sheffield Wednesday was stronger than ever. It was time to take it to a higher level.

2

AN OCCUPATIONAL HAZARD

So often I have heard it said that football hooligans are not real fans; that they are just thugs who use football as an excuse for their antisocial behaviour. That is simply not the case. I have met very, very few firm members who are not committed to their club. It is the reason for their being. Even if there was no trouble at football matches you would still find these people at matches, and when the fickle 'real' fans have had their fill, it will be the supposed 'hooligans' still there hoping for better days.

The English are a race of fiercely territorial people. They take great pride in their home towns, and the differences that set their area apart. Our regional dialect, tastes and cultures made England a country of nations within a nation, even before the tides of immigration brought peoples from around the old empire to our shores in search of a better life. I don't think I truly understood this until I moved away. I now live in Canada, which is a very beautiful country, but it is a place where every town looks the same, where every municipality has the same street names, stores, housing and culture. Travel for 3,000 miles in Canada and you will hear the same accent; travel for 30 miles in England and the differences are obvious. We stand up for our little patch of ground, and want to defend it from those who do not care for our values. I truly believe that this is what led to the rise of football violence; it is certainly this kind of thinking that led me into the lifestyle, and I am sure the same is true for many others. I was of the view – and still am, to an extent – that if other fans wanted to come to Hillsborough and cheer on their team, then they had every right to do so. It is those that want to come and piss on you and your home that needed putting in their place, and there will always be those people, because another trait of the British is their desire to conquer and explore. It gave us the largest empire the world has ever known, and it has given us football hooliganism, and it will, in time, lead to other serious social consequences.

I don't want to dwell on the sociological aspects of why lads seek to misbehave at football – that particular topic has been done to death a thousand times over. My point is that I was a Sheffield Wednesday supporter in the beginning, and I will be a Sheffield Wednesday supporter at the end, no matter what the 'real' supporters think of me, or others like me.

If you are unlucky, leading the life of a football lad can entail a couple of very serious occupational hazards. The first one is to take a kicking from rival supporters, and I would suffer that fate on a number of occasions down the years. The other, and far more serious, problem is that you may be apprehended by the boys in blue. In the ten years that I was involved with hooliganism I was only arrested twice, and on the second occasion no charges were levelled against me. My first experience of the law came at the FA Cup semi-final of 1986. I can sit here and chuckle about it today, but at the time it was no laughing matter – for me or my family.

AN OCCUPATIONAL HAZARD

On 5 April 1986, Sheffield Wednesday were scheduled to face their bogey team, Everton, in the semi-finals of the FA Cup at Villa Park. I was keyed up for this game, and with good reason: not only were we one step from a Wembley appearance, but I also had two tickets for the game – one of which I intended to sell outside the ground before the game for a tidy profit. I knew what time the main firm was supposed to be travelling and Dawesy and I decided that we would get an earlier train. It was also Grand National day, and we figured if we got there early we could place a few bets before rendezvousing with the rest of the lads when they got in. The train to Birmingham was quite full, there were other lads on heading down early, and the mood was one of quiet optimism. On arrival at New Street we alighted, half expecting to see a few Villa or Zulus knocking about, but none appeared to be present. There were a few shady-looking characters hanging around, but this was Brum after all. The next hour was spent wandering around looking for a bookie, without too much success I might add, and my old pal Dawesy, who liked a good flutter, was getting rather agitated. 'What's up with this fucking town?' he complained, sweat beading all over his reddening face. 'Why can't I find a decent bookie?'

I remember looking at him that day and mentally marking his card for a coronary before too long. He was starting to pack on the beef, and was easily stressed, but he was a nice lad, was Dawesy – for a Blade. He was the first person I had ever seen back then to pick up a Blue Burberry, and in my mind this marked him out as a lad who knew the score.

I suggested that we find a phone box and call home to have someone place our bets – after all, the train carrying the main bulk of the firm was due in any minute. We walked round the back of the station and proceeded to make the calls. I was just hanging up the phone when down the ramp from the station came the biggest mob I had ever seen in my life. There were easily 400 lads on their way out of the station.

I looked at Dawesy and he looked at me.

'Who the fuck is this lot?' I exclaimed.

I need not have worried. As they reached the bottom of the ramp I noticed Bentley at the front wearing the grin that would, in later years, become his trademark. It was the Wednesday and this firm was the business. Both Dawesy and I knew that no one would be able to touch us on this day. We also both knew that being in a mob this size was going to severely limit our drinking opportunities, and so we decided to get a few light ales inside us before joining up with the lads. Having a rumble was important, but having a few soda pops was, at that moment in time, even more important. There would be no worries locating this firm later, and so we set off on a separate quest for the amber nectar. Incredible as it may seem in this day and age, there was no real police escort waiting, and a group of 400 lads was allowed to leave the station and head off into town virtually unimpeded.

We spent the next couple of hours drinking in a couple of pubs, and a club up near Villa Park. The rest of the firm was always nearby, and we had seen nothing of any Everton mob. Plenty of Scousers were about, but harmless ones – just there for the match.

Time was getting on, and kick-off was approaching, on the field at least. The mood was beginning to grow restless among many of the lads; the lack of an Everton firm to play with had become a source of frustration. Eventually a move was made to head down to the Everton end, and the Wednesday lads made for the stadium with the intention of taking the fight to the Scousers. A Scouse ticket tout made the mistake of trying to sell his tickets at an overinflated price, which resulted in him being relieved of his supply, and getting a swift clump round the head. Both Dawesy and I were in the mob as we entered Witton Lane. We marched round to the Everton turnstiles and still saw nothing. Now, this was becoming a little bit strange. Everton were known, at that time, to have a very handy firm, but where the hell were they? We made a full circuit of the ground, with no luck. My increasingly breathless chum and I decided that we would go grab a couple of cans and sit in the park near the ground sooner than walk around fruitlessly. If something went off we could easily catch up, and besides it was a warm day and a parched, dry throat was no laughing matter.

We sat on a bench enjoying a couple of cans; the sun was beating down, and all in all it seemed a perfect spring day. Plenty of Wednesday and Everton fans were milling about, but there was precious little hint of malice. I saw a girl who I had gone to school with – she was an excellent footballer herself, and would go on to play for both Sheffield Wednesday ladies team and Doncaster. We chatted amicably for a while, until our conversation was interrupted by the unmistakable sound of trouble. I turned to see one of the Wednesday lads waving his arms and gesticulating to other fans:

'Come on, they are here!'

With that I jumped up, bade my farewells to my old schoolfriend, and headed into the fray.

The Wednesday mob had dwindled in number – many had headed into the ground – but there was still a good hundred of us. It was 2.20pm and finally there was going to be a party.

We marched again into Witton Lane, but this time the atmosphere was dark. As we walked through there was no confrontation, but as we passed the heavens seemed to open, and rain bins, bottles and stones down on us. We turned to see

Everton fans charging toward us; the lads spread out ready for the onslaught, but it was interrupted by the appearance of mounted police bursting through the Everton ranks. Both mobs withdrew a safe distance, but some of us simply stepped out of the way. This was it, and I was having some. I ran into the road, and turned to the other Owls further up:

'Let's have em lads, come on!' I shouted

Some Everton had the same idea as me, and a big scar-faced lad came bouncing my way. I caught him a nice one on the jaw, but was suddenly jumped on from behind. I struggled to throw my assailant off. Then without warning – BANG!

I looked up to see a police horse over me. My unknown foe was in fact a police officer trying to arrest me – but how was I supposed to have known that? More officers appeared on the scene, and I was dragged, proclaiming my total innocence, to the charge room.

Once inside I figured the gig was up, and decided the best bet was to be nice and hope they let me out with a warning. Alas this was not to be, and the charge sergeant laughed when I asked if I had any chance of seeing the match.

'But I have two tickets; can't I at least go out and sell them?'

'You're off to the cells, mate,' was his rather blunt reply.

I was taken to one of those big police bus things with the individual cells. I sat on my little bench, and the door was closed. I sighed and sat back as the prospect of missing such an important match sank in. Looking across I saw a familiar face. It was the Everton lad I had fronted. Seeing as how we were both in the same boat I figured I would try and have a chat.

'All right mate, looks like we fucked up,' I said.

He turned to look at me, from his cell. His face was puffy and red; he was in tears.

'Fuck off, you Sheffield wanker. I'm gonna miss the game because of youse,' he replied.

I have to say I was shocked, not by his reply, but by the fact he was in tears. He had certainly looked the part, and had been game as fuck outside the ground, but now here he was crying like a baby.

I spent the next four hours in a police cell. There was already a familiar face in there when I arrived. Bowen had been lifted earlier in the day, and there were two Scousers in the cell: one sat quietly, and I never heard him speak at all while we were in there; the other was a real mouthpiece to begin with, and was spouting as I arrived. Over the next hour or so the cell started to fill, with Wednesday, and eventually there would be 22 people in there, including some major Wednesday faces such as Mick, and a Blade called Tim, who claimed to be a Chelsea fan. The police kept coming and telling us how the game was going. In all there were three cells filled to the rafters: two with Wednesday and one with Everton. I assumed my scar-faced cry baby was in the Everton cell, and I wondered if he was still crying.

Finally, at around six, the police started to release us. I had got talking to this Tim character and he wanted me to wait for him if I got out first; I wondered if he would wait for me if he got out first, but I didn't fancy trekking back to Sheffield on my own.

I was one of the first out. Charged with threatening behaviour, and bailed to appear before Birmingham magistrates on 16 April. Once outside the station I sat down to wait for Tim. There was lots of Wednesday waiting around for lads off their coaches who had been nicked. After a while the quiet Scouser emerged. I was surprised when he headed my way, and even more surprised when he held out his hand to shake mine.

'Thanks for not filling me in in there, mate,' he said

It was the first time I had heard him speak.

'Not a problem,' I said and wished him a safe journey home. With that he was gone from my life forever.

Eventually, Tim emerged. He was a charismatic character, full of energy, and himself. We headed off to the nearest pub for a pint.

My recollection of how we arrived at the station is quite blurred, but arrive we did at around 9pm. We boarded the last direct train from Birmingham to Sheffield, and settled down for the journey home. Suddenly Tim jumps up and starts yelling at a train full of Everton fans on the platform opposite. Next thing I know we are being dragged from the train by two policemen.

'Fuck me, not again,' I thought. I was pretty pissed off with the situation. Not only did it look like I was headed back to the cells, but as I was led away the last train home was leaving. I decided the only course of action open to me was to grovel to the boys in blue.

'Come on, lads, it's been a long day, we lost the match, and now we have missed our last train home,' I pleaded

For some reason the police decided that making us miss our train was enough, and let us go, but not before a stern talking-to and warning about future conduct. I think that they just couldn't be arsed with having to file an arrest report so close to the end of the shift, and that was what saved us from further charges.

So we were free, but without transport home. We toyed with the idea of a taxi, but decided it would be too expensive, so we went to the information desk and asked when the next train was. They told us that one was leaving shortly, but it would need a change in Derby and the train from Derby to Sheffield was not until 2.30am. We had little choice, and boarded the train.

Upon our arrival in Derby we found the pubs all shut, and so we headed for a Chinese restaurant. There we got talking to a Derby lad and his girlfriend, who told us that a Wednesday firm had been in Derby earlier and that all hell had broken loose, and the police had been called in to escort the Owls followers from the town. On the following Monday the *Sheffield Star* carried the story on the front page. It seemed that about fifty Wednesday had got off the train in Derby. They had entered a pub called Jimmy's Bar, and a mass brawl with locals ensued. The paper even carried reports of fans swinging on light fittings during the fighting. Two local youths received stab wounds, and a number of arrests were made. Amazingly the fifty were put on to the same train that we got kicked off. Dawesy was present during the fracas, and later told me it was like a scene from a Wild West movie.

We finally boarded our train home. It was the mail train and crawled along at a snail's pace, but I have never been so happy to hear the words, 'We are now entering Sheffield.'

It was 5am!

I was in big trouble when I got home, but I pleaded my innocence and swore I would go 'Not Guilty'. Of course, when the case came to court I pleaded guilty. I was rewarded with a fine of £250, the highest fine dished out for the day's events, and walked away with the firm intention of staying out of trouble for a while. Now, the thing that really pissed me off came the day after the court date. There had been about forty other Wednesday in court that day, but the *Sheffield Star* only named *five* the next day, and I was among them. I was pissed off. What's more, they had the story wrong too. The blurb claimed that I had 'punched Everton supporters during a fight in a road near the ground' – what a load of crap, it was one supporter. *And* the paper printed my address.

The following season there was an interesting aside to this tale. On our trip to play Villa there was a lot of fighting outside after the match, and nine people from our coach were arrested. As I arrived at the coach park a voice from the past came back to haunt me:

'Well, well, Paul. I hope you have been staying out of trouble.'

It was the officer who had arrested me the year before, PC Spotworth. I gave him a wry smile and assured him I had. We both laughed and had a chat about recent events, and parted on good terms. A very fair copper was PC Spotworth, and I wish him well whatever he is doing today.

I did manage to stay out of trouble for a couple of weeks, but the lure was strong. A testimonial game against Sheffield United a month later would suck me back in – but more on that particular evening later.

My next period of confinement at the hands of our friends in the police force occurred almost exactly a year later, in April 1987. I have tried to put the events of this particular night firmly to the back of my mind over the past 16 years, and as a result I will not go into too much detail. Mind you, sitting in a cell for 181/2 hours does not really give much scope for description.

It was late on a Friday night, and about a dozen of us had been out on West Street, our usual habit back then. We had decided to try getting in the Leadmill, but had been denied entrance, for some reason which escapes me now.

One of the lads had the bright idea of heading up to Roxy on Arundel Gate. I don't know about today, but back then Roxy was a good night on a Friday. We arrived to find a few other Wednesday, and a few Blades milling about outside. It seemed there was a coach party inside from Derby, and word was that they were DLF. Now ordinarily there would not have been a coalition of any kind with the Blades, but there were only a few of them and they were well known to Tin-Tin, one of our number. We waited outside for quite some time, chatting and having a laugh. Our numbers swelled to about thirty. Half of that number was Wednesday, about six or seven were Blades and the rest were lads with no particular allegiance who wanted to have a dig at Derby.

At 2am the club began to empty, and out came these Derby lads. It became blindingly clear that these chaps were not DLF – in fact, they were a busload of bodybuilders on a stag night. We waited until they reached the ramp leading on to the street – no need for innocent bystanders to get hurt – and then steamed into them. These lads were big, but they were taken completely by surprise and had no choice but to flee. They ran down into the Hole-in-the-Road; a couple were caught and apparently given a few slaps, but nothing major, and so we walked back up toward the kebab shop at the bottom of the ramp. We did not leave the scene – why would we? A few lads had got chased; no big deal. How wrong we were: as it turned out, one of these non-aligned lads had knifed two of these Derby boys. Of course, we did not know this as we tucked into our kebabs and discussed the night's events.

Within minutes the police had arrived, and they had one of the Derby lads in tow. A big lad wearing one of those leather jackets with the tassels hanging from it; the sort that Buffalo Bill used to wear. The main officer turned to the cowboy and asked him if he recognised anyone. There were no football rules of etiquette in play here on this night, and so, instead of deliberately not identifying us he said,

'Yes, I recognise all of them, especially him there,' and pointed at me. Of course, I was a touch perturbed by this revelation, and the prospect of a night on a hard bench down Bridge Street suddenly became very real. Not that I was overly worried – after all, as far as I knew a few lads might have released a bit of aggression but no one had been hurt. The police brought up a Maria, and we were asked to get in. There were about seven of us, five Wednesday and two Blades. The Blades were brothers, and I knew the younger of the two quite well; he worked in the wood shop at the tool factory where I worked.

I don't think I really grasped the severity of what was going on until a police sergeant in the van began to lay into us.

'You fucking animals,' he snarled in his delightful Scottish brogue. 'Two young lads have been stabbed because of you cunts. If I had my way I would build a wall around town to keep scum like you out.' My first reaction on hearing his little rant was to wonder why he wanted to keep us out of town, when he wasn't even from bloody Sheffield.

We were taken to Bridge Street, searched and stripped of our shoes and belongings, and put in cells alone. It was 2.30am.

I must have fallen asleep soon after entering the cell because the next thing I knew it was daylight. Time passed slowly. Food was brought – surprisingly good food, actually. I was allowed to make a phone call – to my mother, asking her to get me a solicitor pronto – but other than that my day was a total loss.

Some time in the afternoon the slot to my cell opened. I could hear people talking, and what I heard made me extremely apprehensive.

'Yep, that's him. Black shirt; he's our man.'

'Oh shit,' I thought. 'What the fuck am I going to tell people when I get put away for six months for something I haven't fucking done?'

The door swung open, and two detectives entered. They introduced themselves, and I was taken for questioning. It turned out that Wild Bill Hickock had identified me as one of the knifers. They told me that one of the wounded lads was critical and looked like popping his clogs. Well, what the fuck do you do in a situation like that? Protest your bloody innocence is what, and that's exactly what I did.

To be fair to the coppers they did seem to believe me, but they were concerned about the blood on my shiny new Reeboks. I was loth to explain it at first, but when it's either confessing to a bit of a barney or going to jail for killing someone, there is no choice to make. We had been to Great Yarmouth after a match with Norwich the week before, and there had been 'disturbances' that resulted in some nasty cuts to my hands. Hence the blood. I gave a statement confessing to my part in the fighting of the evening, but denying any knowledge of any knives. The two CID chappies told me that they believed me, and that I would be bailed very shortly to reappear at West Bar in a couple of weeks when it would be decided whether or not I would answer to the charge of wounding. They would need my trainers for forensic testing to confirm my story, and so I agreed to return the next day with the shoes. Fortunately no charges were ever brought against me, but they did keep my shoes for three months – in fact, eventually I had to enlist a solicitor to get them back for me.

I was finally released at 9pm. I headed home, changed my clothes, and headed back into town to the Limit. It also turned out that the lad who was 'critical' had not been badly hurt at all, and had been released from hospital hours before I was questioned.

A number of people did do some time for the night's events,

including the two Blade brothers, who got, if memory serves me right, three years.

I was never arrested again after that night, although I thought I was a goner after a fight with the BBC in the Yorkshire Grey one night in 1993. Police stormed into the pub, and I was dragged out by the throat. Once outside I was released, much to my delight – and, as it turned out, to Bentley's chagrin. He was arrested later that night, but consoled himself with the thought that I was in the cells too. Except I wasn't: I was down Ecclesall Road having a few soda pops. Sorry, mate.

3

THE YEAR OF LIVING DANGEROUSLY

The 1986–87 season was the best season I ever had as one of the lads. I can also look back on it now and see a clearly defined break from my former life. The previous season had been one of transition, and I had mixed my 'firm' activity with my normal routine and friends. By contrast, the 1986–87 season would see a major departure from my old ways, and an abrupt severing of ties that had lasted for years, in some cases throughout my school days. I don't know if many other lads have experienced this kind of change, though to be honest I think that most haven't. I know many lads who still hold the vast majority of their friendships outside the gladiatorial aspect of football, and as I sit here now and reflect on those days, I feel a certain amount of regret that I let good friendships decline when I could easily have had the best of both worlds. We make such choices, however, and there is nothing that we can do to change them afterwards.

What was so great about the 1986–87 season? Well, for starters it was the only season when I was active that we travelled regularly. And not only did we travel regularly, we travelled and achieved a great deal of success too. Out of all the away games I went to that season we only came unstuck once – though to say we came unstuck is a bit of a misnomer. Amazingly, that day was at Loftus Road. Only 17 of us travelled down to the capital on a damp November afternoon in the back of a beat-up old bread van. It was filthy inside, and to make matters worse the back doors would not open, a fact that would come back to haunt us later when no one could get out the van in the face of a QPR onslaught. Yes, QPR – not West Ham or Chelsea – although to this day I am still not a hundred per cent convinced that the mob who attacked our van were purely Rangers fans. One of our lads had reported seeing a large mob of Chelsea disembarking at Shepherd's Bush tube station while the match was on; still others claim it was West Ham. Either way, I don't think anyone who was there that day could believe that QPR could turn out such a big firm as we saw.

The day had not started very well anyway. We had not had a very enthusiastic showing, which was understandable I suppose. With all due respect, Queens Park Rangers is not the draw that Nottingham Forest or Liverpool is (those two being our opponents on the previous two ventures).

There was also the problem of finding a way to get down to London. The coach that had been booked was sent away when we realised that taking 17 people in a 52-seater coach was not the most economically feasible idea, and so we were without transport. It has to be said, though, that we were a resourceful bunch in those days, and soon established that one of the lads had a brother-in-law who was the proud owner of an old van. Initially, the owner of said van was not interested in carting 17 football hooligans, but after a certain amount of coaxing and offers of large sums of cash, we managed to persuade him to drive us down.

The journey to West London was not the best, or the most

comfortable. The van had no seats and was a real boneshaker. We could not even open the back doors to let a bit of air in, and the floor was covered in oil, which meant that we stood for most of the journey. I look back on that day now with the usual nostalgic glow, but at the time I hated every minute of it. By the time we arrived in London we looked like a van load of mechanics.

We set off late, and arrived late (shortly before half-time, in fact), which meant no stopping for anything to eat or drink – and that did little to raise spirits. Some of our party paid to get into the ground, and some went off in search of food; the rumbling bellies seemed to drown out the intermittent groans from the crowd within the stadium. I headed for a nearby fish and chip shop.

The next hour or so was a complete non-event. We saw no sign of any QPR fans, and headed back to our van, which had been parked down some innocuous-looking side street. At the final whistle the rest of our group arrived back with nothing to report – except for one lad who claimed to have seen about forty lads, who he reckoned were Chelsea, coming out of a tube station. This particular character, a very well-known fellow who, for the purposes of this book I will call Carl Moores, was known for his overexaggeration, and so little heed was paid to his warning. I have also since heard from another member of our party on the day, that a couple of large coloured gentlemen were hanging round the tube station earlier that day claiming to be West Ham. One of them even handed him an ICF calling card, but why the fuck would West Ham be hanging round West London?

With everyone in attendance we shaped to set off in the van to find a decent watering hole. I do not recall even getting a pint that day, though. Someone looked out of the back window and saw a largish mob, numbering around sixty, walking down toward us. As they got nearer they started to jog.

'They're here now!' somebody shouted.

Everyone in the van made to get out of the narrow gap behind the seats. As the first few hit the pavement our driver went into panic mode, and slammed his foot down. The van took off at speed, and we all fell in a big heap.

'Fucking stop this van now!' we all yelled. The van came screeching to a halt, and once again we all lunged to the front of the vehicle in a desperate attempt to escape. The returning lads who had managed to get out in the first place pushed us back inside, however: in burst Steve Baker and Tin-Tin, two extremely game lads, one of who is sadly no longer with us. They flopped to the ground, exhausted from their sprint to catch up with the van. Another lad who had got out, Greggy, had fired an orange smoke grenade into the pursuing cockneys, and had picked a few of them off one by one as they staggered through the fog. We wanted our driver to drive down a couple of streets and let us out leisurely, but he was having none of it.

'I'm getting my van back to Sheffield, there's no fucking way I'm getting it smashed up,' he wailed. Although anyone looking at this battered old wreck would have thought it had already been smashed up.

Our day was done, and we had achieved virtually nothing. I don't think anyone there had really expected much in the way of a tussle, and we were certainly caught out when it did come on top, although I still wonder where that firm came from, and how they knew where we were parked. I'm also still wondering how I let a certain person owe me a bag of chips from that day too, but I digress.

As I said earlier though, that one very minor setback was the only second we took on the road that year. We travelled firm-handed to probably eight or nine matches, and never looked like coming unstuck. In fact, we scored some major successes against mobs that, at the time, had pretty impressive reputations.

On 6 October 1986, Sheffield Wednesday played Stockport County in a League Cup Second Round Second Leg game. The home tie had been won comfortably, 3-0, and the return leg was staged at Manchester City's Maine Road ground. It would be an easy ride for Wednesday that night, with 'the binman' Colin Walker grabbing a hat-trick as Wednesday romped home 7-0. I attended that game, and it was special not only for the scoreline, but also because that night marked the first time we travelled under the name of the 'Owls Crime Squad'. On this night the chant of 'OCS!' would ring round a sparsely populated Maine Road, bringing bemused looks from many.

I don't remember who came up with the name Owls Crime Squad, but I do know it was largely in response to the Blades mob dubbing themselves the Blades Business Crew. It was a shrewd bit of name picking from our neighbours to call themselves after a national corporation. We, on the other hand, named ourselves after a cleaning company. I never liked the name Owls Crime Squad – still don't, if I am completely honest. There was some debate over whether it was Owls or Organized. I preferred the latter, and indeed Mick had some T-shirts printed up with 'Organized Crime Squad' on them. It's just as well it stayed as Owls, though, because we would likely have been liable for prosecution under the Trades Description Act for calling ourselves 'Organized'.

On the night of our historic trip to Moss Side I had been at work and met up with a lad I had known from school; his name was Sav. He was a complete pikelet, but I didn't have the heart to tell him to fuck off, and so I tried putting him off by asking him if he was tooled up.

'Whaddya mean?' he asked, with a daft look on his face. He was a bit goofy was Sav, and in school our old woodwork teacher had described the gormless face he pulled as looking like that of a 'pregnant rabbit'. It was completely true, although I admit that I have no idea what a pregnant rabbit's face looks like.

'Are you carrying a blade? You'll need it when we get to Manchester,' I said, trying not to laugh. The colour drained from his already pasty face.

'No,' he said, 'you never said we needed blades.'

'Fuck me, Sav, we are going into Moss Side – it's rough as fuck.'

'Where's yours, then?' he countered.

Just then a lad I knew, whose name I forget, suddenly appeared on my shoulder.

'All right, D,' he said. 'You lads off to Stockport?'

I nodded in the affirmative. My mind had wandered off trying to wind up poor old Sav. The pregnant rabbit was going to Manchester that night whether I was keen on the idea or not.

'Well, we'd best get moving if we're going to get the train.'

Upon our arrival we were greeted by a much smaller group than I had expected – probably only about 25 of us, and all young lads. None of the old faces would be making this trip. I looked around and it was a good solid 25; by the time we got the train there would be 22 of us. Laver was there, so too was Clocky, Halesy, Bowen, Ash, Carl Moores, John Delaney, Pete Turner, Zagga and a few others who I did not know too well at the time. We were all in our teens except Greggy, who was the old man of the group at 20.

The train journey was non-eventful. There was much talk of the new name, and discussion about having shirts made up with 'OCS' on them, and other speculations on what we were likely to encounter in the evening ahead, but I was content to sit and let the journey pass quietly. Not only that, but I had Sav to keep me company, and his imaginary tales of women chasing him everywhere he went kept me entertained.

We had to change trains at Stockport. I think that most of us were a little disappointed, as football supporters, that the game was going to be at Maine Road and not Edgeley Park, but that disappointment was tempered by the knowledge that we could well run into Manchester City, who were likely to prove stiffer opposition than an unknown Stockport County firm.

We arrived in Manchester to find no one waiting. I doubt that anyone really expected us to show up anyway for such a 'nothing' game, and a decision was quickly made to walk to the ground in the hope of maybe bumping into some other 'likely lads'. Zagga and a couple of his chums were a little perturbed at our decision to walk, and they jumped in a taxi, to much derision I might add. We were not going to worry about marching through Moss Side, and that was that.

The walk was long and slow and dull. It has to be said, though, that Moss Side is a place that you really wouldn't want to walk through on a regular basis. I remembered going to Liverpool for the first time a couple of years previously, and being struck by the scenes of decay. It had looked like another world, even sadder than the post-industrial Sheffield from which I had travelled. Moss Side reminded me of that night in Liverpool, but this time I was walking through the landscape and not simply viewing it from the safety of public transport.

We arrived at the ground late, as usual, and found the Stockport boys scuffling with City right outside the turnstiles. What a find. This was our moment, and with that Pete Turner, work bag in hand, let out the OCS battle cry for the first time:

'OOOOOOOO-CCCCCCCCC-SSSSSSSSSSSSS!' rang out into the chill October night air.

We immediately bounced into view, and the surprise caught the City and Stockport fans off guard. Both mobs immediately split, and ran. An early result for us as both sets of fans tried to figure out what was going on. We were well up for it now, but our arrival had triggered a belated response from the Greater Manchester police, who only moments earlier had seemed happy to sit back and do nothing. Now they came down on us swiftly. We were rounded up and pushed toward the turnstiles; the City lads, having now got over their initial surprise, started to come back giving out the verbals.

'Town after!' they shouted as we were herded into the ground.

We were put on to the Kippax, and Stockport had the visitors' section. We busied ourselves doing nothing while the game was on. Zagga and his cronies had arrived at the ground and missed our little waltz. They were a touch miffed, but the general reaction to that was simply, 'Too fucking bad, you should have come with us then.'

About ten minutes from the end of the game we noticed a group of Stockport fans leaving. Thinking it was their boys we got ourselves together too, and headed for the exits. Once outside, however, we found that the Stockport who had left were simply disgruntled fans, and not firm. No worries, we thought, because we knew City would be waiting back in town. Not wanting to miss that we jumped on to a passing bus that was heading into town.

Sitting on the bus we were full of anticipation. Everyone was getting psyched knowing that we could be set for a good tussle with City – everyone, that is, except for good old Carl Moores. He decided that he would grab a girl's arse as she got up to get off the bus. We absolutely roared with laughter as she steamed into him. I think she got a couple of good punches in before deciding that he had taken enough punishment and left him alone. His face was a picture of embarrassment as he tried to shrug off what had happened. We took the piss mercilessly, and I never saw him try a stunt like that ever again.

Next stop was our stop, and we were off and into town, where there was nothing to see, so we headed for the station. Most of the lads had gone to look on the platform to get times, and Clocky and I were sat on a bench when in walked about twenty or thirty City boys. They were almost all youth with a really ugly looking scar-faced lad leading them. It was the same firm we had seen near the ground, but they weren't alone. Behind them was a large squad of Old Bill. We went to alert the others, and I think that Halesy went and spoke with them. They said that we should try and get out the station and they would be waiting for us. But how could we just march out the station twenty-handed without alerting the police? We headed for a back exit, but were pushed back inside by the boys in blue, and put on to our platform, where a train was waiting. After few moments' thought, we decided that we had to get out in twos and threes, so that is exactly what we did. Looking back it is amazing that the police did not cotton on to what we were doing. They just let us walk out in small groups, and never batted an eyelid. They really must have thought we had got on the train, but we most certainly had not.

Outside the station we grouped up on the forecourt. We could see the City lads about fifty yards further up the road, and off we went. They saw us coming and walked down to meet us. Both mobs marched toward one another. City probably had an edge numbers wise, but we had a strong belief in ourselves. The next thing I knew we were five feet apart. No one spoke. I remember looking round to see a couple of our stragglers running to catch up, then I heard John Delaney speak:

'Right, lads, on the count of three.'

I looked at the City lads standing just yards apart. Scar-face was at their head.

'One.'

Everyone looked calm, on both sides.

'Two.'

Movement ruffled through the ranks. This was the moment of truth. In a second it would be game on, and battle would be joined.

'Three.'

The words came slowly from John's mouth. Like slow motion.

The roar went up, and we steamed into the Manchester boys. Scar-face shit it, and to a man they turned tail and ran.

We headed back to the station. The OCS had opened their account on a good note. We had come to Manchester, we had done whatever we wanted and could return to Sheffield heads held high. Maybe it wasn't City's main mob, but it wasn't our main mob either. We would take the result and say thank you very much.

A few days after our 'birth' at Maine Road we were back in Manchester for a visit to Old Trafford, a ground I had seen Wednesday win at in my two previous trips. Nothing of note happened, except that Carl Moores and I sat on the famous Stretford End and I saw a particularly odious lad who I went to school with. He was with our firm that day, and had been Wednesday all through school. The next time I saw 'Sniffy' he would be shouting the odds with a group of Blades when I was alone, but even then the little no-mark didn't have the balls to actually do anything. Still waiting for you to 'knock me out, Sniffy'.

On 1 November a coach was booked for the trip to Nottingham Forest. I had been to Forest a couple of times before on supporters' coaches. Their firm, the Executive Crew, was well respected and everyone knew the tales about them throwing opposition fans into the Trent. Whenever other lads from the 1970s and 1980s talk about the major firms of the era, the Forest mob always rates highly, so we knew this trip was not going to be a walk in the park. As usual, we met at Sheaf Valley Baths in Pond Street. There was a good turnout when I arrived. All the youthful faces from the Stockport jaunt were there, along with a couple of well-experienced old hands. The idea was to get into Nottingham town centre close to their main boozer. A few of our boys had worked in Nottingham and had got friendly with some of the Forest firm. The word on the coach was to get close to a pub in town called, I think, the Dog and Bear.

Nottingham is a relatively short trip from Sheffield, and we made good time. The mood on the way down was jovial with the usual card schools ongoing, and a few spliffs being passed around. I have always found it to be the same on any away trip. When you start getting close to your destination the mood becomes a little bit more sombre. People can say what they want, but when you go into someone else's town you must show respect, and be ready to fight for your life otherwise there is no point going and you could come badly unstuck.

As the coach got close to the centre of Nottingham you just knew that every pair of eyes on the bus was scanning the streets, looking for signs that Forest knew we were coming. Everything seemed normal; an ordinary Saturday afternoon in the heart of England's East Midlands.

We disembarked close to a pub called the Old Boots. Once

inside the mood picked up, and the beer began to flow. We sang along to the jukebox, 'Walk Like an Egyptian' by The Bangles being a favourite. A couple of lads stood outside scouting – again, this was common practice. No one wanted to be surprised in an unfriendly town, so good reconnaissance was vital.

Time to move out. Everyone drank up and we headed closer to the Forest lair. We marched swiftly through an indoor shopping area; the locals eyed us warily, but there was no hint of any kind of trouble. We were now deep into the town centre, and a decision was made to plot up as close as possible to the Dog and Bear. There was a pub round the corner called the Flying Horse, and this was where we went. I was a little perturbed by this because the Flying Horse main bar was downstairs, which would make it difficult to get out when the inevitable assault came.

Within minutes Forest scouts were hovering. They came, they saw, they fucked off. It was at this point that Clocky and I went for our own scout, and we walked up to the Dog and Bear. We walked in and had a look round; the pub was packed. How many were firm and how many were just drinkers was unclear, but it was a cert we would soon have our hands full. Our visit had not gone unnoticed – but respect where it is due, the Forest lads did not try to pull a shady one and jump us there and then. We headed back to the Flying Horse to let the others know what we had seen. I doubt whether we got too far into the pub when the inevitable shout went up:

'They're *here*!'

Everyone headed up the stairs and out. Looking up the road we saw a large Forest firm headed our way. These boys looked the business and they were tooled up. Some carried bike chains and a couple carried washing-up liquid bottles. This would be my first taste of ammonia.

A roar went up from both sides. The Forest lads had the advantage, in my opinion. They outnumbered us, they were coming down the road, and they were tooled up. This was not going to be easy, or so I thought. As the first punches were traded and the first squirts of ammonia caused people to shield their eyes, the Forest firm looked uneasy. They had expected us to run, and we hadn't. They started to edge backward, and we took advantage. As one a huge roar went up.

'OOOOOOOO-CCCCCCCCC-SSSSSSSSSSSS!'

We charged into them. The ammonia bottles were dumped and they turned to run. The rout was on, and a few of their back stragglers were caught and given a bit of a kicking. Nottingham was in our grip, and we loved it. One of the most respected mobs in the league had been put to flight in their own back yard. Fuck throwing people in the Trent; the Crime Squad had dished out some Executive punishment. The next few minutes were a whirl. We mobbed up and charged through the shopping area, causing shoppers to scurry for the doorways. This was not a bright idea, and the police soon collared us and had us against a wall for a search. I remember Twainy getting extremely pissed off when a copper called him 'son'.

'I'm old enough to be that cunt's dad,' was his retort.

We were marched down to the ground, and across the bridge over the Trent. No sign of the Executive Crew.

The rest of the day was a major anticlimax. A few Forest tried to sort something for after the match, but when we came out to look for them they were nowhere to be seen. We tried to slip the police, and did so to a certain degree, but there was no one to play with and so we boarded our coach to go home. As we pulled away a couple of Nottingham's finest were spotted, and Rippy opened the emergency exit to yell at them.

'Just a bunch of runners and tramps!' he shouted.

The journey home was a good one yet again, but the following season the trip to Nottingham would not go so smoothly. I didn't go along in 1987–88 – in fact, I have never returned to the City ground since that day in November 1986 – but two coaches of OCS were turned over. A number of lads were arrested, and one of the older lads, Wildcat, would finish the day with a broken leg. Some you win, some you lose. We won that day in Nottingham, but Forest did not gain a reputation by being pushovers, and the following year they exacted some measure of revenge.

Next on the agenda was a trip to Liverpool. Now, the Scousers are always tricky customers on their own patch. They have a penchant for being handy with the blade, although they are not alone in this regard. We knew that this was going to be a testy little trip, and we needed to be on top form. Another old boy from that era, Linwell, remembers a tough trip to Anfield in the 1984–85 season:

I don't consider myself to be a hardcore hooligan but I have had my moments. I was most 'active', in the words of the National Criminal Intelligence Unit, during the 1984–85 season, which was Wednesday's first season back in the then First Division. The season previous I had gone to almost all the games and started to recognise the naughty boys. I decided that they had a much better time of it altogether. They always seemed to be having a bit of a giggle, and that's putting it mildly.

Wednesday got off to a flyer on the pitch, and we didn't do so badly off it as well. We had a good turnout for the scabs of Forest, and one of our Doncaster lads did a real number on one of their boys as he came running off a coach. I remember our boy had a checked white shirt on, and decided to go on their end in order to avoid the OB. Unfortunately for him he managed to stand at the side of the friends of the scab he had battered and I think he ended up lamping someone in front of a copper, so he could get nicked and escape the clutches of the scabs!

Newcastle didn't want to know when our top man fronted them outside the away end with even numbers. No coppers, as the game had started and, at that time, the OB were more interested on what happened in the ground rather than outside it. We had a good go with West Brom outside a pub near the ground, although we were in the pub and couldn't get many out, but still an enjoyable little fracas nonetheless. I have always liked the Albion since that day. I also seem to remember we had a good run at the Spurs on Hillsborough corner, up a hill and outnumbered.

Our next little trip was going to be Liverpool. Over the summer of the year we had taken a few 'shopping' trips to Manchester, so we had the trains all figured out, and at this time the 'service' was still the way to go. We met at the station early that Saturday morning and had a quick count: 33! All young lads and well up for it, so off we went. Looking back we must have been mad, but in for a penny in for a pound as they say. First stop Piccadilly. As we got off the train we saw we had a bit of time, so we had a walk to the front of the station to see if we could have a bit of fun with whoever was around. I believe some people now refer to it as dancing, but back then we just wanted a scrap with anyone we came across. As we left the platform we encountered the super firm. Man. United off to West Brom, our friends from earlier that year, numbering at least 350. We quickly decided to split into twos and threes and try to mingle with the Reds until it was time to go. Apologies here to all OCS for not fronting them as we all know the 'Never been done, never been run' mighty Buttered Bread Cakes would have had it with Man U!

I paired off with Steve Bowen. We confidently plonked ourselves down in the middle of the concourse and I started to read a paper. After a few minutes I could feel we were getting some looks, but I wasn't too concerned as I thought with a mob that size they would always have a few first timers every week and after a few seconds the looks would cease. Wrong … the looks got more and more intense, and one or two Mancs started to wander over; Steve and I had clocked this and wondered if we had been sussed from our shopping trips, or were just plain unlucky. For the first time I lifted my head up to have a look and see how deep we were in and I spotted the problem. Steve, who by the way was a Brummie, had a tattoo across the back of his wide neck proclaiming the name of my birthplace and beloved city! All of my life I have known how to pick them and this was another one of my great picks. Fair play to the Mancs, though – a few looks exchanged, two train announcements and we were on our way. It was now clear to me that today was going to be a big one!

We arrive in Liverpool and decide to walk to the ground; no one to spot us at the station, so we waltz out and around Liverpool. I believe that by today's standards that alone is classed as a result. As we get closer to Anfield we decide to go over to Goodison and have a little scout, as we were going there later in the year. After nearly having a brawl in *a local chippy we head off back to Anfield. By now we are all tooled up and ready for it. My favourite friend was the National Express and British Rail window breaker. I am sure many of you are familiar with it! Nothing before the game, so we go in the seats behind the goal and watch Wednesday beat Liverpool 2-0, with goals by Varadi and Shelton. A great day is unfolding. At half-time, as I am talking to some friends, a chap at the side of me gets slashed and has to go to hospital.*

At the end of the game we leave and mob up by the buses that have been laid on for the fruit gum express – our term for the travel club. Here come the Scousers and off we go. We go in to them and do quite well but they just keep coming. I remember scuffling in between two buses with a couple of Scousers and getting a number of slaps before I manage to put the hammer to work – and to be quite honest it didn't work too well. Anyway, we somehow manage to survive, and as the OB corral us on the bus we figure it would be a free ride back to Lime Street, and a chance for another pop at the Liverpool lads. No such luck. The fruit gum is leaving from somewhere else, so we figure we would have to either blag on the train, or pay to get into Liverpool. Blagging the train is not an option as the OB are checking tickets; a great use of their time.

So we hang around for a while, and by now I seem to remember we were in the low twenties, when suddenly a large number of Scousers come over the brow of the hill. We are in trouble as we are at the bottom of the hill and all over the place, and have no clue where we are. It was at that time that I have what I believe to be one of my greatest moments. One bus is just about to pull out. I weigh up our odds: twenty or so of us absolutely fucked against hundreds of Scousers, who by now are charging down the hill having a huge giggle at our expense. The equation reads: two plus two equals four! Quick word with the bus driver, who happens to be an Everton fan, and we are on our way to Lime Street. A scene involving Reg Varney and On The Buses *springs to mind. The best part of it all is that the driver will not take money from us as we had beaten his mortal enemy.*

Back to Lime Street. Nothing doing, so we decide to head back to Manchester and see what we can find. Quick number count and we are a few short, one of them being a school pal of mine who I will call Bryan Ferry, as he liked Roxy Music. Big roar goes up at the entrance to the station. We run back down hoping that we can have it and we are all surprised to see Bryan getting a police escort on to the platform. As it turns out, after the brawl at the buses near the Arkle, Bryan got separated and was legged two miles by a bunch of Stanley knife-carrying Scousers. Goes knocking on a number of doors until some good Samaritan gives him a ride to the station; absolutely priceless. As he gets dropped off there are some Scousers milling around and they clock him, and leg him into the station; poor old Mr Ferry. In the return game at Hillsborough, Bryan fronted some Scousers in Sheffield bus station with his Stanley knife and got nicked. For his troubles he got a big fine, and retirement from the firm.

It used to be like that every week back then: a good day out, usually some action, but always a giggle. Later that season we had many more run-ins with many other like-minded individuals, and always ended up pissing ourselves at the same time as licking our wounds or gloating over victories.

Linwell and his younger brother were very active, one or the other of them anyway, for many years. They made up part of a handy little firm of lads from the Fir Vale area of the city. That group also included Dan Church, Mad Dog Mitch, and Steve Longley, and I think he hits the nail well and truly on the head when he talks of the fun we used to have. Back then, it was more about the fun and games. The friendship and camaraderie that was built up, whether win or lose, can bind people together for the rest of their lives. Unfortunately, for some it was not about having a ruck and taking your lumps. Certain individuals, who I shall not name, lived for it, and had no other proper life. They took a second personally, and would seek out those they viewed as being responsible, and try to exact revenge away from the usual arena. That is bullshit, and those that do things like that know who they are, and what they are: *scum*.

A few survivors of that nasty trip to Scouseland were in Pond Street on this particular morning, and we needed to be as one. That was easier said than done because the night before a running feud between factions of the Woodthorpe mob and the Stocksbridge mob had exploded into violence at the Limit. Owl had fought Owl, and relations would be strained for years to come. To be fair though, elements from both mobs turned up for the meet. Halesy, one of the Woodthorpe mob, was nursing a nasty black eye, and the atmosphere was a little uneasy at first, but it never exploded into violence.

The trip over the Pennines passed without incident. A stop was made at a service station, and large quantities of sweets were misappropriated. Erroll, one of our most respected older characters, had brought his young son along, and the young fella had to be kept happy.

This game was being played on a Sunday, as it was being

shown live on the TV, and so our arrival into Liverpool city centre was trouble free. In fact, the place was deserted. We settled into a pub, and waited. It was expected the Scousers would have noted that we were here, and come for a look. We waited … and waited … and waited. No sign of our friends from Brookside, and so we headed for the ground. Because the match was going out live on national television it was decided that a good show was required, and so a plan was hatched to buy tickets into the Kemlyn Road stand, which was where Liverpool's boys sat.

As we stood queuing for tickets the Liverpool firm finally announced their arrival. They steamed into us at the ticket office, catching us by surprise. One little twat waded in swinging his brolly. They had caught us a bit on the hop, but we went into them. The skirmishing was over in a matter of seconds as the police arrived on the scene. This was only the start and we would meet again – well, not all of us, as Clocky had been nicked. I now half expected the police to shift us into the ground in the Wednesday end, but they didn't and we all managed to get tickets for the Liverpool seats. Into the ground we went. We marched in, and up the stairs near the end. Upon getting out into the seats we realised we were too far toward the centre, and so we went back down the stairs, but by now the Scouse firm had spotted us and knew we were coming. We came back up straight into the middle of them. A huge roar went up, and the Scousers at the front ran on to the pitch. Those at the back charged down into us, and we charged up the steps. I spotted the little twat with the brolly from outside, and made a beeline for him. I managed to get a good punch in on him before disappearing under a hail of kicks and punches. Our lads went into them, and they ran back up the stand. Then something happened that took me totally by surprise. One of the Scousers grabbed my hair, and pulled it. I was totally stunned, and would like to see the silly twat do that today. The chant of 'Wednesday, Wednesday, Wednesday!' went up. We felt like the dog's bollocks. The Scousers at the back were fuming, but by now the police were in and they knew they couldn't do anything. Fifty of us had marched into their seats. We had split them into two groups; running the first group on to the pitch, and backing the main group up the stand, and it was all captured on the television. I watched the tape when I got home: the cameras had lingered on a prostrate Liverpool player laid out during the game, but the chants of 'Wednesday Aggro, Wednesday Aggro, hello hello!' could clearly be heard in the background and we could all be seen being escorted round the edge of the pitch into the Wednesday enclosure. A few of our lads were in prison at the time, and they later told us that they were watching the game on television, and standing on the chairs cheering as we were brought round. The reaction from certain sections of the Wednesday crowd surprised me somewhat. While most clapped us for our audacity quite a few booed us, and cries of 'Don't put those twats in here with us' could clearly be heard. Fuck the spineless cunts was my reaction then, and it's my reaction today. We had gone to do a job for Sheffield Wednesday and it had been mission accomplished; the presence of national television cameras was the icing on top of a delicious cake.

I spent the match nursing my lumps, and complaining about having my hair pulled. I was sat next to Tooky, one of the Doncaster contingent.

'You took quite a few kicks in there, mate,' he said to me.

'Yeah, but give me that every day over having my fucking hair pulled like a fucking lass,' was my reply. For the second year running I had been startled by a very childish reaction from a

Scouser – the crying Evertonian at the semi in 1986 being the first. I was beginning to wonder about these Liverpudlians, and what they got up to in the privacy of their own homes.

Tooky was a good chap, as were all the Donny lads. He would lose interest though, and within a couple of years he was no longer running with our firm, preferring to watch Doncaster Rovers. I would see him at Hillsborough from time to time, but purely as a spectator.

After the match Clocky was waiting for us, and we headed out of the ground expecting a warm reception outside the Arkle pub, but the police had other ideas and had already moved the Scousers before we came out. We boarded our coach, and headed for home. About two minutes after we set off, the Scouse firm appeared. The emergency door on our coach was opened, and a number of our passengers jumped off and into the Scousers. They scattered like pins in a bowling alley, and our chaps reboarded the coach and took their seats, but so too did representatives of the Merseyside police, and Anwar – a curious fellow who I would get to know extremely well – was arrested and dragged from the coach as he tried to change his shirt. Anwar's arrest led to a conversation that still makes me chuckle when I think of it. It went a little bit like this:

Carl Moores: 'All right, Clocky, did you get arrested today?'

Clocky: 'Yes I did.'

Carl Moores: 'I thought so. Were you in the same cell as Anwar?'

Now, seeing as how Anwar had only been arrested five minutes previously, this would not be possible, and poor old Carl just didn't get it. Anwar went back to court a month later, with me as his witness. He walked away with a probational sentence when he thought he was going to prison, so it was a result for him to match the result we got at Anfield that day.

Our next away day was the trip to QPR mentioned earlier in this chapter, so I won't revisit that one. If my memory serves me, the next match we ran an organised coach to was Manchester City on Boxing Day, but before that little escapade I attended a six-a-side competition at the GMEX in Manchester, at which other clubs such as Manchester United and Celtic were scheduled to take part. A few of us thought it might be a bit of giggle to pop over for some indoor footy, and as luck would have it a coach had been organised from the Bradfield Road WMC. Dawesy came back out for this one, and even though the coach was not full there were some good older boys aboard – in fact, Dawesy and I were virtually the only lads on the coach under 25. Some major faces such as Mick Big Wayne, and Billy Taylor were aboard, and most of the others – although not OCS – were lads who would have a dig if the need arose. When we arrived at the venue it soon became clear that it was mainly a family event – apart, that is, from our motley crew of forty or so, and a large Manchester United contingent.

The night seemed to be passing peacefully enough – indeed, we had a drink or two with some of the Mancs – but as the night wore on, and more alcohol was consumed, the atmosphere started to turn a tad naughty. The first sparks flared during an intermission when some Mancs took exception to the 'Wankers United' T-shirt that I was wearing, even though it was nothing to do with Manchester United, and was in fact a poke at our porky neighbours. The design was of the Sheffield United badge, but crossed penises had replaced the crossed blades. Mick was a major producer of T-shirts at the time, and he and a Blade mate of his had created dozens of shirts designed to wind both sides of the Steel City up. It was just a laugh, but of course the thick Mancs think the world revolves around them and took it as a slight in their direction. Words were exchanged and the situation was defused somewhat, but I think we all knew it would just be a temporary respite. I remember turning to Dawesy who, as usual, was tucking into a mountain of food.

'It's gonna come on top here tonight, mate,' I said.

'I know, but we have enough here,' was his rather muffled reply.

I wiped the food from my face and turned back to the games. The Mancs were starting to gather behind the goal to our right. We were down the right side of the pitch, which was surrounded by plexi-glass. A few young Manchester City boys, sensing some fun and games was to be had, had come across to sit with us, always eager for a chance to turn over the Reds.

By now the football had become secondary, and the increasing tension was palpable. Finally the fuse was lit, and anyone who didn't want it was advised to stand back or run like fuck. Of course, running wasn't an option, as there was nowhere to run to inside the arena.

The trouble started when one of ours, an older ginger-haired lad, jumped up on to the plexi-glass around the edge of the playing area. The Mancs rose up from all around, and stormed on to the area between the stands. They came from all angles, and we felt sure we would have a fight on our hands – but as it turned out, we were wrong. Despite outnumbering us at least two to one they seemed strangely apathetic. I recall watching them bounce about and shout threats, but they didn't come into us, so we had to take the initiative. Big Wayne had about three Mancs hanging from him and shook them about like rag dolls. They just didn't have the balls for it, which surprised me. They backed off, all the time issuing threats, but it was funny to watch.

A small team of police moved in, and the Mancs were ushered out of the arena. We were held back, and we watched as more

Mancs vacated surrounding pubs, eager to try and put on a show. At its height I would estimate there were about two hundred of them waiting outside for us, and I have to admit that by this time we really were not so keen to waltz into the centre of Manchester looking for it. Not all our coachload were lads – there were a couple of women aboard, and kids too. Nothing would be gained by putting them in harm's way outside, and besides we would likely have got murdered if we went out into the streets to face that mob. It was much easier in the arena where it was contained, but on the dark streets of Manchester we would have been fighting for our lives, and so we waited for the police to clear the hordes away, which they did with relative ease.

The police escorted us to a nearby pub until our coach could come pick us up. This wasn't a result for us by any stretch of the imagination, but neither was this really our firm, and we had more than held our own against a much larger Manchester United mob. I doubt that this was a main mob of theirs either, but they had called it on thinking they could bully us around, and it hadn't worked out that way. A few years later, in 1994, I would go to Old Trafford and witness the Mancs again try to throw their weight about by attacking women and kids, but not really want to know when it came down to actually having to get their hands dirty. More on that later.

The next trip to Manchester was a Boxing Day visit to Maine Road. I had been up all night playing cards the night before – fuck knows what I was thinking, because I hate playing cards – and so I was feeling a touch dodgy upon meeting for the coach. Once again we met at Sheaf Valley. And once again we filled one coach. This would be the pattern for the season, and it may not seem much to some of the 'superfirms' out there, but it was a tight 50–60 lads that were out every week, and to me that is preferable to having 200 lads who you don't know and can't trust. The trip itself wasn't really very notable for much at all really, and I only include it because it still makes me chuckle recalling the reaction of the 'ordinary' Wednesday fans to our presence.

We all stood together in the bottom corner of the away end. I ventured over to talk to some old friends of mine just before kick-off. As I was chatting I could hear the Wednesday fans around discussing our group.

'Who the fuck are that lot?'

'They look like City to me.'

'What we gonna do?'

It made me laugh to think that the Wednesday fans were worrying about their own, based purely on ignorance. To compound their fears none of our lot clapped or cheered when the team came out, which further heightened the paranoia of our scarf-wearing compatriots.

I remember nothing of the match or anything that was said during the game; I was shagged out and just wanted to get home and have a nap. After the game we tried to slip away for a prearranged bit of argy-bargy with the City lads, but the Old Bill were on to us and we didn't get far. I walked back to the coach with Scribs, who would sadly be taken from us within the year, and he summed up the day very nicely. 'Not to worry, D,' he said, 'can't have it every week, mate; we'll have some fun next week.'

He was a top lad was Scribs. Always up for a laugh, and full of life. His death was a tragedy and he is still remembered fondly to this day by those of us who knew him. Even Blades came out to pay tribute to him after he died, and plaques were placed honouring his memory in the West Street Hotel and the Saddle. God bless you, Scribbler, mate. Gone but never forgotten.

4

STILL LIVING DANGEROUSLY

As 1986 drew to a close and the season reached its halfway point I was full of it, but I did not notice dark clouds starting to gather in the distance. The events of Maine Road marked out for me what the support at Hillsborough was becoming. Throughout the 1970s and early 1980s the fan base of both Sheffield clubs was working class, but this was now starting to change, if not yet at Bramall Lane then certainly in Sheffield 6. The demise of Sheffield's traditional industries had prompted strenuous efforts by the powers that be to try and regenerate the city. The University and Polytechnic were expanding, and the student base in Sheffield was primed for explosion.

Many of the new 'Sheffielders' chose to support the Owls, obviously, as we were more successful than our city neighbours, and these incomers could not really grasp the idea behind organised mayhem at matches. Many of the working-class fan base couldn't either, or didn't want to. Fair play, it's not everyone's cup of tea, but they never poured scorn on our efforts or booed us, as had been our experience at Liverpool. The new breed did, and it was a little disconcerting. Also I think that many fans had grown sick of the trouble, and the Heysel disaster simply fuelled a growing discontent with the hooligan. Many of us engaged in those pursuits really couldn't see the writing on the wall at the time; I do now, looking back, but at the time I just put it down to a few 'student wankers' being ignorant. During the 1986–87 season I was living the dream that I had had since I was a young lad. The buzz of going out with other like-minded individuals and getting involved in confrontation, especially in another town, was intoxicating. I loved the whole scene; even when we had a nobody team at home a laugh could be had. Friday and Saturday nights on West Street and into the Limit were what I lived for at the time, and I know for a fact I wasn't the only one who felt that way. It looked like it would never end, but it did, and soon. Within the year our successful trips would have almost dried up, and the BBC would also start to make life uncomfortable for us, but at the time the dawn of the New Year of 1987 simply seemed to be the signal for more fun and games, and no one was going to tell me otherwise.

Our first trip of 1987 looked like it would be a tasty one. It was Leicester, and their firm, the Baby Squad, was building a very handy reputation at the time, as were many of the Midlands clubs. The visit to Leicester in 1985–86 had been a violent one, and had resulted in Sheffield Wednesday making national newspaper headlines, when a number of fans who had been involved in the trouble were banned for life, so it was with a keen sense of anticipation that we met for this relatively short trip.

That sense of anticipation would prove to be misguided. The trip was a total non-event. We arrived in town, and no one was there to greet us, so we holed up in a pub near the station. Phil – a good friend of mine to this day – and I had a wander down to the station to see if there were any spotters around, but we found none. Even on our walk to the ground we saw nothing of consequence. We entered the ground into the Leicester seats close to the away section, but it was sparsely populated, and a few scuffles, at half-time, and the usual verbals were as far as things went. We went home disappointed, and to make matters worse the team was drubbed 6-1 on the field.

The FA Cup is probably the most glamourous cup competition in the world, and every fan from Carlisle to Plymouth looks forward to the Third Round draw. This is when the league's elite come into the competition, and the small clubs get a crack at the big boys, on and off the field. We had been drawn with our old friends from Derby, but the game was postponed due to inclement weather on a couple of occasions, before finally being played on a cold Monday night a few days before the Fourth Round ties were due to be played. The match passed without any major incident apart from some fighting near Pond Street after the match, and resulted in 1-0 win to the Owls, and the reward of a trip to Chester on the following Saturday.

I was quite surprised when I showed for the meet a few days later. I did not really expect that too many would be interested, and so I was pleasantly surprised that we had to get one of those big double-decker coaches to fit us all in. There were a few of the older lads out, and one very interesting customer who would become known to both Blades and Owls alike – Mr Polak, and I'll call him that because he is of Polish descent. (I think anyone reading this who has ever been involved in the Sheffield scene will know who I am referring to.) He was originally an Owl, but started turning out with the Blades, and would go on to become a major face in the BBC. His presence on this day was not greeted with major enthusiasm by some of our older lads, who regarded him as a traitor, but I didn't mind him back then – in fact, I had a decent relationship with him. He would save me from a major kicking at the hands of the BBC a couple of years later – when I was on my own, I might add – and for that I still have a lot of respect for him, despite some of the very unsavoury incidents that have occurred since and with which his name has been associated.

I think this was also the day that the National Front had planned an anti-Irish march through Sheffield, so while we awaited the arrival of our coach we went and had a drink in the Penny Black. A short time later a number of skinheads were spotted walking through Pond Street bus station; a few of us went out to investigate and found a half dozen or so Tottenham 'skins' who had just arrived in from London for the march. Upon spotting our small band they immediately went on the defensive: 'Leave it out, lads, we're here for the paddies not the blacks.'

They had noticed one of our number was coloured, and being the brave chappies that they were had decided to try for a different approach, but sadly for them a number of our boys are of Irish descent, and one of them, John Delaney, was with us to hear this. We held out our hands in the usual manner, and that was enough for the Tottenham lads. It took us a few minutes to brush away the dust from our clothes as the Tottenham NF fled, and then we toddled off to board our bus. I am reminded of this because I keep reading, mainly from Sheffield United supporters, how racist our firm is. I find that difficult to believe. We have had many lads of colour in our ranks, not to mention the extremely strong Irish Catholic links. In my day, race and religion was never an issue, and even today many of the new lads tell me that it is not. It just happens that we don't have many blacks in the firm at the moment, but that will change. The racist political groups never gained any major foothold in the Wednesday ranks, unlike our neighbours and accusers across the city. I know of quite a few BBC boys who had/have very strong right-wing views and links, but of course that is hushed up by them now.

Our journey to the historic city of Chester was interrupted just outside the town, and our coach was diverted to a coach park where the police were holding all the Wednesday supporters' coaches, with a view to escorting everyone in together. It looked like the game was up, but we weren't just going to sit back and take it, so we set off walking even though we had no idea where we were going. I think it was Trev's idea, and he certainly hit upon a masterstroke this day because we had gone no more than a hundred yards when we came across a petrol station with an empty coach parked in it. The owner of the petrol station happily agreed to drive us all into town for a couple of quid each. We couldn't believe our luck – particularly as this was bound to catch the police out. Into the town we went, and once again it seemed there was no opposition waiting.

We busied ourselves in a couple of pubs. It seemed that having a few light ales in the quaint little pubs of Chester would be the highlight of our day. After Greggy had a little altercation with a youth in our final pub we headed for the ground. We were walking down a small hill that led to a bridge when we saw about seventy lads walking down toward the same bridge, but from the other side of the road that ran under it. At first we thought it might be the lads from the Gate coach, but we soon realised that it wasn't and a roar went up. Almost immediately the police arrived on the scene, and got in between the two factions. A few of our lads tried to run across the bridge and get behind them, but to no avail. The Chester group was escorted away as we were held, and searched, under the bridge. I had a half-sledgehammer handle in my jacket which I quickly hid under a nearby bush. We were then marched up to the ground, and left to our own devices, which I thought was pretty slack, but all the Chester 125 boys had gone in the ground. We hung around the home fans' turnstiles for a while, but nothing was on the cards; we couldn't get in as the game was all-ticket. Most of our lot had tickets, but about ten of us didn't and so we headed off to find our coach, if indeed it was even there. Our intention was to have a drink on the coach, and head up to the ground at the final whistle in order to mob up and go hunting for Chester. The coach was located and we boarded and sat to await the final whistle.

The match finished 1-1, which meant there would be a replay at Hillsborough. We walked back up to link up with the rest of our mob. As we walked back to the coach park – our numbers by now swollen to around a hundred by other lads who had come by other means – we heard a roar in the distance and immediately we all started running in that direction, but we found and saw nothing before the police cut us off and herded us back. I have since heard that Chester claimed to have run us that day after the match. They may have run someone, but it wasn't our mob. That said, they seemed a game bunch of lads from what I saw that night and at the replay a few days later.

We had seen precious little at home that season. In fact, no team had really fetched much of a firm, so it was with eager anticipation that we headed into Pond Street after a match with Arsenal in February. While drinking down in the Rose, we had received word that Arsenal had a firm in town waiting for a train home. About twenty of us boarded a passing bus and headed down to investigate. Six or seven of us went into the station for a look, while the rest waited at the Sheaf Valley Baths. We found about 15 Gooners in the snack bar. Words were exchanged and an invitation was issued for them to go walkies, which they promptly accepted. Once they got to the corner where the baths were the rest of our number made themselves known, and with no police in sight we went into them. The Arsenal boys were no mugs, and stood toe to toe with us for a good few minutes before we started to get on top. They finally lost it when their main actor, a big fair-haired lad if memory serves me correctly, was knocked clean unconscious in the middle of the road. Seeing their ace player go down sent them into panic, and they ran back toward the station. We did not give chase; concentrating instead on removing their prostrate lad from the path of an incoming bus. Luckily he came round a few minutes later, and rejoined his friends. It's always a little bit of a heart-in-mouth feeling when you see an opponent go down and not get up again. It may sound hypocritical, but no one wants to see anyone get seriously hurt – well, not round our way anyway.

A week after the Arsenal encounter we entertained West Ham at Hillsborough in an FA Cup Fifth Round tie at Hillsborough. We expected the ICF to show in numbers, and we had a score to settle with them. In 1985 a television programme following the antics of the ICF had shown a Wednesday firm getting run on High Street. That was fair comment – it did happen – but the whole story was not really shown. There had been some careful editing. One piece of footage showed a group of Londoners walking through Pond Street bus station. The next scene shows an undetermined mob running up the side of the Howard Hotel, at the other side of the bus station. The commentary led us to believe that this was Wednesday, when in fact it was West Ham. They had been caught out near the Queens Head by the full Wednesday firm, and being vastly outnumbered had beat a retreat – and there is nothing wrong with that, it happens to the best of us. The next piece of footage showed a group of ICF confront Wednesday on High Street, and chase them off. No excuses for that, but it was only a small proportion of the Wednesday firm out that day – the bulk of the mob had already left for another pub down Neepsend by the time a member of the BBC fetched the cockneys to the Blue Bell. It still makes me laugh to hear any Blades try to pour scorn on us for the High Street debacle, because there were a number of Blades in that group, a couple of whom are clearly seen on their toes along with the Wednesday lads.

This national exposure of what was really nothing more than a skirmish, and the subsequent bad publicity, had led many older Wednesday boys to show their faces whenever the ICF were due in town. Of course, the fact that West Ham were clearly the premier firm in the country at the time helped to swing larger than average numbers too; everyone wants a pop at the best.

It was with this in mind that I headed up to the Blue Bell on Saturday lunchtime. By midday we had a good hundred lads in; many were older faces, already in their thirties. What happened next came as a complete surprise to me. An older, well-respected lad by the name of Connor stood up and informed everyone present that we were going to London Road on a Blade hunt; Sheffield United were also playing at home against Plymouth, and to this day I don't know the full reasoning behind it, but everyone drank up and headed off into Blade country. I will not go into details of the events subsequent to our leaving the Bell right now – I will deal with that later in the book – but upon our arrival back in town we found the Bell closed, and easily another 100–150 Wednesday drinking in the Dove and Rainbow around the corner. Spotters informed us that small groups of ICF had been seen, but no major firm had made itself known (this obviously contradicts comments in other books about town swarming with ICF while we were on London Road).

Our usual modus operandi back then was to bus it down to Penistone Road and walk to the ground from there, stopping for a beer or three in the Rose. A small fight broke out near the entrance to the Uncovered South Stand seats, the area where we usually sat, when a group of about twenty ICF tried to get in. They were backed off, leading one large Londoner to yell at his men, 'Facking hell, get into 'em, it's only Wednesday for fack's sake!'

The scene inside the ground was impressive. The seats were jammed with lads, many of whom I had never seen before. One group had black dots on their faces and were calling themselves the 'High Green OCS'. It was easily the biggest firm I had seen us have for a home game. The ICF had been spotted in the West Stand, but only a fraction of the number we had expected, although, if truth be known, it wasn't such a big game for them as it was for us.

At the time we used to gather behind the kop after games, on the bridge. This was before the road widening scheme that transformed Penistone Road. Once again the numbers were impressive. Old respected faces from the 1970s were there, alongside lads who spanned both eras, and the new breed. The police eyed us warily, and had just started to try and move us on when a group of about 15 Londoners marched up bold as brass and announced to the gathering throng, 'All right, lads, we're the ICF. Let's have it.'

You have to give those boys their due. It took some front to do that, but it was unwise. They were swamped and ended up running into a nearby concrete aggregates yard, where they took a severe kicking, before being rescued by the police. All of this activity brought a swift response from South Yorkshire's finest, and they became extremely heavy handed in their efforts to move us along.

By now the mob had split into two, on either side of the road, but the police had not sussed this yet, and when one of a couple of brothers from Rotherham tried to cross the road to have a word with his brother on the other side, he was forcibly removed back to our side of the road. The long march into town was on, and predictably the farther we went the more the numbers started to dwindle. I would say we still had well over a hundred when we reached West Bar, but now the police decided to try and stop us reaching the bus station. At the corner of Bridge Street they forced half of us down on to Blonk Street and the rest were allowed to walk into town. Our group of about forty walked down Castle Gate and under the bridge into Pond Street, just as the other group emerged near the Friary.

Immediately a roar went up and everyone started running toward the Penny Black pub. I couldn't see what was going on, but word was that a number of BBC in the pub had burst out at the first sign of our group. Scuffling broke out near the old newspaper kiosk, but before we could get any further the police quashed the flashpoint. We were forced back up into town, and the Blades lads, if indeed it was them, were pushed back into the Penny Black. Quite a few of our number decided that would be the end of their day and drifted off, and we were left with about sixty or so. We headed for a quiet little pub at the back of Cole Brothers department store. Our intention was to try and throw the police off our scent, and it worked. In fact, it worked so well that the police let their guard down, and the Yorkshireman's Arms would very shortly become yet another battleground in the never-ending war for supremacy between the OCS and the BBC – but more of that later.

The game against West Ham had finished in a 1-1 draw, and this meant we would have to take the daunting trip down to Upton Park for the replay. Back in 1984–85 I had travelled to West Ham, and after the match they tried to attack the escort on the walk back to the coaches. At first the Wednesday, including ordinary fans and kids, had started to run, but one lad ran into the road and waded into the cockneys. This spurred everyone on, and the West Ham boys were put to flight. They attacked us again by the coaches, and again they were seen off; this time leaving one half-caste lad alone to take a kicking. Admittedly this was unlikely to be the ICF main firm, but it was still a heartening show from what was not even really a Wednesday mob at all. It was with this in mind that I headed for London the following Wednesday night. The Gate on Halifax Road had filled two coaches for the trip. The make-up of the coaches was similar to the GMEX episode, with a number of lads on board. Erroll, Mick and Big Wayne were among the older lads on board, and as always when you see the old respected faces you feel just that bit more bulletproof.

We disembarked from our coaches outside the Queen's. A quick glance in the direction of the pub showed that it was heaving, but the expected ICF attack never came, and we were escorted around to the South Bank where the away supporters stood. The game itself was good, from a football point of view. Wednesday won 2-0 to book a passage in the quarter-finals, where we would play Coventry. As far as any disorder went – well, that was a nothing. West Ham made a token attempt to breach the police line, but it was half-hearted at best. After the game our escort passed off peacefully and we boarded our coaches and made for home – apparently. In fact, we actually didn't head for home. We went about a mile or so from the ground, and stopped of at some pub in East London. The chaps needed a drink, and all the pubs would be closed by the time we got home. The pub we arrived at was deserted, and the sudden influx of a hundred Sheffielders caught the landlord by surprise. Big Wayne jumped over the bar to help out, and all – including me, even though I almost made myself puke from eating too many bags of crisps – had a good session.

I have never been back to Upton Park since that night. There is not really much doubt that the ICF were the toughest firm in the country throughout the early 1980s, and to have gone there and come away unscathed the number of times I did is something I can feel proud of. Maybe West Ham didn't really feel a need to turn it on against little old Sheffield Wednesday, and I can fully understand that, but it's where I think Chelsea have the edge on them. West Ham were the nastiest firm, but they seemed to save it only for the big games such as Millwall, Manchester United, Chelsea and the like, whereas Chelsea took it everywhere, and could always be relied on. They would show up on a cold Tuesday night and make some noise, but West Ham didn't appear to be so forthcoming. I have nothing but respect for the ICF – they set the standard for so many others, and the books by Cass Pennant really give you an insight into their world – but they were like the World Heavyweight champion who would only fight the No. 1 contender and never give the little fella a shot. Maybe that's the way it should be, but just like in the FA Cup there is always the chance that the underdog can jump up and bite you on your backside.

The victory at Upton Park meant we were in the quarter-finals for the second year running, and I have to admit I really fancied our chances, what with the game being played at Hillsborough, even though Coventry were a bit of a bogey side for us at the time. The week before the cup tie we were scheduled to play the Covs at Highfield Road, and, with the thought of giving them an early taste of what was to come, a coach was scheduled. We should have saved our money; there was no sign of any Coventry mob all day, and despite the fact that they had already sold 14,000 tickets for the cup game, there were less than 12,000 people in the ground for this one. I remember us getting back to Sheffield that night in a snowstorm, and we headed down to the Barrow Boys for a pint. There really was nothing going on in town and so I went out to Derbyshire with Phil, and a couple of other lads from round that way. The snow continued to fall, though, and I decided I would be best advised to jump on a train back into Sheffield. I ended up in Hillsborough before the night was out, counting the days to the big game.

I awoke with a huge sense of anticipation on the day of the FA Cup quarter-final with Coventry. I was firmly of the belief that we only needed to show up to win the match, and claim our rightful place in the semi. This would also help erase the memory of my arrest in the previous season's trip to Villa Park against Everton. The game was close to being a sell-out, and the Covs alone had sold 14,000 tickets – to who I don't know, because they could barely raise their average attendance to that, but I suppose that is the magic of the Cup. A meet in town was not deemed necessary for this game as the Covs were not really expected to bring a major firm, but they were expected to have a lot of piss pots in their ranks who could mix it if provoked, and that was what we were looking for. The weather was warm and sunny as I made my way down to the Rose; in total contrast to the previous week's snow. The Rose, on Penistone Road, had been our meeting place for quite a while by now. Eventually it would become used more before games, but only until the pub changed hands. In fact, our pre-match meets would change venue on many occasions. By 1995 we had moved up Halifax Road to the Travellers, but by then our numbers had declined seriously, and that move was influenced more by drink than other motives.

I walked into the Rose at around 11.30 that morning, and the place was already heaving. All the usual suspects were in attendance, the beer was flowing, and the promise of a great day out made for a buoyant mood. As time passed reports began to filter through of van loads of Coventry passing by on the top road, and it was decided that some of us would go and have a look. Small groups headed out so as not to arouse too much suspicion from our local constabulary. Dicky took one of the first groups out, and they headed up to Langsett Road ready to make hay with the passing Covs. Another group was standing by the Rose door when a group of about twenty Coventry came past. In contrast to all the others who had walked by quietly, this group was shouting the odds. They didn't look like lads, indeed they were all in their late thirties, but they were giving it large and needed to be taught a lesson. We followed them down the road a short way, in order to escape the Old Bill, and then proceeded to pick them off with abandon. By the time they reached Parkside Road they were nervous wrecks, and looking desperately for police protection. They tried pointing us out to the police, but we melted into the crowds heading for the match. Why call it on if you don't want it? It was very confusing to me – after all, it's not as if these were kids who didn't know the score.

Inside the ground it was a cauldron of noise. The crowd was over 48,000 and the Leppings Lane end was a sea of sky blue from the Coventry supporters. Sadly, for most of the match Wednesday flattered to deceive and ended up losing 3-1. I was gutted. I honestly could not believe we had lost and these pathetic shits in sky blue would force us to listen to their ridiculous sky-blue song. I was pissed off royally, and so were a lot of others. We left the uncovered seats en masse and headed down Parkside Road toward the back of the kop. As we rounded the corner we saw a mob of about 200 heading up Parkside Road. Was this the Coventry Ghost Firm? Sadly no, it was more Owls coming from the kop to try and attack the Coventry fans. After a brief exchange of views the whole mob of us, numbering around 400, decided to head for Herries Road to attack the Coventry fans as they headed for the Wadsley Bridge station. The police really didn't pick up quickly enough on this due to the size of the crowd as a whole, and the problems they faced getting 14,000 visiting supporters to their buses and trains. At the bottom of Herries Road is a patch of woodland with a gennel running through it to the bus depot. We sneaked through here, all the while still undetected by the police, and appeared close to the junction of Herries Road and Halifax Road. The police would soon be bringing the whole of the Coventry support through here, and we would be waiting to ambush them. We waited until we saw the bulk of the escort reach the roundabout at the bottom of Halifax Road, and then the roar went up and we charged.

A number of Coventry fans on Herries Road were battered senseless – indeed, I saw one have a large rock dropped on his head. This was well out of order in my eyes, and I went to his aid and asked a Wednesday fan heading to his car to try and get the lad to a hospital. Whether he did I don't know, because within seconds the police had realised what was going on, and sent the horses and dogs into us. They didn't clear us off, though, they only pushed us back on to Penistone Road, which just led to more carnage for any unsuspecting Coventry fans. Cars were being smashed, and fans queuing at hot-dog stalls were attacked. I had never seen Wednesday attacking innocent fans before – and wouldn't again until a revenge mission against Manchester United in 1994 – and I was taken aback by it all. Naturally feelings were running high, but behaviour like that is inexcusable and unnecessary.

I was a little perturbed by the whole series of events relating to the Coventry match, especially the result, but I knew that I couldn't let it shake my focus. There would be other big cup games, and the mindless behaviour was a one-off and was unlikely to be repeated on a regular basis. If I am totally honest I think that losing the game prevented me from exorcising the pain of missing the semi-final of the previous year, and I felt extremely guilty about my part in the violence that followed the match.

This guilt would resurface from time to time, especially after a particularly violent incident in the early 1990s during a fight near the station with Villa fans. A Villa lad had been left face down in a puddle, and we had just abandoned him there. For the next few days I was convinced that every unfamiliar face was a policeman coming to arrest me for my part in the incident. I also could not stop wondering about the Villa fan, and how he had taken it, and whether he had recovered. I knew deep inside that he was probably fine, but my conscience bothered me for a few days.

Of course, by the following weekend I would be back out and about without a care in the world. I think that most lads must have attacks of conscience from time to time – if we don't, then what stops us from killing and maiming? A conscience tells us what is right and wrong and moderates our behaviour accordingly. Without wanting to get into a major debate on psychology I would just like to ask those lads, and there are quite a few, who claim to 'not give a fuck' what they think it is that stops them from going completely out of control? We all need that little bit of control – it is probably the most important weapon in any sane person's armoury.

A few weeks after the Coventry episode we played Norwich City at Carrow Road. Not really a game to spark major enthusiasm, but this would give us the chance for a weekend away in the seaside town of Great Yarmouth, and every footy fan loves the chance of a match and a weekend by the sea. We knew that a coach from the Gate was planning on staying over too. The weekend proved to be a major success and led me to make friendships that endure very strongly to this day. I will talk about the trip in chapter 6, but suffice to say I still view that weekend in April 1987 as being one of the major high points of my life.

We returned from our jaunt to the seaside with a bank-holiday game at home to Manchester City. There was no major meet planned, but about twenty of us met up in the Dove and Rainbow, mostly lads who had been on the Great Yarmouth trip. We were all in high spirits, and only really in the practically deserted town for a drink, and maybe to a snoop to see if any City were about. Steve Bowen and a couple of others went out for a look round, and came back with the news that a firm of Manchester had just been rounded up near the station by the police, and they were bringing them up through Fitzalan Square. He went on to say that there was about eighty City in the escort. Even though we knew we were outnumbered it was decided that we had to confront these interlopers from Lancashire, and so we drank up and headed out the pub. We bounced down the middle of the High Street, and round the Hole-in-the-Road to see the City firm in escort near where the old Classic cinema had stood. Upon seeing us they immediately burst the police lines and ran into us. I always remember the first lad walking casually toward us, removing his sunglasses and letting out a loud 'Come on then, you Yorkshire bastards!'

The rest of the Mancs steamed toward us, and even though we were heavily outnumbered we tried to hold them off before turning and running back the way we came. I couldn't believe it and was in a state of denial. I turned to Waggy: 'We didn't run, mate, it was just a strategic withdrawal,' I said.

Whichever way I wanted to voice it, the fact was that we *had* run. We may have had inferior numbers, but we knew that and should have just sat tight rather than putting ourselves in a position to get swum. Surprisingly though, no one was too downbeat. We knew we would have a few more opportunities before the day was out, and the general consensus was one of respect for these City lads. They had paid little heed to the police presence and gone into us. To us this meant they would be about all day looking for it, and that augured well for future shenanigans.

We met up with more lads down at the Rose and filled them in on the events so far. It was decided that we would walk through Hillsborough and down Leppings Lane rather than around the back. This was felt to give us a good chance of another pop at our rivals. A couple of scuffles did break out, but it was largely uneventful. For some reason every time we had games on bank holidays back then our organisation was weak – or should I say weaker than normal? After the match some of our number headed the usual way back to the Rose before moving for town, but a good dozen or so of us went back along Middlewood Road hoping to meet up with the Mancs. They didn't disappoint us. We had reached the shops near the Hillsborough Park bowling greens when we spotted an equal number of City walking briskly toward us. At their head was a huge man-mountain, but the best of all was the complete absence of the boys in blue. We ran into them and they stood their ground. Both groups were running into one another trading punches for what seemed like ages, and no one seemed about to run. Finally we started to edge them back – but I am only talking inches, not feet. One Manc was down near the park gates, and they were starting to look rattled. A quick glance down toward the ground and police on horseback could be seen heading our way.

A shout of 'Coppers!' went up, and both mobs broke. We headed into the park, and the Mancunians melted into the background. There were more fights near the station in town, but I was not party to those.

Manchester City are always a game bunch of lads up for a row – unlike their city neighbours, who only seem keen with large numbers on their side. I would be involved in a few more fights with the blue half of Manchester in the years to come. One notable brawl happened in 1993. Again, it was a small-scale affair. About eight of us had left the Rose and headed into town. For some reason we headed on to the top road, where we bumped into about six Casuals. Evans walked up to the biggest fella – mind you, Evans is about six-foot three – and asked him in a very candid way, 'Who the fuck are you lot?'

The lad turned and faced him, and in a way that reminded me of the day in Fitzalan Square six years earlier replied, 'We're the fucking guv'nors, mate.'

BANG! Evans cracked him upside the head and the lot went. Before it was up a young Wednesday lad would be put on his arse, and a Manc would find himself planted through a nearby shop window. Game lads, the City; these boys could have said they were just Joe Public and nothing would have happened, but they had more pride than that, which is why I rate them as top boys in Manchester.

The final away game of 1986–87 was at Aston Villa. It had been a long season – I don't think I realised how long it had been until I sat down to write this book. Our coach arrived in Birmingham by about 12pm, and the police immediately ensnared us. They escorted our coach to the ground, and it was quickly realised that they intended putting us inside; three hours before kick-off. We got off the coach, and tried to walk away from our waiting greeters, but they had it completely sewn up. Well, *almost*. Some of us managed to slip away in small groups, and for the next hour or so a game of cat and mouse was on. I had slipped away with Laver, dressed in a long Gestapo-like leather coat, and Carl Moores. We had made our way undetected to the park near the ground, the same place where I had sat drinking a year before, and we were quite pleased with ourselves for giving the Old Bill the slip. Carl, as usual, was moaning and groaning and trying to tell us we should have stayed with the others, when out of the blue two police officers were seen heading our way. Carl didn't see them, and bent down to tie his shoelace. I looked in the direction of the police, and there was not much doubt in my mind that they were after us. Any doubt I did have was erased when they yelled in our direction, 'You lads wait there!'

'Fuck that,' said Laver, and he was off and running.

I was quickly in pursuit, but poor old Carl had missed the boat.

'Lav, what are you doing?' he cried, but we were leaving him way behind. In hindsight the fact that he got captured at that point meant that Laver and I managed to get away again; getting put in the ground two hours before kick-off was not on our 'to do' list.

When we did get in the ground all the rest of our chaps were pretty fed up – and who could blame them? The consensus was that we were going to make sure we got some after the game in order to prevent the day from being a total loss. Wednesday won the match 2-1, a result that meant Villa were relegated. Good news for us, because this meant they would be steaming and looking to get among us. We slipped out a few minutes from the end, and moved to the seats close to the away end. The plan was simple. If the police kept the Wednesday fans in, we would not be among them. As it happened they didn't, and we exited into Witton Lane with thousands of others. The scene was one of confusion as we sought to stick together in the middle of the throng. The hooligans were in place and surveying the crowd, and I really didn't see it coming.

'Come on, you Sheffield bastards,' came the shout.

I turned to see what looked like hundreds of Villa heading our way. I looked the other way; familiar faces looked at each other with that look of surprise, mingled with anticipation. Anyone who has ever been in a situation like this knows what I mean. We fanned out as they came pouring into us. Ordinary fans struggled to get out of the way, and the police, who had also been caught completely off guard, looked to try and get a grip. Neither side ran, but then again there was nowhere to run in the packed road. A Wednesday lad tried to kick out, but fell flat on his backside, and was fortunate to scramble to his feet before he was enveloped by the Villa hordes. One of the occupants of our coach – a lad called Havo, who I had not seen much of before – went straight in. He was banging Villa lads left, right and centre. Even the police couldn't stop him, and when one did try Havo sparked him too. The last I saw of him that day was as he disappeared under the combined weight of three West Midlands police officers. By now truncheons had gone to work, and both mobs were feeling the effects. We were pushed to the right side of the road, and the Villa were forced down the road past us. Quickly realising we could head them off, we ran down the first road to the left.

There then followed some of the worst police violence I had ever seen up to that point in my career. They blocked the bottom end of the street off, and came into us truncheons drawn, lashing out at anything that moved. I was caught on the back of the head, and sought shelter in a nearby fish and chip shop. I saw women and old people battered to the ground by people who were supposed to uphold the law. A well-known deaf and dumb Wednesday fan, who wouldn't hurt a fly, was badly beaten and arrested. I suppose some would say that it was our fault that innocent people got hurt, but frankly I do not buy that argument. I think anyone with a level head can tell the difference between someone looking for a fight, and someone walking to their home, or their coach, eating fish and chips.

Some of our lot had got in with the Villa when the police split us. The sounds of fighting and police sirens could be heard in the distance. I limped back to the coach park, battered and bruised, but feeling pretty good about how we had held our own against a large Villa firm. It was there that I had the interchange with PC Spooner, who had arrested me the year before (see chapter 2). Nine people from our coach had been arrested, and the police refused to allow us to go and wait for them. We were escorted from Birmingham, and told never to come back. We got back into Sheffield and headed for the Alexandra. United had been at home, and we thought we might catch them while we were still jumping, but as usual in those days, they were not in town. We ended the last away day of an extremely eventful season enjoying a light ale or three on West Street.

The final game of the 1986–87 season saw us at home to Wimbledon. We sat outside all day drinking in the sun, and reflecting on a season where we had easily held our own against all-comers. What made it more special, to me anyway, was the fact that the majority of lads who had turned up week in week out were 21 or under. Our away trips would see a couple of older lads on every coach, but never a large contingent. One week it may have been Erroll and a couple of mates, the next it might have been Chappell, or X, but the bulk of the regulars were youth, and game as fuck they were too. Everything boded well for the next season, but storm clouds were gathering – big red storm clouds – and also an unexplained indifference would begin to fog our movements, rather like the orange smoke grenade at Loftus Road had fogged the movements of those QPR fans.

The 1986–87 season would prove to be a watershed. From here on we would start to struggle. We would still have our days, but they would be spread out over years instead of months. Dark days were indeed close by as we sat outside the Compleat Angler drinking and laughing. We didn't know it then, but the laughs would soon be on us.

5

TAKEN TO THE LIMIT

My old man said be a Wednesday fan
And don't dilly dally on the way
We took the Shoreham and all that's in it
We took the Shoreham in less than a minute
With hatchets and hammers, carving knives and spanners
We showed the Shoreham bastards how to fight
They NEVER took the Limit with the OCS in it
Pride of Sheffield

West Street cuts through the heart of Sheffield city centre. In days gone by it was one of the hubs of the cutlery industry that made Sheffield a household name around the world. The little backstreets that cluster around it were home to some of the finest knifemakers the world has ever known. In the 1970s and 1980s the pubs that lined the street became a favourite haunt for the increasing student population of the city. The annual student 'pyjama jump' would end here in a lather of alcohol-induced merriment; it was a fun place to be. It was also a very dangerous place to be, for here was the front line in the battle between the warring Sheffield hooligan elements.

West Street had once been 'Blade territory', but by the late 1970s that was changing. The dominance of the EBRA at that time saw West Street become known as 'Wednesday territory'. Throughout the tough times of the late 1980s and early 1990s that was how it remained. As the BBC grew in numbers they would come away from their usual haunts on London Road, and West Street – with its high Owl population – was more often the target.

Even when we were up against it, and were being swamped from all angles by the United firm, we always knew that there was a safe haven; a safe haven that the Blades could not, or would not, penetrate. That safe haven was the Limit club, close to the bottom of West Street.

It wasn't much to look at from the outside – in fact, it wasn't anything to look at. The only way anyone even knew it existed was the blue sign above its double doors. It was quite literally a black hole beneath one of the old Victorian buildings that run the length and breadth of West Street. Entering through those double doors led to a flight of stairs. You paid your £3 to the right, and then entered through another door to the left. It was dark, damp and stank of decay. The beer came in plastic glasses, and your feet stuck to the floor, but it was home to many, many people, and many of us remember it with a great deal of fondness even today, more than ten years since it closed its doors for the final time.

The clientele of the Limit included people from all walks of life. It was a favourite destination of the goths and punks, of the students and of the football hooligans. The music varied according to the night of the week. Friday was soul and house music, and on those nights many of Sheffield's Afro-Caribbean community would come along. For many of us though, Saturday was the night. The music was largely indie stuff of the time: The Smiths, New Order, Spear of Destiny and New Model Army to name but a few. The lads in the Pringle jumpers danced alongside the goths in their all-black outfits, smoking Moroccan, sniffing poppers and drinking piss-warm, flat beer. The Limit was also a live music venue. Bands such as U2 and The Human League played there. It was just a fantastic place to be. I still believe that the heart of our firm went when the Limit closed. We never found another club to really call our own. Mind you, the Blades never really had one to begin with. They used the Locarno on London Road, but I think if they are honest they know it wasn't a patch on the Limit.

I first went to the Limit in 1985. I had heard it was rough, but ventured in with some old schoolfriends and was hooked. To me there was nothing better in life than a night out on West Street rounded off in the Limit. We stood near the stage, beside mirrored pillars that were warped and reminded you of the mirrors in the fun-house at Skeggy. The music boomed out from large speakers that stood six feet high, and still we thought we could hear ourselves speaking. A couple of nights in the Limit probably damaged my hearing more than 13 years working in the forge. A trip to the toilet was an experience in itself. Invariably the sinks would be overflowing with piss and puke, and if you were fortunate enough to find one that wasn't then you would have to give the hand dryer a sharp kick to make it work, all the time trying to avoid falling down in the process. I was always wary about using the toilets. Usually by about 12.30am I would be very much the worse for wear due to either alcohol, drugs, or a combination of both. I would bang my head against the wall to ensure I was still awake, and not at home in bed dreaming.

I have so many memories of the place it is hard to know what to write, so I think I will leave it to my younger brother, Craig, say a few words. Craig started coming in the Limit a few years after me, and he, too, grew to love the place with a passion.

From the 1980s right up to the millennium, Sheffield – the fourth largest city in England – only ever housed a small selection of nightclubs, but the ones it had – especially during the 1980s and early 1990s – were in my opinion some of the finest around. 'What has this to do with football supporters?' you may ask. Well, in many ways footballing passion – whether blue and white or red and white – often spilled over to Friday and Saturday night around the club scene ... During the years that much of this book is set in, Sheffield was a divided city, with Owls supporters drinking mainly around the West Street district and their Blades rivals about half a mile away in the London Road area.

Towards the bottom of West Street opposite Carver Street was a large imposing building, to my recollection as high as any building around it, but it was the basement that still brings a smile to my face.

I will give you an insight into how I remember this place, although my memory may be slightly out of synch as I was usually slightly the worse for wear by the time I got there.

I don't remember the first time I ever went, but I do remember feeling that I would be back. The addictive quality of this seedy club was immeasurable and would be the venue of choice during my teens and early twenties.

This was the place that I first met many of the Owls' main faces and also witnessed football-related violence on a domestic scene for the first time.

I cannot remember when the night in question was, although I was probably no older than 17, a small, wafer-thin lightweight [Author's note: changed a bit there then, bro!] who although he had seen violence before, during and after football matches, had never seen a nightclub become the target of a siege – and therefore a battleground – before.

I recall being inside the club drinking Red Stripe when fighting broke out at the entry door. As more people pushed towards the door I remember word going round that Blades were trying to get in. All the Owls lads that generally used to mass just in front of the dance floor had headed towards the disturbance. Although the internal entry doors had been closed by the doormen, the sheer weight of numbers on both sides forced them open, and I was witness to hand-to-hand combat on a massive scale inside a club for the first time. Although I was afraid, I also recall getting an indescribable buzz that can be matched only by sex.

As the fighting intensified on the door, one lad was dragged inside and I saw several people surround him and beat him senseless, leaving him a crumpled bloody heap on the floor. The fighting at the door now appeared to stop as the invading people backed up the stairs and on to the street, quickly followed by the defending hordes.

As I reached street level I saw a sight that to this day gives me a great feeling of being involved. Across the road near a wasteland was a sea of people facing us and as we fanned out directly opposite them I realised how vastly outnumbered we were. People were shouting at each other and missiles were raining down on us. Then, with a sudden surge, both groups ran forward; people fell then got up, then fell again; this was mindless football violence and I loved it.

Bodies were everywhere and I remember wondering how anybody knew who was who.

I never heard the sirens, but suddenly police were everywhere, knocking us to the ground. I was decked with two others as the police waded into us. I jumped up and ran down a gennel next to the club just as I was about to be arrested. All in all, from when the club was under siege to when the police had us routed probably lasted no more than ten minutes, but this short passage of time changed my life. I remember looking back to see people being bundled into police vans; this former battleground was awash with bodies being restrained on the ground by police.

I made my way home cautiously, walking as far as the Kelvin flats before finally hailing a taxi, but couldn't wait to tell my friends of my exploits. Remember, this is before mobile phones and the Internet, so the grapevine was by word of mouth only.

During the following week I don't remember anything being reported in the papers – maybe it was so common at the time that it really wasn't newsworthy. Either that or the media didn't want to glorify Saturday night hooligans.

The following Saturday the Limit didn't open. I felt a sense of loss but couldn't wait for the next time I could go there.

Over the next few years I went there many times, seeing many things – girls and fighting, usually. One unforgettable night was the Macc Lads concert. Wow! Although we were crammed in like sardines it was a truly magical experience.

Sadly the Limit closed in the early 1990s and was subsequently demolished, but even to this day as I walk past the buildings that replaced it, I still remember with great fondness some of the best nights of my life spent there.

Reading Craig's recollections, and also thinking about my own, really does bring a lump to my throat. Craig's account describes one of the times that our chums from Bramall Lane made an effort to 'take' the Limit. It was one of a few similar occasions, and they never truly succeeded. Even the Blades in the club, and there were quite few, would help us defend it. The BBC might have had us on our toes all night, but once inside the Limit we felt invincible, and they knew it. Full-frontal attacks on the club, like the one described above, were very rare. Sometimes they would sneak in in small groups. More often than not fighting would break out, but sometimes it didn't, and both groups would drink side by side, eyeing each other warily. The Limit was ours, and they knew and respected that.

The Stocksbridge Owls were always a large presence in the Limit. Mind you, Stocksbridge 'Owls' is a bit of a misnomer because a couple of their number were actually Blades. I got to know the 'Stocky' lads well over the years, and more often than not would go out with them, rather than the OCS proper, in the late 1980s. That wasn't too difficult though, due to the fact that many of the regular faces in the OCS had disappeared from the scene, for one reason or another, by about 1989.

I got on well with the Stocky lads. I had not really met any of them until the Yarmouth trip in 1987. On that day I met Iggy, who would go on to be a major player in the OCS, Wag, another top lad who had drifted away from the scene by the early 1990s, and Gill, who would become a great friend of mine – we were best man at each other's wedding, and to this day still keep in regular contact. There were other lads from Stocksbridge who became big names in the more general firm, including Cowley who had made his name as a 16-year-old at Stamford Bridge in 1984, when he put a road sign over the head of one of the legendary Chelsea 'generals' of the era. These lads made up a very formidable front line for both the Stocksbridge Owls and for the broader Wednesday firm. They were joined by a good back-up of lads, many of whom were not really football firm as such, but who enjoyed a gallon or two of ale on a Saturday night and stood by their mates. By 1989–90 it was the Stocksbridge Owls who had become the primary defenders of the Limit.

As well as fighting with the Blades we also got into dozens of scraps in the Limit with other factions. Shirt-and-tie merchants out on a stag do, overzealous student wankers, lads from other towns – the list went on. I was ejected from the Limit numerous times for fighting. On one occasion the bouncers threw me out on to the stairs, and as they rushed back in to quell more trouble I simply walked back inside to resume my evening. Gill remembers a funny episode during a fight with a group whose identity has subsequently been lost in the mists of time.

There was a big fight one night, and everywhere you looked people were getting brayed. It all ended up as a big scrum on the dance floor. I remember stepping back and seeing John Delaney pulling a shoe off a leg which stuck out from the bottom of the pile. He saw me watching and came over.

'You see, Gill, if you pinch someone's shoe it really pisses them off when they have to walk home in only one shoe,' he said as he pulled the lace out and threw the shoe to the far corner of the club.

About five minutes later I saw one of our lads, Shane, walking toward me. He was griping about the fact that someone had stolen his shoe during the fight. I burst out laughing, and didn't have the heart to tell him that it was John who did it.

The beauty of the Limit was that, whatever happened, it was always a laugh in there. One night I had purchased some trips, and was looking forward to taking them, but unfortunately I bloody well dropped them on to the floor. I stood for a while staring intently trying to locate them in the darkness. John D wandered past and saw me looking down at the ground.

'All right, D,' he said, 'dropped a trip, mate?'

'Yes,' I replied, without looking up.

'Nice one,' he said and wandered off, not realising that I had literally dropped a trip and was trying to find it.

A scarier incident involving trips and the Limit involved a lad called Hermy. In 1988 Hermy and I would often slip off from the main group, and head to out-of-the-way pubs while on acid. It was a lot of fun, and could really throw you. One night we wandered into the Saddle to find it full of Blades. We were 'on one' and Hermy went into the middle of them – they were all standing in the back room – and then came back with a report.

'It's full of Blades,' he said. 'But it's all right because they are all tripping.'

'That's all right then,' I said, totally oblivious to the fact that it was us tripping and they were likely not.

One night, though, he went a little bit too far. We were in the Limit as usual, and he turned to me and said, 'Have you ever seen anyone eat a glass?'

I laughed and thought nothing more of it. We were tripping and would often say daft things in that state. Anyway, the next thing I know he is holding a whiskey glass, and heading into the toilets.

A few minutes later he emerged and his nose seemed bigger, and there was a trickle of blood coming from it.

'Fucking hell, Herm, what have you done?' I gasped.

'Eaten a glass,' he replied in a very matter-of-fact way.

I really couldn't handle this, and felt extremely cold. A poster of Sting hung on the wall in the corner, and as I looked at it the expression on Sting's face seemed to grow hard and malevolent. I was close to flipping at this point, and when I touched Hermy's head and felt shards of glass embedded in his scalp it became too much to bear.

'Somebody is going to die,' I yelled at him, but he didn't seem to care. 'You fucking idiot, what the fuck have you done?'

A girl who was standing nearby had overheard the commotion and she took Hermy into the toilets to clean him up, while I waited outside with the fear of death inside me. She cleaned him up, and sorted him out, but I never really had the same bond with him again after that, and our friendship was never as close. A couple of years later he suffered a very close shave with some dodgy substances. He cleaned his act up after that, and really got on his feet, which shows it can be done, and I am proud of him for that.

I could tell stories about times in the Limit until the cows came home. The night we had a fight with some Blades, and I sustained a knife wound to the shoulder, but didn't even realise until someone pointed it out on the way home. I think that was the same night that Gill was hit over the head with a pool ball in a sock. Every week was another adventure and you never knew what to expect in there.

And it wasn't just events inside the club that made the Limit so special. The fish and chip shop that stood next door was an experience too, especially their renowned greenish curry sauce. It was outside there one night that I saw probably the best punch I have ever seen thrown. The area around West Street was full of little lanes and alleyways from the old cutlery days. These little alleys were ideal for launching ambushes, and we would always be on the alert for what might be hiding in the shadows. One night we saw what we thought were Blades lurking across from the Limit. A few of us went over for a look, but saw nothing. I was standing outside the chippy, enjoying the aforementioned chips and curry, a few minutes later. Down the road wandered Ponno, an older Stocksbridge lad, looking a little bit the worse for wear. Suddenly, out of the shadows stepped a Blade by the name of Jamie Sillars He caught the startled Ponno a perfect crack to the jaw. Sillars was not the biggest lad – indeed, he had to jump up to land one on Ponno. I watched in amazement as Ponno at first wobbled, and then keeled over backwards, sparked. Bit of a sneaky one, but perfectly executed. We ran across, but Sillars vanished as quickly as he appeared. A second or two later and Shane appeared from out of the darkness; he, too, had been scuffling and had put a brick over someone's head. Those little alleyways saw a fair deal of action over the years, and I would guess they still do.

On another occasion we had fronted up some rugby players, and the fighting spilled outside and into one of the alleys near to Carver Street. We were downwind of these big fuck-off rugger lads, and it was starting to go against us when suddenly from behind them stepped old Plug and a couple of others, sending the big lads sprawling and turning the tide in our favour. Plug was a top lad from the era, so-called because of his resemblance to the *Beano* character of the same name; he was game as they come, and an absolute riot to be around.

When the Limit closed its doors for the final time in March of

1992 a part of my life ended. I am sure that many others would say the same – and not just Owls, but Blades too. It was a part of Sheffield popular culture for many people, and no matter how many swanky clubs are opened in the city it can never really be replaced.

This little chapter simply cannot do the place justice – it deserves a bigger stage. If I could be granted just one wish I would simply say, 'Take me to the Limit ... one more time.'

6

A STROLL ON THE PROM

There is something very English about a day at the seaside. I only really realised that when I moved to Canada. For many Canadians their equivalent is to head for some cottage in the northern woods, and sit around eating and drinking, while getting bitten by mosquitoes and black flies. All well and good I suppose, but not really my cup of tea. For me there is nothing better than to walk along the front of a seaside town – Skegness was always my favourite – taking in the smell of the sea, the fish and chip shops and candy-floss stands. It really is wonderful, and it is an experience that millions of Britons look forward to every year.

As a young lad I would count down the days until we headed for that grotty caravan in Ingoldmells or Brid. Nights would be filled with long walks along the seafront, or trips to the caravan park social club. Not the most exciting prospect these days, but good times nonetheless. As I grew older that love of the seaside trip never left me, and as I lost myself more and more in terrace culture, the thought of spending weekends away in seaside towns with a large group of friends after watching the Owls became very appealing. There would usually be a game being played not too far from a seaside resort. If there wasn't, then you had to

103

make a little bit more of an effort – heading for Blackpool after a game at Oldham for instance. One of the first things many fans do when the fixture list is published is to scour the early and late season weekends looking for a seaside match. It would have to be early or late season weekends because no one can really enjoy a trip to Cleethorpes on a cold, wet Wednesday night in February, can they?

I had some great weekends away with the lads, and some not so great ones. The highlight by far was the trip to Great Yarmouth in April of 1987, but before I get on to that memorable weekend I want to let Stevie muse over another seaside trip. This one was for the opening game of the 1975–76 season. The match was away to Southend, and it would be a day that would make headlines:

Probably my favourite of all the away games I've been to was Southend for the opening game of the 1975–76 season, our first in the old Third. We set off early from Pond Street on one of the old SUT coaches, and this 17-year-old was full of excitement and anticipation. I knew we were a shit team in a shit division, but I also knew the away games would be fun.

We arrived in Southend about midday, and the coach driver said he'd pick us up just down from the ground after the pubs had shut that night. Pre-match on the seafront there was a mass of Wednesday, and it was a carnival atmosphere, the odd fight breaking out but nothing serious – we had come to have fun. We made our fairly drunken way to the ground, and after getting there were amazed to see there was a market going on, in the car park outside the ground – things really were different back then.

No sign of any Southend mob at all up to this point, so we got in the ground for kick-off. I seem to remember we took the lead and then lost 2-1, which kind of set the scene for the rest of the season. The attendance was under 7,000, and at least 5,000 were from Sheffield. The atmosphere changed during the game, the fun-filled singing and dancing carnival was turning nasty, and just before the end lots of us left the ground looking for any Southend to take our anger out on. The market had packed up, and a group of about a hundred Southend was at the top end of the car park. The roar of 'Come on, Wednesday' went up and we charged at them. To give them their due about twenty stood and had a go, but they were swamped, a couple taking a bit too much of a kicking. The others were stood at the bottom of the road, gesturing that they'd see us down on the seafront later. We ran towards them and they were off. The game had ended and the rest came out of the ground, some got on their coaches and in their cars and went home, but the vast majority mobbed up and headed for the seafront. The OB didn't know what to do – this was the 1970s, after all, and they hadn't expected thousands of Sheffielders to be stopping in their town all night. I heard later they had to bring in reinforcements from all over the surrounding area.

This was the era of mindless damage to property at football matches, and lots of shops, cars and other property was trashed on the way to the seafront. I'm ashamed to say that I did my share of window smashing, but like I said, it was different back then. The sight on getting to the seafront was an absolute classic, just a mass of Owls everywhere. There didn't seem to be enough pubs to get us all in, and the rest of the night was spent getting totally pissed and fighting with locals and holidaymakers, as the Southend mob never turned up. One Southend skin I spoke to said they'd had a look and on seeing how many of us there were had decided to not bother – a wise decision. They'd only expected a few of us to be staying for the night.

As the night went on and people got more and more drunk it got decidedly more violent. We went in one pub, with a load of Teddy Boys in, and decided that we didn't like the music, so we picked the juke box up and threw it through the window and out on to the road, then wrecked the pub. By the end of the night there were only Owls left in the pubs and on the streets. The OB were clueless, because unlike today where they only have to round up maybe two hundred max and put them in a pub and keep an eye on them, what do you do with two or three thousand fans, most of whom are intent on causing trouble?

After the pubs shut we made our way back to the coaches – again, shamefully, leaving a bit of a trail of destruction in our wake – had a bit of a scrap with some OB at the station who were hassling some fellow Owls, then got on our coaches and headed home. The coach stank, lots of blokes were pissing and spewing all over the place, we must have stopped about twenty times on the way back for people to have a piss.

We got back to Pond Street about 6am and the Sunday papers were outside the newsagent's kiosks, so we nicked a few and on the front pages of some were reports of the previous night's trouble in Southend, complete with pictures comparing the wreckage on Southend seafront to the aftermath of an IRA bomb in Belfast. The local papers made a big deal of it too, various MPs and local dignitaries saying how disgusted they were, which cut no ice with us: it had been a brilliant day, probably the best.

Scenes like the ones described above became regular occurrences during the 1970s and 1980s, involving the fans of many different clubs. And it wasn't just the firm members who got involved. The combination of sea, sand, football and alcohol could bring out the wilder side of even the most law-abiding members of the football-supporting fraternity.

In April 1987 we were due to play Norwich City at Carrow Road, and it had been decided that we would stop off for a weekend in Great Yarmouth after the match. We knew that a coach from the Gate was going, and that they had booked a hotel; depending on how many of us showed up we could always stay there – well, that was how we approached the trip anyway.

We met as usual at Sheaf Valley Baths. As I was walking down with Hermy we spotted a young Wednesday lad of the time. Hermy looked at me upon seeing him.

'That young kid is here again,' he said.

Here we were, barely 19 ourselves, and already berating a 'young' kid – who, as it turned out, was our age.

'Yeah, I see him, but give the lad a chance, Herm, he could be a real nutter.'

If memory serves me correctly we had about twenty or so lads show up that day. It was a good mix: some from Stocksbridge – including Gill, who I met that day for the first time – a good few from the Woodthorpe mob – Halesy, Tommy, etc. – and a few others including Dan Church, Scribs, and Shaun, who would go on to become a main face at Millwall. I would name all the other participants of the trip, but the old memory for faces is not so great 16 years on, and I don't want to offend anyone by leaving them out. I will name them as they play out their parts in the drama that ensued.

The first drama that ensued was to find a means of transport.

There weren't enough of us to make the booking of a coach economically viable, so the hunt began to arrange a van. Memories of the blue bread van from QPR returned to haunt me. This task proved easier said than done: we did not arrange transport until late, and did not set off until after 1pm. The late departure meant that we had no chance of making the match, and so we decided to head straight to Yarmouth. A lad called Lee, from Woodthorpe, drove the van, and the rest of us crammed into the back. It was a step up from the QPR vehicle, but with one small drawback: fumes from the exhaust filtered in. The back doors had to be flung open periodically, though it was all a little bit too much for yours truly, and I puked.

We arrived in Great Yarmouth at about six in the evening, and the first thing we did was hit the local fun fair, which had been set up on the front. Various implements made their way back to van with us, including darts and pieces of pipe, and we set off driving along the front looking for signs of life. We did not have to drive far before we spotted the lads from the Gate coach. They were drinking in a pub along the front, and so we parked up opposite and got out the van. Many of our main lads had gone with the Gate coach, including Mick, Big Wayne and Glen, and so it was quite the impressive mob that we had on show. As it turned out the police had been stopping other Owls from going into Yarmouth from Norwich. The Gate coach only got through because they had booked a hotel. This meant that the problems we had encountered arranging transport had worked very much in our favour.

The next couple of hours were jovial, with a bit of a carnival atmosphere following us everywhere we went. The mood began to turn a little darker during a stay in a pub just off the front. The song 'American Pie' was playing, and some of our party started jumping on the bar, and changing the words of the song to 'this will be the day the Blades die'. This succeeded in working everyone up into a bit of a frenzy, and the prospect of wreaking havoc began to loom large. Upon leaving the pub a group of bikers were attacked and viciously beaten. John D had seen them insulting passers-by, and so it was down to us to teach them some manners. The next pub we entered was the Holkman. It was a kind of disco pub, and was heaving when we entered. As I headed for the toilet I had no idea of the absolute mayhem that was about to engulf the place.

Upon my return from using the facilities I noticed that a large group of lads had started to gather at the edge of the dance floor. About half a dozen of our lot were close by, and this unidentified mob was giving out some naughty eyeball. It seemed I wasn't the only person who noticed this, and John D and Simon started to dance about, deliberately knocking into them.

I moved over to join our small group sensing that it was going to go any minute. Looking round I saw that the bulk of our group was over by the bar. Our potential opponents didn't seem to realise what numbers we had, and their bravery grew. They must have thought their twenty or so lads would have no problem with this little group of half a dozen 'Yorkshire bastards'. We found out later that this little crew went under the name of the Northampton Affray Team (NAT), and were supposedly quite a handy little firm who followed Northampton Town. Well, unfortunately for them, an affray that they could not handle was about to come on top.

I think it was John who started it, but I am not sure. All I know is that suddenly the air was raining glass. I put my hands up to protect myself, and sustained severe lacerations. We backed off at first, but then I remember looking round and seeing Glen heading our way. A huge roar went up.

'Come on, we're fucking Wednesday!'

It was like a bomb exploded in the bar. Suddenly fear replaced the cocky arrogance on the faces of the NAT boys. They didn't realise what they were dealing with until it was too late. Stools, bottles, glasses and chairs flew through the air. Steve Baker pushed over the fruit machine, and it went crashing to the ground, causing more panic. They turned to flee, but there was nowhere to go. We were into them, smashing them all over. They ran to the women's toilets, and I remember Paul Green standing by the door battering them as they ran in. The place was in chaos, and Northampton lads lay strewn across the dance floor. The sound of police sirens filled the air, and the cry went up, 'Outside, Wednesday, now!'

Outside the pub we regrouped on a small patch of grass just across the road. The street was not the front; it was a small side street leading away from it. We surveyed our casualties. Shaun had sustained a severe cut to the head, and was going to need treatment. Blood was pouring from my hands – blood that would come back to haunt me a week or so later (as I mentioned in chapter 2). The sight of a stricken Shaun filled us with rage. Tin-Tin and Baker ran across the road and started to launch stuff through the pub windows. The NAT chaps, who had by now come out of the Ladies, responded in kind, and a missile fight ensued through the shattered pub.

By now the scenes had attracted a large crowd of awestruck onlookers. We shouted for the NAT lads to come out, but they declined and the fire-fight continued. It lasted until the police arrived, along with an ambulance. Shaun was put on a stretcher, and put inside the ambulance. The police formed a line around the entrance to the pub, and started to escort our opponents out. Sadly for them, though, this thin blue line was not enough. We simply went through the police and into them. I remember whacking one lad in the face, and his teeth came flying out. We were taking liberties that would be unheard of today, and panic reigned among both the police and NAT. The Northampton firm had had enough, and ran. A few tried to melt, but Iggy was on top of that, and they, too, had to flee.

The police were struggling desperately to control the situation. They arrested Scribs and threw him in the van, but we simply went over and pulled him out again. Lads were now being brought from inside the pub on stretchers, and they were being dragged off those stretchers and battered, with the police seemingly powerless to stop it. Astonishingly, throughout all the mayhem and destruction only one person was arrested: Nick Rambles, who was nabbed for kicking a car. More police were starting to arrive on the scene, and our mob split up and disappeared into the back streets. I ended up with a few of the Gate lads, and the next few hours were filled with sporadic fights along the seafront. The main bulk of our lads regrouped, however, and were involved in another major confrontation, with a group claiming to be West Ham. This ended with a shotgun being drawn, and a B&B suffering severe damage. I can't really go into the specifics of that incident, though, as I wasn't present.

The night seemed to last forever, and no matter what happened we were easily on top. I retired back to the Gate lads' hotel, and climbed into bed. Whose bed it was I had no idea, but no one cared anyway. It had been an incredible night of mayhem and madness, and most of the Wednesday firm was still out.

The next day we all got back together and went for a walk on the seafront to assess the situation. Scribs had actually thrown a beer glass at the hotel window, and it had lodged unbroken in the windowpane. The chaps were full of the previous night's revelries, and there was a general sense of disbelief that we had got away with so much at such a small cost. Rambles had been arrested, and Shaun had been taken to hospital with a serious cut to the head, but we had dished out far more damage than we had sustained. We had a brief bounce on a bouncy castle, which quickly deflated to the cries of 'OCS!' – much like the fortunes of the fellows from Northampton, really – and then climbed back into our van to head home.

Our first call was at the hospital to get Shaun. He was gutted that he had missed a great night, but proud as punch with the way we had dealt with the evening's obstacles. We stopped at a pub somewhere on the return, and Simon and Lee went for a swim in a canal, to the delight of all present. It had been a top weekend for us, and for me it became the benchmark by which all subsequent trips would be judged. At that moment in time we were definitely a firm on the rise, and a match for anyone on our day. Although the mob in Yarmouth was a good mix of youth and experience it had been the youth that had led the assault at the Holkman and our reputation among the older campaigners was gathering momentum.

The next trip I went on was for a pre-season friendly to Scarborough before the start of the 1987–88 season. It was really an uneventful trip, the only noteworthy event being an impromptu streak across the pitch by Simon and John D.

A trip to Skegness in 1989 was memorable to me for only one thing, and that was that when we left our room to get breakfast Gill crept in and pissed all over our beds, which he thought was hilarious, but he had forgotten that we were leaving that day, so the joke was on him, wasn't it, old chum?

A trip to Blackpool in March of 1994 saw a modicum of action, and a large dose of irritation. Wednesday were playing

Oldham, and a firm had gone to Boundary Park. I was not really that bothered about going there, so Martin and I decided to just head straight to Blackpool in his car, on the Saturday afternoon.

Martin was, and still is, a top lad – not just in terms of his willingness to mix it, but also because his sense of humour was simply top drawer. He is of mixed race too, and to all those who decry Wednesday as a racist firm I would ask that you find me one person who has a bad word to say about Martin – and I include many Blades in that statement too. It has been my pleasure to know the lad over these years, even if he did have an awful knack of getting you to get both the first and last round of the night in.

We set off around lunchtime, and made fairly steady progress, arriving in Blackpool around 2.30pm. It was quiet, and after finding ourselves a scummy little boarding house we had a couple of pints in the Tower ballroom. The plan was for all our boys to meet at the Manchester Arms after the game. One of our old lads also owned a club in the town, which would make a good base for the night's events.

As the day wore on more and more of our number began to arrive, and by about 5.30pm the club was filled with a good sixty or seventy Wednesday, and another ten or so Chelsea lads, who had been at Manchester City. Over the previous couple of years a couple of our lads, Phil and Erroll, had started to frequent the England scene, and they had got very friendly with a number of Chelsea faces. This 'friendly' relationship exists to this day, and reciprocal visits by various lads are common. By about 7pm around 25 of us moved back to the Manchester – this would prove to be a costly decision later in the night when we could not get back into the club, but at the time those of us who left felt that the weekend would be wasted if we sat in one bar all night.

We had not been in long when we saw a scruffy looking mob of youngsters heading our way; they were about thirty-handed, but didn't look too impressive. Two or three of our group headed them off, and had a chat. It turned out they were Carlisle, but they claimed to not be looking for trouble. I suppose the alarm bells should have started ringing there and then: a football mob in Blackpool not looking for trouble? They were allowed to go on their way unimpeded. We had heard rumours of Huddersfield coming to town, and felt it would be a better caper with the Hudders than lowly old Carlisle.

We moved along the front, drinking and enjoying the sea air. There was no sign of Huddersfield, or any other mob for that matter, not even the Carlisle firm. By about 9pm we were in a big pub with more than one level. I forget the name of the place – perhaps it was the Clock Tower. We were only about 15 strong by this time, and nothing appeared to be on the cards. Most of the Chelsea lads had sloped off after a bit of a disagreement with Mick, and now we were starting to drift off back toward the club. I was just finishing my drink and watching a few of our lads outside as they left the pub when suddenly the Carlisle mob reappeared. They ambushed the half-dozen or so of our unsuspecting lads outside. One ran up and smacked one of our Donny lads from behind. The sneaky attack caught the Wednesday lads outside completely off their guard, and that, combined with the numbers, forced them to retreat. I stood inside the boozer, watching in total horror. I turned and saw Cowley looking on too. We turned and looked at one another, and then without a word headed for the door. Shaun Bains joined us, a top lad in the Donny Owls, and a bloke who liked his ale so much he bought a pub. The three of us arrived outside to find a police van trying to round up this sneaky Carlisle mob, who by now had started to abuse innocent passers-by. The three of us bounced right up to them, offering them another little pop. Amazingly, they backed off. Only three of us, and the mob made famous by 'England's Number One Hooligan' didn't want to know. Cowley was livid with this abject cowardice, and seeing another small mob over the street, headed their way. As he reached them one shouted at him, 'Come on then, Carlisle!'

Cowley laughed, and held out his hands.

'We're fucking Wednesday, pal,' he said

With this the unknown mob eased their stance a little, and the lad who had called it on thinking we were Carlisle changed his tune.

'Oh, sorry, lads,' he said. 'We thought you were Carlisle. We're Blackpool.'

Cowley looked round and saw a few Carlisle trying to sneak by. He went at them, we followed, and so did the local boys. A police van screeched to a halt. Cowley was bundled into the back of the van, along with one of the Blackpool lads, while the Carlisle snakes slithered away.

Our attention now turned to the police, but despite our pleas they refused to release the two lads. I would later stand as a witness for Cowley, but before the case came to court I had emigrated. Notwithstanding that, I still saw his lawyer and made a witness statement, which was read in court. He had done nothing wrong, and yet his weekend would end in a police cell.

The night began to go down the toilet rapidly after this incident. By the time we got back to the club the bouncers would not let us in, and I ended up sat outside all night along with about a dozen other stragglers. When Martin came out we headed back to our digs, stopping on the way for a massive four-burger hamburger. A night, and weekend, that at times promised much ended with me feeling rather pissed off, and vowing never to return to Blackpool.

Our other seaside trips never really delivered anything of note. They were a laugh, but that's as far as it went, and there was never another Yarmouth.

Another good trip for South Yorkshire sides is Grimsby Town. Grimsby play in the neighbouring town of Cleethorpes, which is a popular seaside destination for Sheffield folk. I think most lads who live in a seaside town must develop something of a siege mentality. They are never really easy places to go to, even in big numbers. The locals stick together, and any inch of ground you want to take must be fought for. Grimsby are a very good example of this. They may not have a mob numbering in the hundreds, but what they do have is a closeness, which seems to bond them together; even when things go wrong for them they never give up, and will keep coming back for more. I had never been to Grimsby until shortly before Christmas in 2002, but Linwell remembers a typical trip to Blundell Park back in 1984.

Our first trip of the season was a friendly at Grimsby. We arrived in Cleethorpes at about 10am, expecting a bit of a reception from the locals. We didn't get this, so we went off to find someone to play with. By 11am there must have been close to 250 lads roaming all over the place and as you can imagine we were just taking the piss left, right and centre. The Old Bill had a small presence but generally watched from afar as we proceeded to look for any Grimsby then 'swim' them – our term for running our foes – all over the shop. This went on before, during and after the friendly, which was possibly the worst game I had ever witnessed.

After the game we headed back to Cleethorpes for a few beers and slowly our numbers dropped. As we were young and brave we decided we would wave off the last coach and stick around for the 8pm train – all 12 of us! Obviously the local lads, who must have had a terrible day, were watching this and decided to mob up and have some revenge at our expense – fishy Humberside bastards!

At this point we were in an arcade, just killing time – we had seen no one around and were wishing we had left to get back home. The arcade was at the Grimsby end of the front, so we had to walk back down towards Cleethorpes to get to the station for the train. All of a sudden one of our boys comes running in to the arcade to tell us they have a mob of sixty to seventy walking up to give it to us. This unexpected news really made me wish we had gone at 7pm. We went for a look outside and sure enough about fifty fish heads are streaming up the front. Now, the problem for us is that we have to run at them to get to the station and safety – or so we hoped.

We come flying out the arcade and this saved us. They slowed down thinking that we were all nutters as 12 were running at 50; this gave us the time to get into the station – just. We mobbed up on the platforms and they came through the door at us, but because it wasn't the widest of entrances we were able to hold our ground and back them off for a while. We managed to get some rubber tubing and we kept battering them with that – I had always fancied being a cowboy and we all gave it a few 'yee haws!' as we twatted the ones that got through.

Bottles and bricks were flying in our direction and after a few minutes they managed to get a few more on to the

*platform. One of their boys came running from the back
with a big magazine stand raised above his head and none of
us fancied that, so we just back away a little. Anyway, he
goes to launch it at us and trips, lands face down and the
magazine rack goes about two feet towards us! Quick as
flash one of our lads goes forward, picks up the rack and
beats the living daylights out of the cod head as we fall about
laughing on the edge of the platform. This was enough for
Grimsby and they gave it up as a bad job.*

*We did well there, but if they had got us out in the open it
would have been curtains, as they had us big time with
numbers.*

*All in all a jolly outing to get us ready for the return to the
First Division. I know for a fact that the friendly did more
for our firm's preparations for the upcoming season than it
did for Howard [Wilkinson] and the lads!*

I met up with Linwell back in Sheffield for Christmas 2002. He
is now living in Canada too after stints in New Zealand and the
United States. I tried to persuade him to come to Grimsby again
over the festive period, but sadly his schedule would not allow it.
I did go, however, and although there was no real trouble, just a
few small skirmishes, it was a fun day out, and good to finally go
there for a match.

I had made arrangements with Fringe, a good lad from
Burncross who I had never met before, but he was good friends
with Dickie, and Dickie and I went way back. He had booked
himself, and his brother, and myself and Dickie on a mini-bus
leaving from Chapeltown, on the Saturday morning.

It was nice to finally meet Fringe, and good to see Dickie once
more; his Mick Hucknall looks still shining through his

advancing years. We set off promptly, and all was well. There was no intention of getting involved in any 'naughties', this was just a pre-Christmas piss-up by the sea. I knew that a coach of the lads would be going. I was no longer interested in the troubles as a participant, but I knew I would find it interesting to view our 'new' firm strictly as an observer.

Things started to take a turn about 15 minutes outside of Grimsby. Our bloody van broke down, and it didn't look as though it was going to be fixed any time soon. There was nothing else to do but call one of the lads on the coach, and ask that they pick us up. This they surely did.

It felt unusual boarding the coach. This was about the first time I had climbed aboard a coach of OCS lads in almost ten years. I climbed aboard, and looked around. Of the forty or so lads on board I knew just three people, and two of those I had only met for the first time the evening before.

The first person to come and greet us was a lad who I thought I vaguely recognised. It turned out he had just been getting into the scene as I was making plans to emigrate, but he remembered me, and that was quite a boost to my old ego. His name was Sundy, and over the next week or so I began to find out that this lad was now the real deal, and a main face in the new generation of Wednesday hooligans.

The coach arrived in Cleethorpes and parked near to the railway station. Incredibly, there were no members of the local constabulary to greet us. We disembarked and walked to a pub called the Submarine, which was just opening up. I didn't go straight into the pub; I looked around and soaked up some sea air. This was the first time I had seen the sea since 1994, and all my childhood memories came flooding back, as my senses took in this grey winter scene on the east coast. For the next two hours we drank between the Submarine and nearby Schuberts with no sign of either the police or the local firm. I was a little taken aback to be honest, because I had heard all the stories of the heavy police presence, and yet when it came it amounted to a single van parked outside the pub. There were a couple of spotters from South Yorkshire, but everything was decidedly low key. A single car load of Grimsby came by, and numbers were exchanged, but they claimed that they didn't have enough out as yet to call a party. The next day I would read a Grimsby account of the day's events, and it claimed that they had walked mob-handed past Schuberts. All I can say to that is that they must have been the invisible men because I never saw it, and neither did anyone else. By 2.30 it was decided to walk down toward the ground with the hope of finally seeing the elusive Grimsby firm, but we had no such luck. Some of us even stopped off at a pub called the Leaking Boot, and Glad asked a police officer if the locals had been about mob-handed. He was told that they were all in the ground.

Most of the lads had tickets, but Dickie, myself and a handful of others did not. We decided that we would head back into town and wait in the pub rather than shell out £20 to sit in some cold football ground. Four of us headed back to Schuberts, and settled in for a few light ales. We heard a few reports of the whereabouts of a Grimsby mob, but nothing materialised in town, and we turned our attentions to having a good session.

Just before the scheduled end of the match, which we lost 2-0, a text was received saying that the police were escorting about thirty of ours back toward the station, and that a mob of Grimsby was rumoured to be on their tail. There had been a bit of handbags in the car park of a nearby burger chain, and the police had swooped to marshal both teams away. We walked down and met up with our group. The police escort was fairly good natured, and banter was exchanged. The police had the intention of taking everyone to the station, but we had come by coach, and amazingly we persuaded them that they would be better off allowing us to return to the Submarine to await our coach. While they were making their minds up, I finally saw the Grimsby firm. They had indeed been shadowing the escort, and as our group started to fragment and head to the Submarine by various routes they made their presence known. Somehow I found myself in the middle of them with some of our lads seemingly unaware that they were around.

One youth marched up to me, and before he could speak I said, 'All right, fella, we're Wednesday.'

He looked taken aback at first before replying, 'Leave it out here, mate, too many filth about.'

I laughed and headed across the road to the pub. A couple of scuffles broke out, but the police quickly snuffed them out. From the Submarine we could see about thirty Grimsby hanging around, but by now the police were about in numbers, and nothing was going to happen. We had a drink and boarded our coach.

As we were being escorted from the town we saw the Grimsby mob. They were mainly younger lads, and their frustration showed in the gestures that they made to our coach as we passed. That would quickly change as we stopped at a red light. Everyone on our coach stood up, and made out as though they were getting off. This had the effect of panicking the young Grimsby lads, and some started to run. There was no way we could have got off with the number of police around us, but it looked good and made the locals think.

We were escorted to the edge of town, and then made our way back to Sheffield. A few drinks were had in the Harley upon our return, and phone calls reportedly from the BBC were received. About forty of us then walked through town to the Dickens, and TP Woods, but there was no sign of anything going on and so, after having a final drink at the Old Monk, we went our separate ways. I headed to Hillsborough to link up with Mad Dog, Gill and Linwell. It had been an interesting day – maybe not in the league of other trips that had been made to Grimsby in years gone by, but it had felt good to be out and about once again.

In 2001–02 Sheffield Wednesday had gone to Grimsby on Easter Monday. This game was a real six-pointer, as both clubs were embroiled in a relegation dogfight. The importance of the game, and the fact it was played over a bank-holiday weekend, saw a huge firm of Wednesday descend on Cleethorpes. Reports put the number at over 300. Grimsby were out in force too, but they were simply overwhelmed by numbers.

Jambo is a young member of the new Wednesday firm, and this was one of his first away games. He and a few of his friends had gone over on the Sunday, and had a bit of fun. Here he tells the story of his weekend:

The first time I remember actually being on our own and having to have a go was Grimsby on a bank holiday. We had headed down on the Sunday and planned to have a heavy session. We had been with about15 to 20 lads in the afternoon and the beer was flowing. As four of us made our way back to our digs to get changed for the night session we bumped into one badly dressed Grimsby lad. He was wearing a bright-red Lacoste jumper with tracksuit bottoms of the four-stripe variety! He was eager to swap numbers and get something on, saying they would bring 15 to 20 lads to meet us at 8 o'clock in a boozer on the seafront.

Confidently we agreed, thinking, 'If they're all like him, then no problem.' At 8 o'clock six of us were in a pub waiting for a few more of our lads to appear.

The next thing we know, thirty-plus Grimsby have walked in. These lads weren't like the scruffy young lad we had seen earlier, but were older, well-dressed lads. At first they saw there were only six of us, so they basically told us to fuck off, but due to a mixture of drink, inexperience and young bravado we didn't fuck off, and for what seemed like ages – but was only seconds – we were dodging pint pots and bottles, and one of the lads' mobile phone case!

Eventually we got out. As I was just getting out of the door I made the mistake of thinking I had done well to get out unscathed when, out of the blue, some cunt hit me over the back of the head with a pint pot! We all managed to get out with a few cuts and bruises between us, but it was our own fault. The scary thing about it was how much I enjoyed it. The adrenaline that was pumping round my body was amazing. People will think, 'How can you enjoy being hit by a pint pot?' but it's the excitement of having a go that makes it worthwhile.

The next day was the day of the match, and I have never seen a mob like it. In fact, it wasn't even one mob, it was three or four. The Grimsby lads were game, but they were simply outnumbered, and if it hadn't been for the police they would have been massacred.

With the decline of Wednesday's fortunes on the pitch there have been numerous other opportunities to visit the seaside. Matches against the likes of Blackpool, Brighton and soon to come Torquay have given the Wednesday faithful many opportunities to sample the sea air. This tale of the Brighton game in 2003–04 comes from the 'Terminator'.

We met up in Brighton town centre on the Friday night, and had a night out with no trouble. I had had a few fights already, but had not been with the main lads until that night. Chris Turner and a few others turned up at the club we were in at about 1.30, but he would end up having to be escorted out after Mooney asked him to get a round. Turner turned and said, 'No, now have a good night and behave yourselves, lads.' This pissed Mooney off and it looked like he was going to do him; close behind him was Miller. I went back to my hotel with the knowledge that we were meeting in Greens Bar at 11 am, and all eyes were on me when I arrived at the pub at 11 with Neil. All the other lads were already there and there were about 15 of us. 'Is this it for lads?' I asked Mooney.

Mooney replied that a few more were on their way but that the 15 already there were all top lads, and we would have no problems. At that point a lad came out of this tattooist next to the pub covered from head to toe in tattoos. I shouted out to him, 'That will teach you to fall asleep in there, pal!'

At about 11.30 the police spotter from Sheffield came in to the pub and did a head count. He passed the usual comment of 'Behave yourselves today, lads, they have got a few out', but did not really give us any hassle, to be fair.

At about 12 Joey sees a couple of lads having a look out the back door of the pub nearby, so it was decided that we would drink up and have a stroll over. Joey went first, with me second, then Neil, Bentley and the rest. After we got in I was thinking to myself 'This is it, we are going to have it.' Joey walks in and about eight or nine lads back off. Joey stares them down and gives the obligatory 'All right, lads?' Quick as anything the OB have run in from the front door, and are pushing us back out of the pub back across the road.

It was a red-hot day and Bentley was a little bemused that I kept hold of my jacket. I explained to him that I had my car keys, house keys, match ticket, petrol money home and phone all in a couple of zip-up pockets, and there was no way I was going to put my coat down just in case it got nicked.

At about 2.30pm one of the older lads and his missus called to say they had found Brighton in a pub near the train station, so calls were made, and off uptown towards the train station we went. Unfortunately the OB soon surrounded us, and roped us into an escort. There had still been no sight of Brighton. Then, just as we were about to get on the train, about twenty or so came into the station, but there were loads of OB about, so no joy. As usual, Wednesday lost the match, and about ten minutes before the end we phoned the Brighton boys to let them know we were on our way out. Ditto – they headed out too. I was now buzzing with excitement – it was such a rush to see their lads at the top of the hill, about thirty of them and about twenty or so of us.

The police were lined up to stop us going up the hill, so the long walk around to the station began on the main road to the station. There were lots of side streets that led up to where their lads were. Then, from nowhere, a couple of their lads came bounding down.

Bentley distracts the OB and gave a few of us the chance to get away. I have still got my sunglasses and jacket on, and my programme in my jacket pocket. About 400 yards down the road I see their lads running up the road. I shout, 'They're here!' and with that Mooney and me start jogging down the road. Mooney is saying, 'Straight into them, pal, no danger.'

I am yelling at the top of my lungs, 'Wednesday! Wednesday! Come on you fuckers!'

There are about four or five of their lads at the front and about another fifteen behind them. The first lad gets swiped away by Mooney. I knock over the next one, but the third lad is more game than the first two. Suddenly from nowhere Boyd arrives out of thin air and puts him down with one punch. It was such a rush; we were getting more organised and had managed to get the upper hand. I went left at the back of a Land Rover and found myself against two lads. I could not get the better of these two lads, just exchanging kicks and punches. The next thing I know Boyd has grabbed hold of me. I felt a whack on my right shin then another. 'Oh fuck,' I thought, 'they are all over us.' I turned to see a copper. I quickly jumped into the newly formed escort. We had been fighting for two or three minutes before they had restored order.

Boyd looks at me and says, 'You're mad, I told you the OB was here.' I never heard him – all I could think about was not letting the Brighton lads get the upper hand. Mooney came over, shook my hand and said, 'Well done, brother, there is always a place for you, kid.' He then went over and told the other lads that I was crackers, and a good lad to have about. On the way home the lads were chatting about the day's events and that new lad who had his jacket and sunglasses on. Mooney gave me the nickname Terminator in honour of my efforts that day.

I made other seaside trips with the lads, but I have only mentioned those that stick most vividly in my mind. The Grimsby trip in 2002 was nothing special in terms of misbehaviour, but it was special to me because I was back at the seaside, and no matter how old I get I will always be drawn to a stroll on the prom.

7

THE WILDERNESS YEARS

At the end of the 1986–87 season we were feeling pretty cocksure of ourselves. We had travelled extensively, and been more than a little successful. Admittedly, the warning signs were there, but it is really only now when I look back that I see them clearly. The biggest indicator was apathy. If I added up all the lads that showed at least once in that season, we would have had a huge firm, but we didn't because for the most part it was the same core faces week in and week out. Once those faces started to drift it was going to be an uphill battle, and drift they did as the 1987–88 season progressed.

No one took much notice of the threat of our neighbours from across the city either. Many old faces believed, as many of us younger lads did, that their mob was a flash-in-the-pan, and we would have no trouble putting them in their place should the need arise. The problem was that the need did arise, and nothing was done. We had continued to drink in town problem free all through the 1986–87 season, but as the year dragged on our turnouts in town became smaller and smaller. By contrast, the BBC shows in town became bigger and more threatening. I'm sure that many Blades would love to say that they took the town from us, but that would not be true. In my mind we gave it away. We could have put on shows of strength when the BBC started turning up, but we didn't for the most part. Now and then there would be a token show, but it was too late, and our ever-decreasing firm started to slink out of town, into back-street boozers and up West Street.

Away from the intra-city strife we lapsed into cosy oblivion. Town was dropped as a meeting place because it became too much 'hassle' to go into the centre and then to Hillsborough. We moved our base of operations to the Rose on Penistone Road, and over the next five or six years it moved again and again. Firstly to Hillsborough Corner, then up to the Travellers on Halifax Road, and then back to Hillsborough Corner, and all the while opposing firms went unopposed.

After the matches, card games in the Rose became the norm. We would sit there and hope that someone came along to give us some sport; instead of going looking for it. In essence we became an invisible firm. We were around, but no one could see us apart from a few infrequent appearances.

Away from home the trips that had been a regular occurrence virtually dried up. In 1987–88 I can only remember two major away days being organised: Derby and Forest. Many of our lads began to find other activities to pass their time. The rise of the 'acid' era took its toll on our mob, as it did with most of the clubs in the country. Another huge problem, which wasn't apparent in 1988 but would begin to show heavily a few years later, was lack of youngsters following us through. By 1993, when I was 25, we were still the 'young 'uns'. Only a handful of youth was coming through. In that five-year period it had become 'fashionable' to be a Blade – if you were a hooligan, that is. I even knew a few

Wednesday who started following United simply because their chances of getting some bollocks were better. The on-field success of Sheffield Wednesday during that period pushed the hooligan element farther and farther into the background too.

By 1988 our firm was a shadow of the Wednesday mob that had rampaged through the 1970s. The rules had changed and it had become difficult to adapt and play the game, so many had simply thought 'fuck it' and gone into an extended state of hibernation. It was difficult to imagine by season's end that less than a decade had passed since the hooligan element of Sheffield Wednesday had made national headlines when they had rioted at Oldham. That day in September 1980 was the pinnacle of the old EBRA.

Stevie remembers the day's events as though they were yesterday:

We arrived early and went in a couple of boozers; as usual back then Wednesday had taken over the place. We saw no Oldham at all before the game, and got in the ground just in time for kick-off. I can't recall anything going off before the incident; it seemed like just an ordinary game of football, when all of a sudden Wednesday's Terry Curran and Oldham's Simon Stainrod (later to briefly play for us) clashed at the Wednesday end. To be honest my memory of it is of a bit of handbags at dawn. Curran lashed out and the ref sent him off.

Now, TC was a big hero at that time, and the Owls fans were incensed that he'd been sent off. We were on the side terrace, along with about thirty other Owls, to the right-hand side of the away end, and we saw big surges from the thousands of fans behind the goal. The Wednesday fans were trying to climb over the fences and get on the pitch. The OB tried to calm things down but made it even worse, and the players were taken off. By now the terracing was being ripped up and thrown at the OB. Crush barriers were pulled from the ground and hurled on to the pitch. We decided to join some other Owls in ripping up the snack bar on the right-hand side of the terrace at the corner of their kop. We completely demolished it, and threw it over the fences at the Oldham fans. We tried getting into the kop, but a combination of the big fence and OB forced us back. To be honest we were at a bit of a loss as to what to do next; we'd trashed the snack bar, and there were no Oldham fans to fight, so we made our way back to the corner of the away end to add our tuppenceworth to the proceedings.

The riot probably lasted about half an hour, and everything but the kitchen sink had been thrown on the pitch. At one point Jack Charlton (the Owls manager at the time) even came out to plead for calm, but he was ignored, and someone hit him on the head with a missile, which didn't please him, but fuck that, this was our day – we're always going to be there, and managers come and go. Eventually order was restored, but more because we got fed up of throwing things and fighting with OB than anything the police did to bring back calm. At the end of the game we all walked out to be greeted by numerous OB, dogs and horses, but it didn't really matter because the moment had gone. There was an almost eerie calm outside the ground.

The FA banned Wednesday fans for the next four away games as punishment, giving us no tickets and stipulating that there'd be no tickets on sale on the day of the match, but we had no problems getting in. People just travelled to the ground midweek and bought them in advance. Swansea *was the first one and not many went. A combination of distance, money and the fact there were no trains back meant only about fifty made the journey, but the locals gave us loads of respect for travelling down and there was no bother.*

The next game at Derby we took about 2,000. Many teams wouldn't have taken that many even without a ban, and there was a bit of bother going back to the station, but Derby were no match for Wednesday back then. Next up was Bristol Rovers, who we had heard were a bit handy. We arrived early on the train and had a good drinking session before making our way to the ground. We had tickets for their kop and about 25 of us went in about 10 minutes before kick-off and stood in the bottom right-hand corner. We were soon spotted and there was a surge down at us from their mob, the majority of whom were skinheads, so we ran back at them and they didn't want to know. They went scampering back like scared rabbits; their bottle had gone in a big way. Then the OB jump in and say they're going to throw us out of the ground, to which one lad said something like, 'You're going to have to physically do it then, because we haven't come all this way for nothing.'

The OB relented and took us to the away end, where there wasn't supposed to be anyone, but there was already a good hundred Owls there, and by the start of the match there were around 250 of us. After the game Rovers didn't want to know and the long walk back to the station was very uneventful.

Last up was Grimsby. This one was a night game, where the pubs before and after the game, and the seats in the ground, were full of Owls. No bother though, but plenty of OB, as they had been expecting us.

The legendary chant from those four games of 'We're Not Here, We're Not Here, We're Not Here' went down in Wednesday folklore.

Looking back, I think the decline started soon after the Oldham game. I certainly noticed a difference in the atmosphere at Hillsborough in the seasons following. The Casual era was dawning, and many of the old faces, who had become household names among us, began to drift away. Others stayed on, but the entire culture was about to undergo a major change, and for many of the campaigners from the 1970s it was game over.

Trouble at Hillsborough began to decline, and I think I really noticed the change at its starkest in April 1982 when I returned to Millmoor to watch a 2-2 draw with a promotion-chasing Rotherham team. This was the infamous night when Tony Towner appeared to take a dive which won Rotherham a penalty, and a point which would ultimately doom Wednesday to another season in Division 2; it was also the night that HMS *Sheffield* went down during the Falklands conflict. There was sporadic fighting on the Tivoli that night, but nowhere near the scale of previous visits. Sheffield Wednesday were now a club on the rise, after years of decline, and the hooligan element fell into a terminal decline.

By 1983–84 the Casuals – or 'Trendies' as we called them back then – had taken over from the old rampaging thugs of the 1970s. Designer label clothing was the rage, and every man and his dog were wearing Pringle jumpers and Puma Vilas trainers. To be honest I don't think it was a style that really gelled well with the Wednesday culture, and I know that quite a few older lads wanted no part of the new breed. The policing was also getting tougher, and large fines and jail time for football violence-related incidents began to deter the old terrace rowdies. By the time I came across the scene in all its glory the metamorphosis was complete. We could still turn a large mob when required, as the 1986 semi-final showed, but by and large tight groups of fifty or sixty became the norm, for Wednesday at least.

The season 1986–87 had been a great time to be part of the new OCS, but the following year really saw us go into freefall. There would still be some top-notch battles, but they became fewer. Instead of being out for every match hunting down our foes we would save it for three or four big games. The after-match trips into town happened later, and later, and sometimes not at all. Many of our number also became involved in the acid-house phenomenon that hit the country in the late 1980s, and would evolve into the rave scene. Many firms saw this happen too, not just us, and the days of the firm looked to be over. The only mob I can recall doing much in this period was that of our neighbours, and that would have serious ramifications for the OCS – but more on that later.

The next couple of seasons saw me involved in very little. If there was stuff going on I wasn't really involved. I had been on the pre-season trip to Scarborough in August of 1987, but I don't really recall travelling very far that year. I would still be found in the Limit on Saturday night, and often on Friday too by now. Precious little was happening on the OCS front, and I needed something to wake me up.

In January 1989 we drew Second Division Blackburn Rovers in the FA Cup. The game was to be played at Ewood Park, and for some reason a major buzz developed around this match. The

Blades had been lording it round town for the past year or so, and it was decided that a trip to Blackburn then straight back into town to sort the Berties would be just what the doctor ordered. Not only did we run a coach ourselves, but the Stocksbridge lads took a mini-bus, and so did the Donny Owls.

This trip was memorable for many reasons. For starters, it was the first time I had travelled for quite a while. Secondly I ended up meeting a 16-year-old character by the name of Evan. This big, lanky youth would go on to become one of my closest friends after Gill and I took him under 'our wing'. The most memorable thing about the entire day, though, was my old chum Gill. We had been out up Stocksbridge the night before, and Gill had got so plastered that he ended up sleeping on a bench near the clock tower. He awoke the next morning with the grand sum of 17p in his pocket, and headed to where the Stocksbridge lads were meeting. He managed to blag his way on to their bus, and went off to Blackburn. Once there he drank all day. He went into the ground, and I last saw him at 10.30 that night – with a fiver in his pocket! I just had to admire the sheer cheek of the lad, and still do.

We met as usual by Sheaf Valley, and it was good to see a full turnout, with more than just the usual couple of older lads. We also stopped near the Howard, and picked up more, including Evan. We had a good sixty or so aboard, and knew that there was likely to be more of our lads milling around in Blackburn town centre.

Upon our arrival we walked straight through the town, down some sort of paved pedestrian area. As we walked, the Stocksbridge lads must have been in a nearby watering hole, and they came out to join us. A couple of spotters were noted as they scooted off. The Stocksbridge chappies told us that they had seen a few likely-looking lads nearby, and we marched eighty-handed toward what we thought was their pub. At the bottom of the pedestrian area we came to a pub with a large glass window. We walked in thinking this was their place, but found it to be empty. A couple of lads went for a wander and came back with the news that the Blackburn firm – well, it was more of a large group – were in the pub opposite, but numbered no more than a dozen. We decided to stay put. Eighty of us attacking twelve was not deemed acceptable at that time, though sadly it seems quite the norm these days with many mobs, from what I hear.

The two pubs were divided by a busy section of road with railings at the side of the pavement. There was a fish and chip shop next door to the Blackburn pub, and our lads started heading over to get food. The large glass window gave us a good view of any potential flash point, but none was forthcoming. In fact, it was looking like a quiet day.

I had not noticed much of a gathering of Rovers supporters, but something must have stirred them into action because out of the blue a few of them came out of the pub, and attacked Steve Bowen, Sash and a couple of others in the chippy. Quick as a flash we emptied into the street. The shout went up, and the Blackburn lads looked like deer caught in headlights. I still don't understand why they did what they did in full view of us all. Surely they knew we were mob-handed across the street?

They broke back toward their pub, but a couple got cut off. One got caught and took a bit of a kicking. The other was not so lucky! He leapt the railings and landed in the road, just as a Post Office van rounded the corner. SMACK! The sight of this unfortunate youth being hit by the van cooled proceedings. A few of ours went to try and help him, because no matter what people may think, we do not wish anyone to be killed. The majority of us decided it would be wise to vacate the scene, as sirens were heard in the distance. Sash and a couple of others waited with the lad, and ended up being arrested for their trouble. A story went around that he had died, but thankfully that turned out to be just a rumour.

We moved up to another pub near the ground, and some of our more opportunistic characters decided to liberate the pub cellar of its contents. The booty was shared liberally around outside, and Gill was particularly keen to show me his jacket full of beer. As kick-off neared we decided to head for the ground, and enter the home end. This was actually a first for me, because although I had gone in Luton's end with Dawesy a few years previously, I had never gone in with a group of lads looking to pull a few strokes.

We entered the end and made our way through the crowd, coming to rest about a third of the way up. The old Wednesday wave was then given to the away end, but the nature of Wednesday's support had changed so much by 1989 that no wave was returned. Many Blackburn fans looked on, but did nothing. Here we were, 80 strong in their end, and they just watched us.

The teams came out and we cheered the Owls on to the pitch. By now a few of the more alert Lancastrians had moved down toward us. Timmy went over for a few words, which I would imagine went something along the lines of, 'We're here in your kop. What you going to do about it?'

I watched as Timmy turned round, laughing at the Rovers fan's reaction.

'He says to wait till half-time because they don't have enough to do anything!'

We all started laughing at the poor old Blackburn 'firm'. We may have gone severely downhill in the past couple of years, but nothing could compare to this limp response. A number of Blackburn 'shirts' were now yelling to the police that we were Wednesday and to get us 'oot'.

The police duly arrived and escorted us around the pitch. OK, we didn't do anything either, but there really was no one to fight with. As we were taken round the pitch Blackburn had the temerity to score, prompting one young lad from Stocksbridge to try and run on to the pitch. He was promptly arrested.

I saw Phil and a few other lads from out Derbyshire way in the away end. He asked what had gone on, and I had to give him my truthful reply.

'Fuck all, mate, they were wank.'

After the match we headed straight for home, our destination being West Street. The Beeb had been making a nuisance of themselves up there in the weeks preceding, and a show was called for.

We met up in a pub just off West Street when we returned, but the police were on to us and turfed us out. As I was walking with Gill toward the Mailcoach, a police car pulled up and a uniformed officer beckoned us over. 'If I see you cunts tonight we won't nick you, we will kick the fuck out of you.' I can remember thinking, 'If PC Plod had spoken like that to Noddy it would have turned Big Ears' large lugs bright red.'

Gill had had enough by now and headed off home. I hung around for a couple more drinks, but the police presence was absolutely stifling, and by ten I, too, had had enough, and headed off for Hillsborough Corner.

There was some fighting later in the night I believe, but I didn't see anything. It had been an interesting day, with a number of talking points, and we had shown that we could still turn out a half-decent firm when we put our minds to it.

To be quite honest, though, that was about the only real day out that I can remember for the couple of seasons after 1986–87. It's hardly surprising: the football on offer was rapidly deteriorating, and the bright new dawn of Howard Wilkinson was turning into a drizzly afternoon. The music scene of the time brought with it the lure of easily affordable drugs, and I was not going to turn the other cheek. During this time I became very disillusioned with the entire football scene. I would still be out with what lads there were on Saturday night, but I needed a new chemical stimulant, and I wasn't alone. Ecstasy, acid and speed became very good friends of mine. I remember one night around this time when thirty of us were sat waiting in Silks for the lad who supplied many of us to come in. He was usually in for 6pm, but this night he was late. We sat waiting, and the mood grew impatient.

'Where the fuck are our drugs?' was the general cry, as the promise of a miserable drug-free night stared blankly into our faces. His arrival, an hour or so late, was greeted with such a sense of euphoria that you would have thought he had put a thousand pounds behind the bar for us all to sup on.

Eventually I even stopped going near Hillsborough on a Saturday afternoon. My run of never missing a game in seven years came to an end in October 1987, and I didn't care. The young lad who hated to miss a game, and even attended silly County Cup matches, had grown up, and football was fast becoming an irrelevance.

While researching dates for this book I looked at the fixtures for the seasons 1987–88 and 1988–89, and I can hardly remember a single match. Maybe stuff did kick off, although I doubt it, but I had lost interest. My major concern was finding something a touch more powerful than alcohol to fuel my

Saturday nights. One funny little football-related story that does stick in my head concerns a match at home to Arsenal during this period. I had dropped a trip with Laver in the Bell at lunchtime. Instead of going to the match I headed down to Gill's – he lived a stone's throw from the ground – and sat in his front room all afternoon, no doubt talking absolute bollocks! After watching the result come in we decided to have a wander down the Rose to see who was out. As we came down Parkside Road I remember seeing Sash going past in a car, waving. He was shouting for us to get down to the Rose, which was fair enough because we were going that way anyway. When we reached Owlerton Green, Sash was suddenly there with us.

'A big firm of Arsenal is attacking the Rose,' he gasped.

I peered along Penistone Road, and didn't notice anything out of the ordinary, but I thought I'd best humour him.

'Let's fucking get down there then,' I replied.

I looked at Gill and he was as puzzled as I was. I think we both thought Sash must have been on something, but we headed off at a brisk pace toward the pub. About twenty yards away we saw about ten Arsenal fans in shirts being turned away from the doors. Quick as a flash Sash was bending over and picking tiny stones off the floor.

'Lets brick the cunts!' he shouted.

This was too much, and Gill and I just fell about laughing as Sash ran up the road throwing pebbles at the bemused Arsenal fans. A few seconds later Sash came racing past us as a police van pulled up along the kerb. We followed him back toward Owlerton Green, and had a breather on the bridge.

'What the fuck were you doing, Sash?' I asked

'Trying to brick the bastards!'

'Why were you throwing pebbles then?' said Gill.

No reply was forthcoming. Then, Sash spotted a group walking by.

'Where the fuck are you from?' he asked the likeliest looking lad.

'Worksop, mate,' said the youth, in a broad cockney accent.

Upon hearing the accent Sash kicked the youth up the arse. Dust seemed to fly out, and I covered my face, before collapsing into hysterics. He was good company, was Sash. Spoke perfect English until about nine at night, by which time he had usually descended into gobbledygook, but he would do anything for you and was Wednesday through and through. He still is, and will be until the day he dies.

Drugs took a heavy toll on our mob. Both Scribs and Tin-Tin would meet untimely ends indirectly from drug use. Others would suffer overdoses, or bad experiences, and the heart of our firm was torn out as hunting E's became more important than hunting Blades. My football memories from that two-year period are few, but my memories of heavy drinking and drug taking are plentiful. There were many, many fun-filled nights back then, but at what cost? I don't think it really registered with me until the night I found myself lying in an alleyway off Trippet Lane after a day of booze and acid. Even then, though, it didn't slow me down; I simply made an effort to not overdo things so much. It was a crazy time and the music reflected that. Songs by artists such as D Mob, Jolly Roger and Inner City fuelled the acid fires that were burning in so many of us at the time. I remember being mesmerised by the song 'Voodoo Ray' when I first heard it in a Southsea nightclub. Upon my return to Sheffield Gill and I hunted high and low for the record, but to no avail until Maggot, an old leather-faced Blade from down Hillsborough, told us the name of the song and the artist. We had been hunting round the record shops humming the song to people, so it was no wonder we had little luck.

Another favourite tipple of the time was magic mushrooms, and these grew in plentiful supply round Sheffield, especially in the fields around Stocksbridge. One night, while stoned on mushrooms, Gill and I walked into the Freemasons on Hillsborough Corner, and Gill freaked out upon hearing that bloody Womack and Womack song that was popular at the time. For no good reason, he then decided we had to walk all the way to Oughtibridge, which was a good three miles away, in the pouring rain. I managed to divert him into the Horse and Jockey at Wadsley after we had stopped at a nearby fish and chip shop, where I found myself greatly confused by the shop policy of not selling chip butties. That, added to the fact that the guy behind the counter seemed to move around on wheels and had no face, made us realise that we needed some human contact to convince us that we were not going mental. This would turn out to be a big mistake. Inside the pub we ran into Dick, who was one of our older lads, and Crookesy, a non-hooligan Wednesday fan from Wisewood. They were chatting with an old geezer, who kept rattling on about how he had been in the Boer War. Dick and Crookesy hung on his every word, and also talked about ... shoes. Gill and I could not stop laughing. I swear I almost literally pissed my pants, I found the entire situation so funny.

We rolled out of the pub and laughed all the way down the road to Gill's house, where we proceeded to laugh some more while staring at the ceiling. There were many more nights of supreme hilarity during that couple of years, although there were also some very sad ones too. I look back now with a great deal of fondness on those days, but would never encourage anyone to take drugs. I was very lucky that my body could stand up to it, but many young people cannot handle drugs, and should steer clear. The toll taken on youths across the world from drug-related incidents, both from taking or dealing, is far too high. One drug-related death is one too many. Good times come from the heart, not from a pill.

What of the football, though? The sporting pursuits, which I had yearned after since I was a nipper, were now very much placed behind drugs and music. Mind you, like I said before, the football on offer was mediocre to say the least. I had forgotten that the likes of David Hodgson, Tony Galvin and David Reeves had made fleeting appearances in the blue and white stripes during those seasons. It wasn't long before Wilkinson took his bag of tricks up the M1 to Elland Road, and we got Peter 'Useless' Eustace for a manager. He didn't last long, though, and soon it was time for 'Big' Ron Atkinson to take the helm. He kept us up in 1988–89 with some astute signings, and when Steve Whitton headed the winner against Middlesbrough everyone believed better days were on the horizon.

We had something of a firm out at that Middlesbrough match. Greggy and Bowen had confronted their mob on Parkside Road. Middlesbrough have always been a very handy mob, easily up there with the big boys, but even they were going through a downsizing at the time. The 'Boro lads held their hands up before the match, telling us to wait until after and they would come down for us. An agreement of sorts was reached, and we headed into the uncovered seats. Some 'Boro firm were in there, and small-scale scuffles broke out continually. After the match they were true to their word, and we eventually ran into them down on Penistone Road. They only had a small mob, which was fine, because so did we. At first we had them off, but by the corner of Rutland Road they made a stand.

Far away from the trials and tribulations of the endless OCS–BBC struggle, Paul soaks up the Canadian sunshine Easter 2004.

Top: An OCS-ITI calling card from 2002.

Above: The Rose Inn on Penistone Road was the base of operations throughout much of the mid to late 80s. The pub finally closed in 1995 and was demolished.

Top: The trip to Grimsby in 2002 saw a large OCS firm descend on the seaside town of Cleesthorpes. Running battles with locals and police made newspaper headlines. Here is a picture taken from one of two police escorts that were running concurrently.

Above: The large travelling support at Grimsby meant that fans were lined around the pitch.

Top: No love is ever lost between Wednesday and United in the steel city. Here we see an 'altered' advertising hoarding close to Hillsborough to show a pig sporting United's red and white strip.

Above: Returning from a very eventful trip to Great Yarmouth in April of 1987. Now where did I leave that hat?

Inset: Our graphic talent turned towards ourselves – this design adorned t-shirts produced in 1986 by one of Wednesday's top boys.

Top: En-route with Stockbridge Owls to Skegness – 1989.

Above: Outside the Manhattan Bar later on in Skegness.

Top: Wednesday boys soaking up some Portuguese sun during Euro 2004.

Above: The Old Blue Ball in Hillsborough. This pub was Paul's local from the age of 16.

Top: Wednesday and Bristol youth goad one another inside Ashton Gate.

Above: Wednesday lads attempt to break the police escort in Bristol 2003.

The Detroit skyline now makes a perfect backdrop for me. Here's to the past, present and future and a speedy return to the Premiership. Up the Owls.

Greggy was straight into them, and they came straight back and kicks and punches were exchanged between the groups. For a few moments the fists and boots flew between the traffic heading to town. It didn't last long, though, as the police quickly arrived and ushered the Middlesbrough fans along. Our little group was held at a bus stop, and we were all searched and made to show our hands to the boys in blue.

'This is them lot that have been throwing rocks,' said the big fat sergeant as we held our mitts out. He walked down the line examining our hands. It felt like we were back in school. We were eventually told off like little boys, and made our way into town where a nice cold pint of Sam Smiths awaited us at the Compleat Angler, safe in the knowledge that the Owls had dodged the bullet and the only way was up from here.

During the summer of 1989 Gill found himself kicked out of his home after headbutting his dad. He came to stay with me for a while, but the situation was not ideal. Then one day we happened to bump into Anwar. He was now working as a labourer for some lad who owned a paving company. Amazingly Anwar claimed to be a co-owner of the business, and we believed him. He was quite the character, was Anwar. He had attended Myers Grove School like me, but was a year or two older. It seemed as though he had sat in every desk in the school, because his name was on them all. I had not seen him for a couple of years after he left school until I found out he was now a member of the Wednesday firm, even though he supported Leeds. As I mentioned earlier, I had got to know him quite well, and had even stood as a witness for him in Liverpool after he had been arrested a couple of years previously.

Anwar was also looking for somewhere to rest his head, and had seen a nice flat above a hairdresser's on Toyne Street, Crookes. He couldn't afford to live there on his own – well, he said he could, but it transpired that he couldn't. The three of us moved in together, and so began my association with that amazing anomaly of Sheffield football violence: the Crookes Service Crew (CSC).

The CSC was practically unique in the terrace culture of Sheffield in that its members were a mix of OCS and BBC; to my knowledge only the Springwood mob could rival us in that regard. I even had a tattoo done in blue and red to reflect the two groups. All the lads in the CSC either lived around Crookes or travelled to drink there. From the OCS side we had the Delaney brothers, Dob, Laver, Tyzack, Anwar, Steve Bowen, Jay Taylor, Gill and myself. The Beeb supplied Black Lloyd and his brothers, Baz, Shots, Pricey, Mitchell and Joe among others. The cast often changed, however, and on many occasions other OCS or BBC lads would venture forth. Evan, for example, became a regular visitor to the Punchbowl. Joe was undoubtedly the main face up there though, and rightly so. He was an older Blade of fine repute. Indeed, he was held in such reverence that he had regularly come out down town with Mick and the older Wednesday lads for years. He had been coming out with us for some time before I even realised he was a Bertie.

That summer was a blast. We would regularly sit up all night skinning three-foot-long joints, and laughing at the shite served up on the fledgling Sky satellite service. Anwar came in one day with big bags of weed, and hid them behind a picture that he had hanging on the wall. He thought that no one knew about them, but everyone did, and regular dips were made by all and sundry when he was out. The poor lad was totally bemused by the fact that his 'hidden' weed was disappearing faster than a Rotherham firm at Millmoor.

The sense of camaraderie we enjoyed up on Crookes was

unmatched – we were a tight unit, and even though I was fairly new to some of the lads up there they really made me feel welcome. The nights we spent in the Punchbowl and Ball were some of the best I have ever had, and even though I didn't get to bed until 4am most nights I enjoyed every minute. The only real blip during the months I spent on Crookes was when a main face in the BBC got a little perturbed that Baz was hanging around with Gill and I. Baz got a clip in Silks one night from this individual, and was told that a mob of Blades would be coming on Crookes to sort us out. To his credit Baz didn't let it affect him, and no mob ever showed.

As the first day of the 1989–90 season dawned I doubt many people in Sheffield expected to see the two city clubs swap divisions, as United became Sheffield's higher-ranked club for the first time in a decade. That first day I didn't go to watch Wednesday play Norwich. I was out with the Crookes lads, and a day of mayhem was on the cards. Much of my memory from that day is fuzzy, due to the vast amounts of alcohol consumed, but I know that the day had been largely peaceful until we appeared on the Wicker sometime after 4pm. As we walked up toward Bridge Street a similarly sized group of greasy bastards passed us. As they went by I looked round, to see one spit in the direction of Tyzack.

'Hey up, Ty,' I said, 'that greasy twat just spat at you.'

Tyzack was incensed, and ran over to stick the nut on the offending greaser. The others started flapping and didn't know what to do. I spotted a big bastard, ran up and – jumping up to reach him – planted him a beauty right on the chin. He wobbled and I hit him again. This time he went down like a sack of spuds. The other lads were busy mopping up the rest, and all had had a fun time. All except the greasy bastards, but then again they should know not to do things like that.

We then ventured down to the Rose. Wednesday had lost 2-0 and it was fairly quiet in there. Baz had been a little wary about going in, which was understandable, but we only stopped for one before heading out again; this time to the White Rails at Upperthorpe. Eventually we reached the Old Grindstone at Crookes and settled in for a session. Everything was going well in the Grindstone until the landlord tried to throw Baz out for spitting on the floor. I began to remonstrate about the unfairness of such an action, but then things took a turn for the worse. Out of the blue a group of lads standing next to me at the bar decided to have their say, and this greatly offended me. What made it worse was the fact that they were all dressed up in musketeer costumes. I remember considering my options for a second or two, and I then made a clear decision based on the circumstances as I saw them. I won't go into specific details, but let's just say that the musketeers were well and truly put to the sword.

A number of people were arrested for the night's activities, including Gill, Stan and Baz, but I don't think any charges were ever brought, and the matter faded away over time.

I decided I had best lie low for a while. Not long afterwards I moved away from Crookes, and I have never been back to drink, but I remember those days like they were yesterday, and the Crookes Service Crew will always be a part of me.

Dougie comes from a small estate a stone's throw from Hillsborough. The Winn Gardens is a hotbed of Sheffield Wednesdayism, and even though it is only a small estate, it has quite the reputation. Gill had moved to Hillsborough from Stocksbridge in the early 1980s, and he had formed friendships with many of the Winn Gardens lads, so from that point of view he is probably better suited to talk about Dougie and his mob, but I know of them by reputation, and finally got to know some of them in the early 1990s.

Over the last half of this book, I'll allow Dougie to recount a few tales from his own years of following the Owls. Many times the lads from the Gardens would be within the OCS, but many times they would not. They liked to do their own thing ...

Skunk and Leicester: 1991

We're out with the firm today, half a dozen Gardens lads mixing with the rest of the OCS, or what's left of the dwindling numbers, but there's a good crew of forty or so, and even though Leicester are top ten, or even five, the nerves aren't jangling. Mind you, the old skunk might have something to do with that.

Early train to Leicester, and it's got a bar. Fucking expensive, though – are my dollars going to stretch the distance? I'm out of work and my fashion sense is slipping, clothes and beer are a luxury, but I've manoeuvred a ten spot from our gurt's purse and I'm sure she will understand.

We've no arranged meet with the Babies but I'm sure they will find us. They know we're coming and heading straight for the town centre. We're off the train and there are no police in sight, so we freely walk up towards the town, where we are met by some quaint little drammers and it's all eyes on the South Yorkshire drinking firm as we make our way through the Saturday shoppers. By now, though, I'm certain that some spotter from Leicester is on our case, from boozer to boozer, and spliff to spliff. We land in an empty drammer, and my first thoughts are that it's strangely quiet for a Saturday, especially so close to the ground.

We're inside swilling ale and playing the odd game of pool,

totally unaware that the squad was on our tail, until four of the cunts come through the doors and politely ask us to take to the streets. Obligingly we chase them through the doors and up a quiet little backstreet, only to be met by a well-organised firm with sticks and bottles. I don't recall the numbers involved, but it was alive with the fuckers. Leicester at their best, and we're running towards them, but we're not all out of the boozer doors, and the few numbers that make it towards their front line are no match for their quality lads. I look round to see our lads running back to the safety of the boozer, and with Leicester nearly toe to toe it's time to leave the scene and join the rest in the dram shop we had left. There are a few skirmishes in the doorway, but we're always backing off until we group up by the door. They're not coming in, but then again we are going nowhere.

By now the landlord is becoming a bit concerned, but I think the cunt is part of the ambush. He appeals to us, 'Please don't smash my pub up', and on that note a large lump of concrete comes flying through the window and lands near my feet. Normally at this point I would be fully on my toes, but the weed's kicking in and giving me false impressions of the day's events. I'm generally confused and just want to chill out, but there is a firm outside that's game and dangerous. The safety of the four walls feels calming until yet another window comes through, and one of ours decides that pool balls make for good target practice. He starts throwing them through the window aiming at the heads that keep glancing through. They are coming forward in numbers now, so we decide to go through the door.

We are all up and pushing forward, and shouting whatever springs to mind, but it's a negative move and their onslaught keeps us in the building. They keep running at the door, but we've got some good lads standing and they make no progress.

After a few onslaughts the police arrive, split the crowd up, and enter the boozer. They decide to give us a police escort to the ground, where our 4-2 victory stood for nothing as off the field Leicester got the result today.

Leaving the ground, and after a short walk, we almost had the chance to change the result slightly. We see their lads leaving a wedding register place, obviously not attending the game, but still turned out to have a pop at us, so we make our way towards them. We shout the odds and run towards them, but the police are on the case. They block the entrance, and beat us back towards the train station, where they prevent another skirmish with a few hangers-on. Leicester, with numbers or without, seem keen to get a result and I've got to hand it to them they're a well-organised firm not to be taken lightly. I'm sure that on my next visit to their fair city they will get the respect they deserve.

Barnsley: 1991

The 11 o'clock train should give us plenty of time for a drink; a full crew can't resist this one. License to thrill, I think. It's a nearly home game with boozers that don't know us. We're at the station and it's days of all round as this is a midweek match, and deserves nothing less than a piss-up with the chance of a skirmish or two. About eight of us board the train, and we're off to Barnsley with a plain-clothes police presence – easy to spot, as they were the smart types, and we thank them for their concern.

No time at all and we're on the platform in sunny Barnsley. Marching towards the town centre and we find a nice little boozer, only its one of theirs, and the landlord politely puts us in the picture. It's early, and he gives us directions to another address with the same facilities on the Sheffield Road, where we spend the rest of the afternoon. It's all ours. It's seedy and it's nice, with all the home comforts: beer, crisps and nuts. The nuts you couldn't eat, as they were old Barnsley types who had been drinking since they were born, and had about a week to live. They are the oldest folk that drink and piss normally, but they make us welcome and keep feeding the jukebox. An hour later and a few of ours are dancing with the ladies among them, with the gents not caring at all until one of ours takes a fancy to the 80-year-old with her dress pulled up to her liberty body bottom. Who could blame him? Twelve Newky's does strange things to the mind – it's got to – and he's in there, full-blown necking and dancing. For a split second a small amount of sick appears in my mouth as I view the free show, but with that I swill it down with a drop of the brown stuff, and the party continues with all her fucking mates up giving us the eye. I haven't had a wank for a week and my balls are busting, but I decline the offers as my mate pushes me aside and takes to the floor with his bride to be. It's got to the stage of show us your tits for a half, and the hats going round; at this point a few more Wednesday lads appear, and sit for a while not quite understanding the afternoon's events. It doesn't take long and we're all singing, a mixture of jukebox and Wednesday songs.

Out of the corner of my eye I see a small group of youths walking across the makeshift dance floor. They're not with us and they are not Wednesday. One lad stands out more than the others. He's got long blond hair in the curtain fashion cut. They disappear through the back door, and as they do our young 'un shouts 'Move!' I'm sat under the window, and I just manage to leave my seat as the glass rains in. Barnsley are here, nice, as we head for the door. There's only eight of us as the other Wednesday move towards the bar area. They're outside lobbing stuff from the grass bank across the road, and the odd brave fucker keeps running up to the door, with fifty or so behind him, so we're outsideish. About six lads get through, and the bouncer and the landlord manage to get the door shut, I'm inside and I can see Barnsley across the road through the broken window, and our lads are beckoning them down. There is no way out, so I decide to put the window through with a stool conveniently to my right. This changes things slightly and the doors are open. Now there are eight of us outside and we're running at the cunts. It's pitch black, raining, we're bolloxed, and the silly bastards are backing away. After a few swings, the odd fall-down, and plenty of shouting, they're off. I look round and there's a nice little crew of our lads 'proper' running down the road towards us. They had just had a go with these cunts earlier. We head back to the boozer, but it's a big fuck-off from the landlord. We argue our case that we were the innocent party, but he's having none of it, and points out the reason why: half the boozer, chairs and all, is strewn across the street.

Oldham: 1991

Last game and we're up, but I think with the help of maths we could possibly win it. Tickets for this one haven't been the easiest, and I reckon there's a fair few travelling without, but with the aid of a season ticket I'm virtually guaranteed one, and our young 'un has the same pleasure. The travel arrangements have changed slightly as we decide to jolly boy with the local boozer and their older following but still game as fuck, and up for any Oldham firm that may get in our way. I'm outside the Park Hotel with the usual firm that travels together week in week out, waiting for the 56-seater. I'm armed with a ticket but not all our lads are sporting the full away version, and with this news I'm trying to swap mine with the odd neutral type that's just showing off, but me and my brother are shown the door and have to except the legit ticket which is slightly disappointing, as a walk on the Oldham side could have been the order.

All aboard and the Woodhead beckons, there's a lot of chit-chat on the bus – I think the odd one or two are bottling it and are not as confident as they were in Sheff now we're reaching Oldham, so I walk the mile and get the result I wanted: a nice pair of tickets for theirs. No disrespect to Oldham, but I fancy this one and so does the rest of the WGA. Some Park Hotel-type organised a boozer visit for us – it's a mate or somat and we've got to behave. No blow – now, this is going to be difficult, as our youth's little firm are constantly burning and the aroma gives it away slightly, so there's a bit of a fall-out as the snooker room fogs over – but with respect and all that, the lads and occasionally myself vacate the building to appreciate the finer things in life. It's getting nearer to kick-off and the adrenaline is starting to go a bit. The atmosphere is calm, and in my head I've got a plan: get in and near the front because its going to go and you've got to admit you need accesses – I know this from a bit of previous.

By now the drink's kicking in and the moods getting a bit more heated. As we leave the boozer it's a case of 'Bring on Oldham'. We're all staying close as we approach the turnstiles in small groups. Personally, now I just want in and to see the lads run out. I hand over the contraband ticket. It's too late now, we're in and walking through the top of their kop, probably twenty or so – the full WGA membership – and a few guest members. It's strange – seven thousand or so regulars standing in their own little spot and I'm making my way to the front to the right of the net. In front of me is one of ours who doesn't give a fuck, who fears no one or anything. I can't say enough about this lad – he is the main actor and 'respect' isn't a strong enough word for him.

We're now at the front and I look back at the Oldham heads – they haven't a clue as the numbers grow at the front. I look to my right as a Donny accent gives a lad away – and he's got a few mates. I can see him putting his pin badge on, and after the odd nod and a wink it's obvious that there's a small army of ours on here now and we're shoulder to shoulder. It's clear to me that the odd one or two keep looking round, as we're swamped by the slightly intimidating Oldham fans in full voice. The whistle blows and we're off.

Oldham's singing, but we're not. I swear to God at some point we're going to score, and we do. You had to be there to appreciate the celebrations a quality group of OCS going fucking mental can whip up, and there's nothing anyone can do about it; it's like Sham 69, late 1970s, Top Rank with all the same danger levels. We've made ourselves welcome without the invitation. There are gaps in the crowd now as people push together; it's them and us. I'm trying to gather my thoughts as another goes in and we repeat the celebrations, only this time we've got company, and one of ours feels the full force. We're still jumping, and yes, they're into us. Only the wall at the bottom is five feet high. My access plans are a bit out of the window and we're trapped at the bottom.

At first things seem to be going our way, as they back off, but that's premature. If you fall down now you're dead. I'm trying to get my head down as the punches rain down on us. I'm windmilling like the rest and at some point I'm out of here. I jump at the wall and bounce back. Queensbury rules apply, which is the crawl version of swimming, and then another attempt at the wall, and I'm over with the rest. Fuck me shitless they've ruffled my hair, and so I politely rod them as I walk away. I forgot there's a game on and the ref's stopped it. We're walking across the plastic pitch, and both sets of players are giving us the evil eye. The ref looks worried as we're walking across the pitch to the chorus of 'We're proud of you!' and the famous 'Wednesday aggro!' I'm heading for the fence with the rest, as I see the police trying to vacate ours out of a side entrance, so we run for the fence avoiding the awaiting police, one big leap and I'm halfway across, my arms on one side and my legs on the other, the helpful Wednesday lads win the tug of war against the OB and I fall into the crowd – only to see our lads dip and Oldham take the spoils.

Back to haunt us – Villa: 1991

The big lad's back and I'm worried, but at least we had the pleasure. Big Ron's at Hillsborough, but the dugout's changed, from blue and white to the claret version. Colours mean nothing, I still love the lummox, but the favours that I think he owes us are going to be few and far between. Big game today and our lads are out on the march with a point to prove: WE HATE VILLA.

We're all out for this one and only the best seats will do. South Stand next to the Villa-faced cunts. We're milling about before the game, but there's no action. I'm a little disappointed, but we've got company today: one of our lads moved to Boston (Lincolnshire) a few years ago, and has turned up with a few of his flower-picking mates; they're not ITK, and not quite normal. They seem a bit straight-laced and down to earth, which takes a bit of getting used to, but they like a drink and that will do. Park Hotel takes most of our well-earned, and then the match.

We're walking down Leppings Lane and Villa's hanging around. They look a bit menacing and definitely up for it. By now they're behind us as well as we approach the bridge. Fuck it, they're on our patch, so we're into them, and they return the favour. It doesn't last long due the police presence; one of ours is locked up, and I think a few have got knocks, but at least I've clocked a few faces, for later. They've got some lads out today; a good firm of probably a hundred, which doesn't really surprise me.

We're in the ground, and we can't lose this one; it's not allowed. It's 2-0 and we're giving it them. I can't see their lads properly – I think their in the top tier, well at least that's where the chorus of 'No Surrender!' was coming from, and in them days, you had to be top to sing it. It's 3-2 Villa, and the noise from the west is unbearable. Ninety minutes is up; thank fuck. I know it's my duty to knock one of these cunts out.

We leave the South and head straight to Leppings Lane, where I can see Villa leaving, but the police are everywhere, so being patient today could mean we get a result. Halfway up Leppings Lane and I can't wait. There's a small army of Villa singing with their back to us, and one lad's got a pot on his arm. He's not looking my way. It's not brave, but I let the bastard have one, and he's not gone down.

'What a fucking wank punch,' I think to myself.

I had too much time to think about it. I hope the others are having more success, as I see one of ours tussling and falling about a bit. They're on the run and, yes, so are we. Eight of us now, but we're ready for anything, so we chase them up Wadsley Lane where we are met by a small army on the end of Dixon: a mixture of shirts and lads. They're standing, so let's have it. They're not quite aggressive enough and can't cope with the onslaught, and they disappear.

We're walking up Wadsley Lane and our lads decide to leave.

The Boston types are a bit confused by now and just want to go home. I decide to get in their car for a nice little lift to the Penguin. We're in a jam on Wadsley Lane; I'm on the back seat with my mate on one side and his Boston pal on the other, the driver is an old Wednesday lad also living in Lincolnshire, and his younger brother beside him. A few feet later and me and my mate are out, threatening a few loud-mouthed Villa boys, but they don't want to know, so we leave it. Two hundred yards later and we're near the Horse and Jockey and outside are three or four white transits, not to mention fifty or sixty lads. The little crew that we had run about quite easily, only this time they had multiplied, and worse of all they had spotted our Peugeot hire car from Boston. We're bumper to bumper, and going nowhere.

'Bollocks.' They've seen us, and guess what? They're running our way!

By this time my thoughts would be obvious to anyone who's been involved in this situation: 'I am going to die.' But I'm laughing, probably out of fear. By this time all I can see is a swarm of wasps all round the car, and we're going nowhere. First thing to go are the windows, every fucking one of them. Glass is everywhere, and then shoes and fists appear. They look a bit pissed off. I look forward and the driver, who's no lightweight, is yelling, and asking why he's receiving a large velocity of punches to his right cheek. I can't believe his innocence, and this makes me laugh a bit more. By now they are trying to drag us out; I swear to God I owe my life to the driver, as he copes with the punishment and managers to manoeuvre the car out of the traffic back down Wadsley Lane.

I look over my shoulder and see the frantic crowd of Villa disappear. Can you imagine the relief? I'm alive, but the hire car from Boston is on its last legs. We get to the Park Hotel car park and stand next to the wreck. It's not drivable, especially not for 80 miles plus. Every panel and window has gone. A few phone calls later and they've got a replacement. Trouble is, it's going to be two hours. I persuade them to drop me off at the Penguin, and change the car over there as our lass is waiting outside having a drink with her family, and our newborn child. It turns a few heads from the numbers outside the dram shop, as the car from hell pulls up, and the lucky five walk free – the three from Boston shocked as you like. I can remember thinking about leaving the car, still three hours till closing …

8

LONDON CALLING

As one of the largest cities in the world, London is home to a teeming melting pot of cultures and races – a reminder that this old town was once the centre of an empire on which it was thought that the sun would never set. Today it is a vibrant metropolis with a history to be proud of. Say what you may about the city and its inhabitants, but it is the capital city of England, and we are grudgingly proud of it.

It is also a major centre for professional football with no less than eleven clubs plying their trade in the English football leagues at the present time. I do not include Wimbledon (now Milton Keynes Dons) in that list since they have gone the American way and franchised themselves out to Milton Keynes, and the day they did that another nail was hammered into the coffin of the game that we love.

Historically the two clubs from north London – Arsenal and Tottenham – have been powerhouses of the English game, followed not far behind by the west London aristocrats of Chelsea, and the graceful footballing style of the East Enders, West Ham United. From the 1960s right through to the present day London clubs, particularly Arsenal, have conducted successful footballing campaigns at home and abroad.

Off the field the name of a certain club from south London brings a sweat to many a brow. Millwall is a club that has been synonymous with the darker side of football for decades. They have terrorised even the stoutest of men who have dared to venture into the Lions' Den. Throughout the 1970s and 1980s Millwall conducted successful campaigns off the field, and along with their hated London rivals – West Ham – they made up one of the two most feared football firms in the country. Sadly, or perhaps fortunately, my path rarely crossed either of these two clubs.

I have recounted my encounters with the mighty ICF of West Ham, and to be frank they were easily a different class to us on their day, as they were to the majority of firms the length and breadth of the country. I saw us do well against them in little spats here and there, but I am not foolhardy enough to believe that if the full weight of the Inter-City Firm had come against us that we could have lived with it.

My experiences with Millwall have been even less frequent. During the 1980s we were in different divisions, and by the time we did meet up with them again, toward the end of the 1980s, a rivalry that had simmered during the 1970s had cooled off as we headed into rapid decline. It hadn't always been that way, and during the 1970s Wednesday had fought out some major battles with Millwall. Even the Millwall lads I met in Majorca in 1983 admitted to a healthy respect for the Wednesday firms of the mid-1970s.

Many older Owls lads still speak today of the day Millwall tried to take the kop at Hillsborough, and the battle that ensued as the Sheffielders fought to hold on to the East Bank. Millwall had gotten in early, and set themselves up right at the back of the kop, and it took a massive effort from a far larger Wednesday mob to eventually shift them out. I hand it over to Stevie again to tell the story of another major clash between the Owls and Lions, but this time on neutral ground:

We had some great days out that first season in Division Three. The game at Brighton was like a mini Southend, with about 500 of us stopping the night, but probably the most violent one I saw was Saturday, 3 January 1976, Charlton away in the FA Cup Third Round. Again we travelled by SUT coaches (only the 1970s versions of Scrapers travelled on the Supporters Club buses), though the fact that the coach company was called 'Sheffield United Travel' used to raise a few eyebrows among opposing fans. We got there about noon and went in a pub about ten minutes down the road from the ground. The pub was memorable only for providing the worst pint of bitter I've ever had in my life.

We walked up to the ground and went on that massive side terrace that they used to have at The Valley. Charlton were behind the net and there was a rope and about ten OB separating them from us on the side terrace. We ran at the cordon of OB and most of us got through. There was a battle for about a minute, but to be honest Charlton weren't really up to much and were soon sent packing. And that was it, we'd taken their kop, which, back then, was what it was all about inside the ground. Just before kick-off we noticed a group massing at the corner of the kop and the terrace where we'd previously been, maybe 100–150 of them. We soon recognised them as Millwall due to the fact that their notorious black lad Tiny was there, and these looked different class to Charlton. We ran down to join other Wednesday and it went off. We had the numbers and weren't short on quality either. Wednesday of the 1970s were IMHO, a very handy mob, and ran Sheffield with ease (a bit like the BBC did from the mid-1980s onwards), but Millwall in those days were the dog's bollocks and had a fearsome reputation.

The fists and feet seemed to be flying for ages, though it was probably only five minutes or so, and we backed them off farther and farther away from the kop, until eventually the OB managed to get in between us. I'd say we did them, but they'd probably disagree. Any which way you look at it, I reckon it was a great result against the top mob of that era. After the game we saw them over the road. We charged over and the bricks and bottles started flying. We heard later that Tiny had lost an eye in the trouble, but thankfully that turned out to be untrue.

That certainly was one of our better days in the capital, though, because in those days we were used to going to places like QPR, Orient, Fulham, etc. and taking the piss, so this was a good day out, even if we did lose 2-1 again. It was really galling that a couple of months later for the league game at Millwall we only took four coaches, and when we parked up on the Old Kent Road half the people wouldn't get off. Worse still was the fact that, after we got off, the coaches fucked off and said they'd pick us up there after the game.

I've probably never been as scared at a game in my life. My mate Chris and I decided to go for a walk, mainly to get away from the ground. We looked in a couple of pubs but to be honest after looking at the people in them decided it wouldn't be wise to go in. We walked back to the ground *and went in; we immediately got chased over the pitch into the seats by a group of complete lunatics. We got slapped for about five minutes and eventually sat with the Supporters Club lot. The five-minute walk to the coach after the game the was the longest I'd ever done, and just before reaching the coach about five or six Millwall jumped me. Luckily a couple of OB managed to drag them off and I ran the last 200 yards to the coach, which had about 4 windows smashed and the back one went on the way out. Scary times indeed.*

Others tell similar stories of their trips to Millwall. Tommy, a member of the Wednesday mob of the 1970s, remembers a particularly hair-raising trip to southeast London in 1976:

It was 27 October 1976 and a dozen or Wednesday lads had organised a day out in London, before going on to the League Cup game at Millwall. The lads in the party were a mix of hooligans and locals out from a south Sheffield pub who fancied a day out in the capital. It was well known by every member of the party that Millwall was a dodgy place even on a pleasant Saturday afternoon, so there was a fair amount of trepidation about what this dark, cold October night would bring.

The journey down was full of laughter inside the bus; an early start had been made in order to spend a full day sampling the delights of London. The day wore on and the beer flowed but an uneasy atmosphere settled in as the time of the match crept closer.

The boys were not going at the ale with the usual gusto, probably because no one wanted to get rat arsed knowing they would need a clear head to deal with what may well lie in store. As the time moved on the mini-bus was well behind schedule and it was fast approaching kick-off time.

It is very likely that if the bus had not turned up until midnight many of its occupants would probably not have been bothered, but unfortunately it did, and as it trundled on its way down the Old Kent Road, you could hear a pin drop.

The driver parked the bus under a railway bridge behind another mini-bus. Many of the Owls fans who disembarked were far too busy rushing to get in for kick-off to realise that those two buses stuck out like a fire engine at a funeral.

The turnstiles were reached with about five minutes to spare to kick-off, and most of the natives were already in the ground. Wednesday had brought a fair following, but all around the atmosphere was dark with a feeling of choking intimidation. Missiles were being thrown into the terrace that housed the Owls. One or two had made the fateful choice of opting to transfer to what they thought was the safety of the seats; fighting immediately broke out, and many of those who had made the journey down from the Steel City must have begun to imagine that this was how Custer had felt at the battle of the Little Big Horn.

The events on the field of play had little relevance for fans or team, as Wednesday were soundly beaten 3-0. As the final whistle sounded three of the lads from the mini-bus got together and decided to exit the ground together. The coaches that had brought most of the Owls were situated to the right of the exit, and the trio were walking in the opposite direction. There were mobs of fans everywhere, and as they turned the corner they came upon about a dozen youths leaning against the wall opposite the bus.

The three Sheffielders carried on walking past the two buses, but they had been sussed. One of the lads immediately fell to the floor clutching his face; another disappeared under a hail of boots and fists. The remaining Owl suddenly found himself at the mercy of the mob. He immediately set off running, and managed to vault the barrier that ran the length of the road, with the mob in pursuit. If truth be known he probably came close to breaking two world records that evening – the high jump and the 200 metres. As he ran people were trying to bring him down but he managed to stay on his feet and dashed the last few yards to the open doors of a public house. Once inside he stood at the bar exhausted, but the Millwall thugs were not giving up just yet, and, when one of the gang picked a pool ball off the table, the lone Owl covered his head, awaiting the impact. It never came however, and he turned upon hearing a loud crack as a pot-bellied cockney, wearing a white shirt and braces, brought his cue down on the aggressor's head. The startled Millwall youth picked himself up and scurried from the bar. The man with the cue calmly picked up the ball, deposited it back on the table, and carried on as though nothing had happened.

The landlord ushered the Wednesday lad out of the back door, which backed on to one of the most uninviting housing estates he had ever seen. He was in no mood to take his chances out there and declined the invitation; preferring instead to wait a while before venturing out on to the deserted streets.

A passing police officer informed him that the rest of his party was in the pub opposite the bridge. He quickly joined the rest of the lads, all of whom had stories to tell. Two other lads had already been in the van when the other three were attacked, and a large mob of Millwall had tried to turn the van over with them inside.

Most of the others had escaped unhurt except for one lad who had sustained a few cuts and bruises, and another who had been taken to Guy's Hospital after having ammonia squirted in his face. The boy was in a bad way, but the excellent hospital staff managed to remove most of the chemicals. The journey home was exhausting, as they needed to stop every half-hour to administer drops to each of the lad's eyes. By the time the van limped back into Sheffield it had been on the road over 24 hours. The driver of the other mini-bus had also been attacked with ammonia, but thankfully it had been diluted. If it had not been, then two men could easily have lost their sight. The lad who had been sprayed with ammonia made a full recovery from his trip to the Lions' Den and most of the chaps still talk about their joyous day out at Cold Blow Lane on a cold dark night in October 1976.

The intimidating atmosphere psyched out many, and not too many firms can shout from the rooftops about their trips down to Cold Blow Lane.

That season saw us make three rapid trips to the capital early in the campaign. Visits to Chelsea, Arsenal and Millwall saw three defeats, and I was at all three games. A group of us went by National Coaches (formerly Sheffield United Travel). We were all lads, but we weren't really looking for trouble at any of these matches. Our intent was to have a laugh, and a good day out in London. Say what you will, but I do believe it is true that your average northern bloke likes nothing better than a day out in the capital, and I was no exception.

A year or so earlier we had gone by car to QPR and stayed

down in the Smoke overnight. We had sat smoking the good stuff in Hyde Park until the small hours after the pubs had shut. One of the Stocksbridge lads, Steve Curry and I slept under a tree in a couple of sleeping bags that he had brought, while the others crammed their collective fat arses into the back of a Mini Metro. A good night out on the piss and ganja was spoilt somewhat by Deano, one of the Stocksbridge lads, having a wank in the back of the car on our journey home. It completely floored me that he would pull a stunt like that, and I was almost sick when he offered up his 'adult' book with the goop still sat on it.

The first trip, I think, was to Chelsea, and about eight of us made the journey, including Bentley and his younger brother. After West Ham and Millwall, Chelsea have historically been another major force in the hooligan world. I had been there a number of times before, most notably for the League Cup trilogy of 1984 when a constant barrage of coins and golf balls rained down on us for much of the game. We arrived in London by about 10.30am and drank in Soho before moving up to the King's Road. It was pretty quiet in the pubs and the weather was warm and sunny. I didn't hang around long after the match started, though, because it soon started pissing it down, and Wednesday quickly found themselves three goals behind, so after about half an hour I thought 'fuck it' and made for the exit. The other lads who had come down on the National stayed on, and I ended up leaving with five or six of the Stocksbridge lads who had come down in a car. The other lads ended up leaving not long after, but I would not see them until we met up again at Victoria for the journey home.

We quickly headed back down the King's Road to escape the rain, and had a few more drinks before walking into a Pizza Hut near to Sloane Square. The restaurant was filled with loud

American youths, and one of the lads, Poopy, took umbrage at their behaviour. 'I fucking hate Americans,' he said, easily loud enough for our friends from across the Atlantic to hear.

Their noise level quickly dimmed, and even though there were about 15 of them, and only 6 of us it was clear they felt uneasy.

'Fucking wankers,' shouted Poopy.

This had the effect of making our little group collapse into fits of laughter, but it had a quite different effect on those fellows from the Land of the Brave. Quietly they drank up, and headed for the door; not one of them looked round at our table. They filed out and I got up to see where they were heading. As I got to the door I saw them running down the King's Road, heading for Sloane Square tube station. A group of big-mouth Americans put to flight by the harsh words of one individual. That sight has stayed with me all these years, and living as close as I do to the US border I always allow myself a wry chuckle when I hear Americans boasting in bars about how tough they are.

After that another lad, Ponno, decided that the food was no good, and he called the manager over to berate him.

'I have been in Pizza Huts all over the world,' he told him while drinking from the beer pitcher. 'This is the worst I have ever had; in fact it's absolute shit.' This despite the fact that he had polished off a large pizza. It had the desired effect, however, and no bill was forthcoming.

After that episode we drank a bit more, and I eventually left them to hop on a tube back to Victoria. The only problem with the coach was that the last one back was at 8.30pm.

I really had no qualms about travelling around on the tube alone. In fact, I have to say that the underground was one of the things I enjoyed most about London. I arrived back at Victoria at around 7.30 and went for a drink in Shakes, which was supposedly a main Chelsea pub at the time. The ICF had been shown launching an attack on the bar in the infamous documentary about them. It was pretty dead inside, but it was somewhere to drink while I waited for the rest of the fellows.

They arrived back shortly before the coach left, and from the sounds of it they, too, had had an eventful afternoon. After the match they had been standing on the platform at Sloane Square, and a mob of Chelsea had arrived. It had kicked off, and from what the lads told me it was a fair old ruck. Bentley had nearly been thrown on to the tracks, and the fighting had been quite fierce before the police arrived to break it up. To my mind that is what the scene is really about. Two small mobs seeking one another out by whatever means and going at it hammer and tongs, not the large mobs clad in Burberry hats who won't shift unless they have a hundred plus of their mates about, and the police not far away. How can you be sure of the others in your mob when you have large numbers? It's nice to see a massive mob, but over the past ten years or so these bigger mobs have been far too unwieldy to actually do anything of any consequence. I would always rather have a good 50 lads who I know and can rely on at my back than 200 unknowns. Mind you, at times during the 1980s and early 1990s it would have been nice to have had a good thirty in our mob.

The Chelsea match was lost 4-0, and next up was Arsenal at Highbury. I don't really remember much about this game, to be honest. A visit to Highbury for the FA Cup semi-final with Brighton in 1982 was the first time I had ever attended a match in London and I remember more about that day than I do about my visit in 1989. I do know that Anwar came, and he had some tickets to pick up at the ground that had been left for him by someone. Other than that all I can recall is that we lost 5-0 and we were in the World's End at Camden when I heard the score. I have never had any trouble with Arsenal, well, not real trouble anyway. I have already recalled Sash's pebble-throwing assault on the imaginary hordes, and the brief clash in Pond Street circa 1987. There was fighting on Wembley Way at the League Cup final between the clubs in 1993, but I didn't attend that game, preferring to save my money for the FA Cup final a few weeks later.

About sixty of us journeyed down by train for that final, and met up with a group of Chelsea lads. Also on the train that day was a certain flame-haired chappie who would go on to find fame and fortune on the most famous cobbled street in the world. At that time he was just starting to make a name for himself in television adverts, and I will always remember Martin giving him a hard time, in the nicest possible way – as only Martin can – about a certain washing liquid advert he was appearing in. He has since gone on to bigger and better things, and all of the Wednesday lads are proud to see what he has accomplished.

We headed straight to Baker Street, and met up with another famous face, the celebrated Nottingham Forest character Paul Scarrott, complete with novelty police helmet. Drinking on Baker Street was very uneventful, with not a single sighting of Holmes or Watson, although one of the Chelsea lads did set fire to a large Arsenal flag. We saw nothing this time around at the stadium, and the match finished in a 1-1 draw, which meant that a replay was required. I simply could not afford to take the time off work for the replay a few days later, and sat in the Freemasons on Hillsborough Corner to watch that match. I missed the fateful moment when Chris Woods palmed the ball into his own net in the final minute of extra-time, because I went for a piss before the penalty shoot-out. What a fucking nightmare that was. I came out from the bog to see people with their heads in their hands, and the REM song 'Everybody Hurts' playing on the jukebox. A season that promised so much, and that saw so much drama, ended without a sausage, and it's been downhill all the way ever since.

My third London trip of 1989–90 marked my first and only trip to Cold Blow Lane, the former home of Millwall. It was largely an uneventful day. Anwar stole a dildo-whip from a gay-sex store, and we ended up going home with Greggy and his brother, who had driven down in the car. I do remember the awe I felt standing inside that stadium. It didn't seem like a football ground to me; it was more like a prison camp. Barbed wire topped the thick steel mesh fences; weeds and grass grew from the terrace, and the feeling of dark, heavy depression hung so thick in the south London air that you could have bottled it – and that was before Sheffield Wednesday took to the field. It really was a strange feeling to know I was standing inside the infamous Den. The ghosts of the past haunted every step of its crumbling stands, and I was glad I had come, though yet another lacklustre Owls performance rather dampened my enthusiasm.

That season saw Wednesday relegated on the very last day. Some inspired signings by 'Big' Ron Atkinson had seen the team play some stellar football, but an end-of-season collapse saw them dragged back into the relegation dogfight after they had looked safe. The final day saw Wednesday needing just a single point to stay up; Luton needed to win at Derby and needed us to lose. That is exactly how it transpired. We lost 3-0 at home to Nottingham Forest while Luton clung on to a priceless 3-2 win at the Baseball Ground. After the match the police tried to use dogs to disperse a large crowd outside the Rose, and they came under a hail of glasses and missiles from the disgruntled Sheffield public. The local paper on Monday reported that a police officer had received a gash to the neck in the trouble. What made the mood worse that day was that Sheffield United had won at Leicester, and would be taking our place in the top flight. I didn't stay out that night – I didn't have the heart, and slipped off home despondent. I didn't know it then but I would be down London within the year to see Sheffield Wednesday lift their first major trophy in 56 years.

Over the years I visited most of the bigger London grounds. As of the time of writing, though, I have not been to Brentford, Orient, or Charlton. My one trip to Selhurst Park, the home of Crystal Palace, was noteworthy on a couple of fronts. First and foremost was the fact that when we went there, in 1991–92, a win would have seen us stay in with a slim chance of pipping Manchester United and Leeds to the championship. As it turned out we drew, and lost our chance of the title, but that point did earn us a place in Europe for the first time in thirty years. A lot of the lads took the opportunity of making a weekend of it, and a couple of mini-buses headed for Southend on the Friday. I travelled down by train on the Saturday with Phil and Matt. Phil didn't hang around with us for long when we arrived in London. He met up with a group of Chelsea lads, and went off to Stamford Bridge to watch the London derby between Chelsea and Arsenal. I have to say that Matt and I were a little perturbed by Phil's choice as we headed for south London. The plan was to meet up with the rest of our lot at a pub near the station. This was rumoured to be Palace's boozer, but when we walked in it was wall to wall Wednesday. To be quite honest I don't recall seeing a Palace fan all day, apart from in the ground, which was a shade disappointing. Even though Palace are not a Millwall or Chelsea, you still think that they must have a few nutters roaming around, but if they did they kept clear on this day.

After the match we decided to head for Camden. This had become a key meeting spot for us when we went to London over the previous couple of years, and the World's End was becoming a bit of a local. There were a good thirty or so of us up Camden that night, and the beer flowed in celebration of Wednesday securing a taste of European football. Everyone was on a high, and there was not even a sniff of any trouble. We moved effortlessly from pub to pub. Most of the lads were heading back to Southend, but Matt and I had to get back to St Pancras by 11pm. As we all marched down toward a pub near the tube station a shout went up.

'Oi, look who it is!'

I turned to see the lead singer of a famous group of 'Nutty Boys'. A few of the lads began to shake his hand and wish him well when suddenly he disappeared from view. Evan had heard the commotion and, not realising what was going on, had planted the strange face. To the singer's credit he got up, and went on his way. Slightly quicker than he had maybe expected, but he went without a word. Most of us just fell about laughing, but a couple of older lads were not so pleased. Evan stood protesting his innocence.

'I didn't know who the fuck it was,' he proclaimed.

'Get fucking ale in now, you big cunt,' somebody shouted, and off we went.

I had decided to have a last pint before heading for the train. I was also starving to death, and as luck would have it there was a fish and chip shop next to the pub, and Matt, Little John and myself headed over to get ourselves some snap. It's a well-known fact that fish and chips in London is not a patch on what you get up north, but beggars can't be choosers. There were five youths in the shop when we entered. They looked like students – no threat – but Little John immediately took offence to them, and started trying to goad them. I personally thought it was out of order, and told John so, but he was pissed up and about to go on one. He picked up a chair and launched it at the group. They were not about to stand there and take it, and they steamed into our rather foolish mate. Of course, even though I thought he was out of order we couldn't leave him to fight on his own, and so with a collective sigh Matt and I joined in. The students really stood no chance, and we absolutely battered them – excuse the pun. I really didn't feel good about it, though, and along with Matt decided to fuck off for our train. John went back in the pub, and a few minutes later the police entered and arrested him. His stupidity would cost him a custodial sentence.

We arrived back at St Pancras to find Phil skulking about round the bar. A large mob of Leicester had been seen roaming the area, and he was lying low. As we boarded our train I found a full can of Guinness on the platform. It had been a day of mixed emotions, but at least it rounded off nicely.

I want to tell of one other trip to London before I end this chapter. I wasn't even there, but this particular night ended in an extremely brutal fashion, and almost cost two young Wednesday fans their lives.

Wednesday had played at Millwall in an FA Cup Fourth Round tie at the Den in the 1991–92 season. The game finished in a thrilling 4-4 draw, and I remember sitting at home in Loxley listening to the match on the radio and watching bloody *West Side Story* on the television. It truly must have been those Jets and Sharks that brought the term 'dance' into casual culture because those boys sure could dance up a storm, and never lay a finger on each other. I heard nothing about whether anything had gone off down in London, although I doubted that it would. A mini-bus of lads had gone, but with no intent other than to watch the match and have a drink in the Smoke. I saw Big Wayne on the bus on Monday morning, and he asked if I had heard about Saturday. Of course, I had heard nothing, and what he told me next sickened me to the pit of my stomach.

The mini-bus load of lads had got out of Millwall without a hitch, and headed for our usual Camden haunts. Phil and a few other regulars were among the group. Everything had gone well until they entered a pub up the High Street called the Queen (not the real name). The landlord welcomed the lads in, and they settled in for a good drink. They did not notice as he locked the exits, nor did they notice the quiet build-up of Londoners around them, and most chilling of all, they did not notice as the landlord tooled the locals up with bats, knives and machetes. They noticed none of this until it was too late. A 50-strong gang launched a savage attack on the 15 Wednesday lads. To this day there is confusion about who the mob was. I have heard both Arsenal and Millwall mentioned, but it does not sound like Arsenal, and it would be well away from Millwall's manor. Either way the Wednesday group had to fight for their lives, and when they did finally get away one lad lay in a coma; another, who was at his first match, had suffered a deep stab wound. The battered and bleeding group headed all the way back to Sheffield before seeking out first aid. I never saw the lad who received the stab wounds again. The lad who was put in a coma recovered, but he was never the same again. I saw him in Meadowhall a few months later, and the lights had gone. His name was Stricky, and he had been around the scene for a few years. He wasn't really into the violence side of the culture, he was more into the nightlife. He would always be in the Limit dancing up a storm. I never saw him at the football again. I would see him around from time to time, but I don't know where he went or what he is doing now. I hope and pray that he is well, and leading a normal life.

What those cockney cunts did that night went beyond the pale, and revenge would be swift. When we reached the League Cup final in April of 1991 a large mob of Sheffielders re-entered 'the Queen' on the evening before the match. Even the police, who knew why Wednesday were in Camden, 'lost' the Owls fans that night, and the landlord of the pub received some payback. Again, I wasn't there that night, but those who were tell me that his face was a picture when Diggers and the boys walked in, and asked him the simple question, 'Remember us?'

Even the Sheffield United firm made sure to pay him a visit soon after as well, and by the time we had gone up Camden after the Palace game, the pub had a new landlord.

There is something about travelling down the M1 to watch a match. It could be the bright lights, and the famous surroundings, but I think that is most likely the fact that on any given Saturday during the football season there could be large mobs of lads roaming the streets of the capital. You would never be sure where or when it might kick off, and you were always on alert. To the follower of the hooligan scene, that is surely what it is all about. I myself never encountered any serious problems down there – the odd scuffle, but nothing major – though the threat was constant. Who could be lurking in that tube station, or drinking in this obscure boozer? There was never a moment to relax and I loved it. I always looked forward to my trips to London, and I hope that one day I will return again.

9

MY CUP RUNNETH OVER

The embarrassment of relegation at the end of the 1989–90 season was difficult to take for the blue half of Sheffield. The fact that Sheffield United had replaced us in the top flight further rubbed salt into the wound. I doubt that many people who attended the Forest game, and who listened in stunned silence as the results that sent us down came in, would have believed that our relegation that day would be the catalyst for a remarkable period in the club's history. Over the next four years Sheffield Wednesday would bounce back, and become a major presence once more. We would see our first trophy in over fifty years, in addition to a string of Wembley appearances, qualification for Europe and a sniff at a League Championship. To be quite honest as I sit here writing this, after yet another dismal day for the Owls in the depths of Division Two, I too find it difficult to believe how far we have sunk since those days. The dissatisfaction of the Forest result, however, was tempered somewhat by the expectation that our declining firm would rise again during our stay outside the top flight. I was in the Limit the night of the match, and there truly was a sense of optimism that we could pull our numbers together and start to challenge the big boys once more.

In reality, that didn't happen – well, not on a regular basis. The promotion season of 1990–91 saw very few firms come to Hillsborough in the league, but we did have a very entertaining toe-to-toe with Chelsea in the League Cup semi. We had decent numbers out for most games, but there was nothing to do except drink. I can only recall two firms showing, if I am honest: Oldham and Barnsley. Both of these mobs brought it right to our door by showing at the Rose.

I actually missed the Oldham performance, as a few of us had already set off for town. The word was that Oldham were coming, but as time dragged we started to wonder if they had by-passed the pub, and gone straight to town. A number of us set off for a snoop, and ended up missing a real performance from the Latics. Those who were there say they put up a good effort before being overwhelmed somewhat by superior Owls numbers. Those of us who missed it were quite rightly kicking ourselves, and a bit of a rivalry developed between Oldham and ourselves from that day. Respect was earned, and over the next couple of seasons some of our better efforts were made on the day of an Oldham fixture. The Latics responded in kind, and amazingly a few reciprocal visits developed between the two mobs.

The following season, after both clubs were promoted, Oldham once again came calling, but this time they caught a severe cold. Their numbers were weak, but then so were ours, and they still brought it to the Rose. They showed very late in the day, probably no more than 15-handed, and didn't manage to get within 20 feet of the pub; unlike the previous year, when they got right to the door. We saw them coming and went straight into them. Only about ten of us fronted them, but they were off without a second glance, and they kept running back toward the ground. It looked like no fun was to be had until those of us in pursuit decided to outflank them. We noticed a bus coming, and so we hopped on in order to get behind them. It worked a treat. The Oldham lads couldn't believe it when they saw us coming from the other side, and they realised they had to go back past the Rose, where another mob was waiting. The gig was up, and they knew it. One of their lads put his hands up in surrender: 'Leave it out, lads, you've done us,' he shouted as he saw Wednesday closing in from both sides. Some firms would still have shovelled them in, but we are not like that, and the Oldham lads were left untouched to get on a bus to town.

I have the utmost respect for the Oldham boys that day. They saw they were going to come unstuck and put their hands up to it. I think some of the keyboard warriors of today could learn a lesson from that. Go on any of these 'football hooligan' websites and message boards, and no one *ever* holds their hands up to getting done, but then again most of those who post on these boards are nowhere near the action – me included. My final run-in with Oldham came in the 1992–93 season, and it was nothing, but it did show the respect that had developed between the firms. They were due to come on a cold Wednesday night in the run-up to Christmas, but the weather was a little inclement. They had the decency to phone the Masons and let us know that they couldn't make it due to the snow, which was totally unheard of back then. Many of us were a little sad when Oldham fell from the top flight, thinking it could be many years before we locked horns with them again; how little we knew, although the Oldham firm of today has developed a reputation for being a bit of a rent-a-mob, constantly bringing in lads from other firms to help them out.

Barnsley were the other mob to bring it to our doorstep in the league that year. I had been to Oakwell in the promotion season of 1983–84, and Wednesday had basically run the show all day. Two separate mobs had come by train, and the mob I was with never took a backward step all day, but in the intervening years the 'pit moggies' had developed a bit of a reputation for mixing it with the big boys, which was in stark contrast to the reputation we had built up in the same time frame. A good show was therefore expected from our local rivals, but sadly it didn't really hit the heights we expected. Nothing was seen of them before the game until about 3.15pm when we saw, from our vantage point on the East Bank, a mob walking down the road outside the ground. This mob was about thirty- to forty-handed, and we recognised a couple of Barnsley Reds in the group. Disappointed that they had shown late, for whatever reason, we were cautiously optimistic that they would make themselves known after the match. A Wednesday side playing some scintillating football won a good game, and with another three points safely in the bag we headed back to the Rose. The word on the grapevine was that the Barnsley lads had made it known they would be coming to the Rose after. It looked like quite a few of our lot didn't really take the threat seriously, and everyone quickly settled into the familiar routine of cards, pool and downing the ale. Without warning a spotter came in with news that Barnsley were on their way. Now, usually when this type of word goes out everyone heads for the door, but the reaction was very slow and unhurried for some reason, and I have to say I was a touch perturbed. By the time we got outside the Dingles were almost at the door. A roar went up from both sides, and then everything stopped as police seemingly appeared from nowhere. Half-hearted efforts were made from both sides before the police tried to push us back into the pub and guide Barnsley past.

Myself and a few others bypassed the Rose, and headed for the Masons Arms on Capel Street. The police pushed Barnsley toward town, and that seemed to be it.

I was standing on the corner of Capel Street with Marty Hayes when I saw another dozen or so heading our way. They got to about ten feet away when another roar went up from the lads outside the Masons Arms, but no charge. Not that it mattered. The roar had the effect of sending the Dingles scurrying off, until they turned and saw just Martin and myself stood in harm's way. Bravery was suddenly their bountiful friend, and bouncing back they came, spewing insults and vitriol. The two of us never budged an inch, and we stood waiting for the assault, but it never came as more police could be seen heading our way, and the Barnsley boys immediately went into marathon training mode. Jaz and a few other OCS lads caught up with them at the station, and they got chatting. They told Jaz that they wanted to join up with us to have a dig at United, but Jaz declined their kind offer, and they hopped on their train back to Dingleville. I am not trying to belittle our lovely neighbours just to the north. I know they have some very handy lads, and have done some serious damage down the years, but I have never seen them do anything against us, or even heard of them doing so. A couple of seasons ago they arranged to meet a Wednesday mob in Wombwell after a match at Oakwell. Eighty OCS made their way there, but Barnsley never did. In the return at Hillsborough a small firm of Barnsley phoned ahead to tell the Wednesday lads on Hillsborough Corner that they were coming in on the tram. When the tram docked outside the Deep End the Barnsley mob were obliterated, and afterwards cried foul! Why make the call if you didn't want it? Barnsley say they don't rate us, and my answer to that is: big fucking deal – nobody does.

The big fun and games of the season was in the Cup. A glorious run in the League Cup saw the Owls bring home their first silverware since 1935. I travelled to the quarter-final tie at Coventry on a coach that went from the Woodthorpe. As in my previous visits to Highfield Road the opposition was feeble. We drank in their pubs before the game, and saw nothing. We had a block of seats in their end, and they did nothing. It was embarrassing how poor Coventry were. Our own stock had declined to mere pennies over the last few years, but still we had way too much for the Sky Blues. I have since talked to numerous older lads, and a few of them do say that Coventry was a dodgy place to go during the 1970s. Dennis, who is an old lad from that time, told me of a visit to Highfield Road for a Cup match in the early 1970s. He said about 200 Wednesday got in the Coventry end, and it went ballistic. The fighting went back and forth before finally the Wednesday fans were ejected. It was, in his own words, the worst trouble he had ever seen at a match, and he can tell tales going back to the 1960s. Maybe the Covs could put on a show when they wanted, but unfortunately I never really saw it.

The semi-final pitted us against the might of Chelsea. A coach went down, but nothing happened except word of a fearsome-looking Chelsea mob. In 1991 Chelsea were once again turning out some serious misters. The farcical Headhunter trials had been consigned to the history books, and from our distant viewpoint Chelsea looked to be getting back to their glory days. Amazingly Wednesday won the first leg of the semi at Stamford Bridge, and when Chelsea came to town for the return we were a mere 90 minutes away from our first visit to Wembley in 25 years.

I arrived in town at around 5.30 on the night of the match. It was rumoured that Chelsea were coming by coach, but would be stopping off in Chesterfield and training it in. Our meet was the Howard Hotel overlooking the station, but when I arrived a large group of our lads were heading away from the Howard toward the Penny Black. I saw one of the young lads, Munch, and wandered over to see what was going on. He explained that an advanced group of Chelsea had arrived early, and were in the pub. The Penny Black was divided into two halves by a bar in the middle and the only way from one bar to another was via an area to the rear, where the toilets and an exit door stood.

Our plan was to get in one side and try to suss the Londoners' numbers. An all-out assault was not considered wise at this point – well, not by the saner members of our group, but obviously no one told one of our Doncaster lot, Rick, because no sooner had we walked in than I saw him through the other side laying into anything that moved. It was going off much sooner than we had planned, and the small group of Chelsea fans took a ferocious pounding as they tried to escape through the exit to the rear. They were hit with stools and bottles in a sustained assault before they could escape. I was not happy at all. Attacking this small group of Chelsea was out of line, and would likely bring it on top before we were ready. They had headed back toward the station to await the big Chelsea firm coming in from Chesterfield. It had also brought unwelcome police attention, and we split up to make our way toward Hillsborough. I stopped off in the Mulberry for a pint with a couple of other lads, before heading for the Rose. It was only one pint and then we left. We heard later that about five minutes after we departed the scene, a large mob of Chelsea came in looking for the perpetrators of the Penny Black assault. Even though I would not class myself as one of the perpetrators, I doubt those gentle souls from Stamford Bridge would have seen it that way, and we were fortunate that we didn't stop for a second pint.

For some reason by the time we got down Penistone Road we could not get in the Rose, and had to settle for the Masons Arms round the corner. The trouble with the Masons was that it was very small, and even having thirty people in made it seem crowded. (By the way, this Masons of which I speak is not to be confused with the Freemasons Arms on Hillsborough Corner, which for many years has been a meeting place for Wednesday fans.) The Masons was absolutely jammed to the rafters, which probably meant there were forty people in it, and a whisper came through that Chelsea had been up on the top road, and had been shooting flares near the Kelvin flats. I decided to go have a look at what was coming down Penistone Road, and wandered down Capel Street, where I was joined by Trev. Almost immediately we saw a group of lads turn and shoot off back up by the side of the New Barrack Tavern. I turned to Trev.

'Who the fuck was that?' I exclaimed.

We didn't have long to wait. Within a minute or so a coach appeared, and more lads appeared from round the corner. This was a Chelsea mob, and they meant business – but so did we. A shout had already gone up, and the Masons was beginning to empty – just as the coach began to empty too. It was going to go, and it was going to go big with not a copper in site.

Bentley was first into the Chelsea fans. He ran straight into them, and sparked one clean out. The next day's newspaper said the Londoner had been injured by a brick, but I can tell you it was no brick. A roar went up, and we steamed into the Chelsea mob, who were trying desperately to disembark from their coach. We backed the first few off, some tried to get back on the bus, but were forced out by those getting off. The fighting began to escalate, and continued down the road. If I am completely honest I would have to say that Chelsea were starting to get the upper hand as we reached the park, but we never budged, and skirmished every inch of the way. The police finally moved in by the entrance to Hillsborough Park. They pushed Chelsea up Parkside Road and we were moved toward the kop entrance. We were pretty pleased with ourselves as we entered the ground. We had taken on a very handy Chelsea mob, and given as good as we got. We had endured some piss-poor turnouts over the previous few years, and interest had dwindled, but tonight we had put up a show of which we could be proud.

That was about the last time that Wednesday and Chelsea came to blows. Relations between the two mobs warmed considerably over the next few years, and visits between lads from the two groups became increasingly frequent. A combined Wednesday– Chelsea mob fought a pitched battle with Sheffield United thugs at Berlins one night in 1992, and Wednesday faces were present at a famous confrontation between Chelsea and Sheffield United in London that same year, when 70 Chelsea put over 200 of the BBC's elite mob to flight. The visits continue to this day, and I think that because of this, and the fact that Chelsea are viewed as being right-wing, the myth about the OCS's far-right ties has gathered momentum. I have never seen any evidence of it myself, and never saw anything out of the ordinary with the Chelsea lads either.

Sheffield Wednesday cruised past Chelsea that night to book a place in the League Cup final against Manchester United. We had not been to Wembley since losing to Everton in the 1966 FA Cup final. The emotion seen that night was unbelievable, and reminded me of the Carlisle game that clinched promotion in 1980. This was what being a Wednesday fan was all about. It made all the heartache worthwhile, and we celebrated deep into the night.

The final was to be held on a sunny Sunday in April, and was played the day after I was best man at Gill's wedding to Joanne.

This meant that I was unable to head for London on the Saturday. Ash and I were the lone Owl representatives at Gill's reception, but we took over the microphone, and made a number of drunken toasts to the 'Wednesday lads doing battle in London tonight'. I went down in Dick's car with Phil, and another lad from Derbyshire. I never saw a hint of trouble all day, and to top it all the Second Division Owls overcame the heavily favoured Manchester United side by virtue of John Sheridan's sweetly struck volley. We had finally won a bloody trophy, and the feeling was unbelievable. After the match we were waiting for the traffic to ease, when out of the stadium came Carlton Palmer carrying the cup. I was totally gobsmacked. Then came Graham Taylor, the England manager of the time, along with his assistant Lawrie McMenemy, and the hero of the hour, our own 'Big' Ron Atkinson. I was suddenly 12 years old again as I queued up to have these three stalwarts of English football sign my programme. I still have that programme in my bedside drawer, and it is without a doubt one of my most prized possessions. And to think some people say that football hooligans don't care about their team. What a load of old bollocks.

The League Cup wasn't the only competition that provided a few sparks in that glorious season. We were drawn against Mansfield Town in the FA Cup Third Round. Mansfield is a tough little town in Nottinghamshire. It is reasonably close to Sheffield and so a fair few of the lads decided it would be worth the trip. The original plan was to go by bus from Pond Street, but that changed in the days leading up to the game. Nobody told me of any change, however, and when I turned up for the meet there was only myself and Tony waiting for the bus. Tony was a coloured lad, and completely game as fuck. He was around on the scene for a few years in the early 1990s before he dropped out and concentrated his mind on the football. We were both a touch surprised to find that no one was around, but decided that since we were there we would go anyway. That bloody bus trip was a real pain. The bus stopped at every little town between Sheffield and Mansfield; towns I had never even heard of. It took about 90 minutes to travel the 25 miles or so to the Nottinghamshire town and were we glad to get there.

Our first port of call was a pub that had been pre-arranged as the meet. I forget the name, but it was just outside the station at the top of a pedestrianised shopping area, similar to Fargate in Sheffield. We went in to find the pub packed with shirts of both teams. Tony looked at me, and I looked at him.

'No fucker here, we may as well go have a look round,' he said.

I agreed with that sentiment and we stepped outside. As we stood contemplating our next move, we saw a number of familiar faces walking up the precinct. I immediately spotted Dickie, Bentley and Moores. It was our lads.

'Nice to see you made it,' somebody shouted.

'Nice of you to tell me the transport had changed,' I replied.

We stood and chatted a while, and it transpired that the first van load of our lot had gone to the pub early, and got legged back out. The police had come, and our lot had laid low in another pub nearby. The Mansfield that had put the first 15 or so to flight were not around now, so where had they gone? We set off toward the ground. Our numbers had by now swelled to a good hundred or so; a mix of barmies and lads. Within minutes we had been pulled up and surrounded by the local militia, or as they prefer to be known, the Nottinghamshire Constabulary. They put us in escort and marched us in the direction of Field Mill. As we walked down by a dual carriageway we saw a group of Mansfield pile out of a pub across the way.

'That's the cunts that chased us!' someone was heard to shout.

The Mansfield lads stood quietly outside their pub watching us being marched by on the opposite side of the road. I didn't have a ticket, and a few others were in the same boat. We spent the match wandering around trying to blag our way in, but to no avail. About twenty minutes after kick-off we saw half a dozen lads walking toward us. No one recognised them, and we were all set for our own little kick-off when the front man of this group, a big lad with red hair, walked straight up and held out his hand.

'Any of you lads know Gill?' he said.

'I do,' I replied. 'How do you know him?'

'I used to work with him.'

The mood immediately eased as we began to chat. These lads were Chesterfield Bastard Squad, and 'Red' was one of their main actors. He had worked with Gill a year or so before, and thought that if they had a wander down on this day he might run into him again. The CBS hate Mansfield too, so it could have been a case of two birds with one stone, but as it turned out it was no birds at all. Gill wasn't there and, apart from a scuffle near the vans after, there was no trouble outside the ground to speak of. I found 'Red' to be a top lad, and would bump into him again a few months later in Sheffield. He was with four or five others that night, and Tony and I chased them up Division Street. We didn't recognise them until we got up close, but eventually ended up drinking with them for much of the night before they headed back to Derbyshire.

I headed home in one of the vans. I had expected a lot from this day, and had seen precious little. Some lads did get lucky inside the ground, however. Mark and his little mob infiltrated the Mansfield fans, and had a fun time, as he explains here:

The 1990–91 season was undoubtedly the best season most Wednesdayites can remember in recent history, and for me it produced some of the best memories I have of following Wednesday, both on and off the field.

Probably due to this success the violence seemed a little unimportant to me as we drank our way round the country watching the lads gain promotion to the First Division and beat Man United in the Rumbelows Cup final.

There was trouble throughout the season, but I tended to drift in and out of it for that year, and went to many matches with friends from my local area. These were lads who would much sooner have good ale than a good scrap, but would stand side by side if it went off.

One such occasion arose in the FA Cup. We had drawn Mansfield Town away, and their ground, Field Mill, was only small – meaning that Wednesday's ticket allocation was by no means enough, and they sold out within hours.

A mate and me decided to travel to Mansfield and get six tickets for anywhere in the ground, which we did without too many questions being asked.

On the day of the match we travelled by train, and from the moment we got off in Mansfield the atmosphere was ugly and I was expecting a busy day.

Mansfield were obviously up for it and appeared to have turned out in numbers. By 1pm the trouble had started, and there was sporadic fighting all the way to the ground, which we somehow managed not to get too involved in.

We entered the ground on a small terrace down one side of

the ground, with the Wednesday fans on the other side of the tunnel and behind the goal. We were stood among the Mansfield fans and I must admit that I felt a little uneasy because there were so few of us. Things eased a little when we spotted another group of ten Wednesday fans who we knew, so we went to stand with them.

I can't remember now at what point of the game it went off, but a scuffle started in the Wednesday area, which ended with Danny Wilson [Owls player] dragging a Mansfield player about, by his boot. This produced a shout of 'Wednesday aggro, Wednesday aggro!' from one of our crowd and the touchpaper was lit.

The terrace immediately opened up and left the 15 of us facing a massive chasm, which was about to be filled with Mansfield fans.

'This is it,' I thought. 'A proper Seventies-style terrace brawl.'

The Mansfield fans surged at us and with our backs to the tunnel we got ready to have a go. One of the first to come at us ran down the terrace and ducked under one of the old-style crush barriers and I saw my chance. One step forward and I put my size nine right in his face just as he came under the barrier. In what looked like slow motion to me his nose just exploded, with claret spraying all over.

Sadly that was as good as it got for us, though, as we were now coming under a heavy barrage of boots and fists. We gave as good as we got and luckily for us we were getting pushed towards the front of the terrace.

The Plod was on the case now and we were still trading blows as they pulled us one by one over the wall. We were lined up at the side of the pitch and then walked round the *ground to the Wednesday end and put in there to chants of 'We're proud of you, we're proud of you!' from the Wednesday contingent. Big Ron was shaking his head as we were marched right in front of him.*

From what I can remember that was it for the day's events, apart from Wednesday winning the game 2-0.

We eventually bowed out of the FA Cup that year with a dismal 4-0 defeat at Cambridge, but, as Mark said, this was a year to remember for all Wednesday fans, apart from that blemish at the Abbey Stadium. This was the year that we began our quest to become one of the big boys again, and over the next couple of years we came so very close, before a rapid decline kicked in.

At the end of May 1991 a civic reception was organised by Sheffield City Council to honour the club's feat of winning promotion and the League Cup. The day before that reception I became a father for the first time, and Ron Atkinson resigned as Wednesday boss to manage Aston Villa. My added responsibilities meant I did not turn out very often during the 1991–92 season. I didn't even go out for the Steel City derby with Sheffield United at Bramall Lane. I did go to the first match of the season, though. Incredibly, that first fixture threw up a Hillsborough return for Big Ron, along with his Aston Villa side. A big mob met in town, and marched down to the Rose. I had gone straight down there, foregoing town, and was amazed to see a lot of old faces back for the day.

We attacked the Villa fans on Leppings Lane. In fact, they got caught in an unintentional pincer movement – as we came down Leppings Lane another Wednesday mob from the Park Hotel arrived off Catch Bar Lane. The Villa boys were game as fuck, but they were swamped and took a heavy beating. One suffered a broken leg, and some of the Villa fans even went squealing to the police, and pointed people out as we walked past. The game started well, and we went in 2-0 up at half-time, but Villa came back to win 3-2. A sizable mob drank in town after, and it looked like our firm was going to make a comeback. Sadly it was not to be for most of the season – and I was as guilty as many in this respect. We had some good turnouts, especially for the home match with Sheffield United, but in the main we showed little, although this may well be explained by yet more internal conflict that surfaced between two factions within the mob. The season itself went very well on the field, and as I mentioned in the previous chapter, we went into the match at Crystal Palace with an outside shot at the championship. It truly was a great time to be a Wednesday fan, although maybe not so much if you were looking for off-field shenanigans.

The 1992–93 season saw the return of European football to Hillsborough for the first time in almost thirty years. It also saw a certain Chris Waddle move to Hillsborough. The scene was set for an all-out assault on the league title. Waddle was scheduled to make his debut for the Owls in a pre-season friendly at Rotherham, and interest was extremely high. A short train ride was the order of the day, and about forty of us headed off to see the 'Waddler' in action – and also hoped that we, too, might see a little bit of action. It was my first trip to Millmoor since 1983, and the memories of my first trip there in 1979 were fresh in my head. This was where I had made a choice all those years ago, and now I was back trying to emulate the Wednesday boys of yesteryear. It really did feel like a spiritual homecoming.

Rotherham is another tough little town built on the steel and coal industries, but now on its uppers. Its close proximity to Sheffield meant that it was seen as a sort of satellite suburb. Throughout the 1970s mobs from both Sheffield clubs had gone to Millmoor, and basically taken the piss. In 1976–67 trouble at the Rotherham-Owls fixture saw over sixty arrests, and numerous people taken to hospital. I had witnessed scenes of chaos at the game in 1979, and the people of Rotherham must have breathed a collective sigh of relief when they no longer had to put up with the idiots from next door, both blue and red. How was it that successive mobs from Sheffield could wreak such havoc on this tough little town? That was fairly simple: many of the town's rowdier inhabitants followed the two Sheffield sides. I have known many, many lads down the years from Rotherham and surrounding villages. The Rotherham Blades were well known to us, and trouble in many Rotherham area townships was invariably Wednesday–United feuding rather than anything to do with the Millers. If I am completely honest I would have to admit that much of the trouble that followed visits to Rotherham by Sheffield teams was a simple case of bullying on the part of the big-city boys.

For this visit I felt no trepidation whatsoever. No matter how inactive our firm had become I could not believe that we wouldn't be able to handle little old Rovrun! We also had quite a few old lads aboard, such as Erroll and Mr X. There was no cause whatsoever for concern. As the train pulled into Rotherham station I turned to Dickie, our Simply Red lookalike. 'I can see it now, Dickie,' I said. 'If you get nicked today the headlines of tomorrow's papers will read 'Mick Hucknall arrested in soccer riot'!

'Fuck off,' he laughed in reply, but it would end up being no joking matter for Dickie.

We wandered through Rotherham town centre seeing nothing, and encamped at a pub just up from the Turf Tavern. The word was that Rotherham used the County Borough, so a few spies went for a sniff, but came back empty handed. A simple walk in the park was on the cards. At about 2.30 we decamped for the ground. We went completely unescorted by any police. Close to the ground we had our first encounter with their lads – well, I call it an encounter, but it was simply Bentley walking into them and knocking them about. We arrived at the ground, and saw Big Wayne and Jonny from Donny. After a brief chat we headed straight for the turnstiles at the Tivoli end. No one spoke a word as we filed in. I don't recall any consensus to enter the Rotherham end, it was just taken as normal practice. Once inside I saw a young lad called Brett looking around.

'What's up, Brett?' I enquired.

'Its full of Rotherham fans in here!' he exclaimed.

I laughed. 'That's 'cos it's their end, mate.'

We walked up on to the terrace. There were another half-dozen or so Wednesday already in, and their faces lit up when they saw us. The away end was full of Wednesday fans who had come to see Chris Waddle make his Wednesday debut. We set ourselves up right in the middle of the kop just in front of the entrance. If and when the Rotherham mob came in, we would see them.

As the teams came out just before kick-off we let our presence become public knowledge. 'Wednesday, Wednesday, Wednesday!' went the cry.

The Rotherham lads that we had seen outside suddenly appeared behind us, but again they looked as though they didn't know what to do. Bentley, once again, took the initiative and smashed their front man in the face. The end exploded in uproar. We rushed up the terrace, and began to drag the Rotherham fans down toward us. I pulled one lad down by his collar and he disappeared in the scrum of people that had developed. We had drawn in their small mob, and a huge gap appeared behind us.

The police really were struggling to get control, and as the melee subsided I saw a police sergeant on his hands and knees scrambling around trying to find his helmet. The police pushed us toward the front of the terrace and got in behind us. I can't say that they got between us and the Rotherham fans, because they stood about six feet of open terrace behind the police line. Both Dickie and Jonny had been nicked, so my 'prophecy' had partially come true. Just as the police had regained control Rotherham scored. We turned, thinking maybe they would try to rush us, but they didn't. They simply danced about behind us, and never looked like trying anything.

The police were taking no chances, though, and they surrounded us. They then told us that they could not put us out of the ground, and that they were taking us to the away end. We were ushered out, and as we left the Rotherham fans suddenly found their voices again. 'You'll never take Tivoli!' they chanted at us as we were taken out. What a bunch of mugs. We had gone into their end, and even had to kick it off with them, but they were singing like they had forced us out. It was a scene of pure comedy from the Toytowners.

We ended up back in the away end, but we didn't intend staying too long. Poor old Shane had once again lost a shoe, and he was mightily pissed off about it. A Wednesday fan from Rotherham told us that the Rotherham lot liked to mob up in a nearby underpass, and at the end of the game we headed straight for it. Shane was on a shoe hunt, and no one was going to get in his way. We found no one at the underpass, but our numbers were swelling, and Rotherham really were on a hiding to nothing. I even heard regular fans saying, 'I'm going with these lads for some aggro.'

It was known that the Rotherham lads usually headed for a

pub called the Angel after a match. This pub was at the bottom of a shopping area, and was opposite the County Borough. We walked parallel to the shopping area, which made it appear as though we were heading back toward Sheffield Road, but this was just a ruse to throw off the police. At the top of the road we made a sharp left and appeared back on the precinct, but this time heading down, and out of the view of the Rotherham fans and police.

A few Rotherham were outside the pub when we arrived, but they soon bolted for the doors. A couple of lads were caught in the doorway and got filled in before someone threw something through the pub window, This was the cue for hordes of police to race around the corner. We took off sharpish, and headed back up the way we had come. At the top of the road was a big church, and a wedding was underway. We ran through just as the pictures were being taken. I can only imagine how thrilled the bride and groom must have been to have a large group of lads being chased by police on the photos of their special day.

I swear I could hardly run for laughing it was such a funny scene. I turned to see Linwell's brother at my side, and he, too, was in stitches. More police arrived to cut us off, but thankfully they just wanted us out of town, and we were escorted to the station.

It was a good start to a season of fun and frolics. We didn't turn huge mobs out that year, but we had begun to develop a close-knit group that stuck together. We travelled more than in previous seasons too. Of course, we had four trips to Wembley that year, and that helps.

There were a few flare-ups that season, mainly in the cup competitions, but my favourite of the season, and perhaps ever, came against Sunderland in the Fourth Round of the FA Cup.

Sunderland had been building quite a reputation at the time. I always thought of Newcastle and Sunderland as being fat, beer-swilling rowdies rather than a Casual firm, but Sunderland seemed to be breaking that image, and their firm – 'the Seaburn Casuals' – had made a few people jump. The rumour mill even said that fifty of them had taken it to the BBC on London Road, so we were not underestimating them in the slightest. The game was to be played on a Sunday, and I met up early with Phil expecting a tough day ahead.

It was quiet when we arrived at Hillsborough Corner, and I headed for the bank to get some money. We moved over to the Freemasons Arms on the bridge. This pub had taken over from the Rose as the meeting place in the previous couple of seasons, and the fact that it was run by an ex-Wednesday player really helped to make it our pub. The bar began filling rapidly after opening, with supporters of both sides helping to make the atmosphere extremely jovial. There were many Sunderland fans in the pub, but they were shirts, and they were under no threat from us. Again I was a little disappointed by the turnout; we had only about forty to fifty tops, and we fully expected a good show from the Seaburn mob, but to be fair the mob we did have was very tight, and we would take some shifting on the Corner.

At about 2pm a rumour went around that the Sunderland firm were just twenty yards up the road, at the La Plata Social Club, but this proved to be false. It did galvanise us into some sort of action, though, and we all spilled out on to the bridge at the bottom of Walkley Lane. A certain Sheffield actor, who was at the time was starring as a nasty market inspector on *EastEnders*, was enjoying a pint outside the pub as we left. He turned to Evan.

'You lads off for a rumble?' he said

'Too right,' replied Evan. 'You want to come?'

He laughed, and politely declined the invitation.

Then, completely by chance, we stumbled on the Sunderland mob, and they were right under our noses – not in the La Plata, but in the Shakey. As we stood around we noticed them coming out the pub.

'They're here now,' I shouted, and half of us set off in their direction. As we reached the corner we shouted to them, and they stopped and faced us. They fanned out across the road. There were about 50 of them, and as I turned to look at our mob I was surprised to see only about 15 of us crossing Middlewood Road. The rest were coming, but not at pace. We got to within feet of them. They did not run, but neither did they counter and run into us. It was strange, and reminded me of the night the OCS was born. With that in mind I turned to Evan, knowing we could do with the rest of our mob catching up.

'After three, Ev,' I said.

Our reinforcements were coming, and I turned to look at our opponents. They seemed unsure of what to do. I reached the number three, and we went straight into them. They scattered, and took off down Bradfield Road. One lad was caught and was taking a pounding. Another of the Sunderland came running back to help his mate, yelling at the cowardice of his other friends. He was run into the side of a passing car, but nothing more. The famous Seaburn Casuals had gone. We followed, but as one old timer who was passing when it kicked off said, 'Those Sunderland fans sure can run fast.'

We entered the ground split between the kop and North Stand. I was in the North at the Leppings Lane end, and felt a little conspicuous due to the fact that I was wearing a bright red jacket. Remembering how the Villa fans had tried to grass us up I felt it wisest to move over to the kop end. The game was won in the final minute when the Sunderland keeper Tony Norman dropped a cross on to Mark Bright's head, and he made no mistake.

After the match we headed up to the Spot On snooker club on Langsett Road. It was a good place to be, with views down on to Penistone Road. We had been in about half an hour, and there were probably only about thirty of us in, when Brian came in with the news that about eighty Sunderland were on the move down Penistone Road, with no police. We piled out of the back door, and sure enough looking down the hill we saw a large mob. They easily had the numbers on us, so we had to be careful if we were going to launch an attack. It was pissing it down with rain by now, and to reach them we had to run down a steep banking. I admit I didn't really fancy running through three foot of mud, and turned to Evan with the intention of saying, 'Get 'em to come up here.' I was too late, the big lad had gone barrelling down the hill, and was already engaging the enemy.

'Fucking hell,' I muttered to myself before setting off in pursuit.

To the Sunderland boys it must have looked like loads of us were coming down the hill out of the darkness. It was too much for them, and again they ran. I swear they outnumbered us two to one, and still they ran. We continued to chase them, and now and then they stopped to try and get something back, but each time we went straight in and put them on their toes. One lad got caught near Rutland Road, and he started crying. One of our lads was in his car, and he ran it straight into them. The Mackems were absolutely terrified, and they just kept running. I honestly think they must have thought there were loads of us, but there were only forty tops, and they easily outnumbered us. Finally at West Bar the police arrived and wrapped up the exhausted Sunderland mob. Once they were in the safety of the loving arms of South Yorkshire's finest they started showing off. They also probably appreciated at last how few of us there were. We laughed at their pathetic posturing, and headed up toward the Golden Ball for a celebratory drink. As we did so the cathedral bells began to ring. Quick as a flash, Fenian Dan turned and said, 'Erroll must have heard we finally got a result and he's ringing the bells.' The point was not missed on any of us as we walked up West Bar laughing.

The FA Cup Sixth Round of that season pitted us against our old friends from Derby. We had quite a bit of history with the DLF, going back a few years. It was always tasty mixing it with the lads from the Baseball Ground, and, having never had any bother with Birmingham, I can honestly say that to my mind they were easily the best firm in the Midlands. They never let you down, and no matter what the size of their mob, be it 15 or 500, they were always game as fuck. They would pop up when you least expected it, and had appeared in Sheffield a number of times unannounced. A lot of people don't like that, but to me it shows craft. The object of the game is to put one over on your opponent, and they were masters of it in their prime. I do admit to having a soft spot for Derby. Since the club moved to Pride Park the DLF has fallen on hard times, which is a pity, but I have a sneaking suspicion that they will pull it around.

The tie was played in Derby, and ended in a thrilling 3-3 draw. I watched the match in the Freemasons with Martin. I don't know that we took much of a mob down that night, but we knew that the replay would bring something, and it certainly did.

The rematch saw about twenty of us meet in the Mulberry Tavern in town, which is usually a Blades pub. I went off for a wander and found a good thirty or so older DLF drinking in the Penny Black. They were virtually all big lads, and looked quite impressive. I headed back to the Mulberry with word. Even though they probably had a slight numbers edge we went for a look, but we dallied too long, and were disappointed to find they had gone, so we jumped on a bus for Hillsborough. We figured they may be walking, and that we might catch sight of them on the way, and that's exactly what happened. As our bus passed we saw them coming out of a pub called, I think, the Cask and Cutler just past Shalesmoor. Quick as a flash we were off the bus, and ran straight into them. They seemed surprised, and backed off at first. We pushed them toward the Ratteners Rest pub near Green Lane, but then they countered, and their superior quality showed. We turned tail and ran down toward Penistone Road, with the chant of 'DLF!' ringing in our ears.

Once again our haste had been our undoing. We only had about twenty lads, and out of that at least half had barely got off the bus when it kicked off. Our small mob was now split, and we could not regroup. Half went on the top road toward Hillsborough, and the other half, of which I was one, trooped down Penistone Road. We knew more of our lot would be on Hillsborough Corner, and tried to lure the Derby lads up there, but they were wise to us, and keen to protect the advantage that they had stolen. In the pub the inquest started, and it was agreed that we were stupid, and should have been a bit less eager. This would have allowed us to get together properly, and launch a proper assault. After the match it would be different.

Many of us didn't go to the match. We stayed and watched the Owls win 1-0 on the TV in the Freemasons. That win booked a semi-final spot with our dear city rivals. As the game ended, those of us who had stayed in the pub drifted out toward Hillsborough Park. A large number of our lads came excitedly our way, and they had news. The same Derby mob from before was headed our way. Now was our chance for revenge, and everybody was up for it. Instead of going silly we kept calm and headed back toward the corner. Then it was on top. Derby came at us like banshees – one lad was even swinging a bike chain – but we didn't run, we went into them. This time we had superior numbers, and it would turn the tide our way. The fighting spilled down some side roads, and one Derby lad was heaved halfway through somebody's front window. They fought hard, but our numbers told, and eventually they splintered and ran.

Honour had been somewhat restored, and we headed back to the Freemasons for a pint. Only for one, though, because we knew Derby would be headed for town, and so we hopped on buses. A small group was spotted on Shalesmoor and chased off. Their main mob must have split, and we didn't see any more of them. We camped out in the Venue on Arundel Gate, but nothing more was seen of them. Again Derby had come and caused us problems, but we had salvaged some pride, and a Wembley semi-final with Sheffield United now beckoned.

I will deal with the events of Saturday, 3 April 1993 in the next chapter, which I have dedicated solely to issues regarding our neighbours from the murkier parts of town.

The 1992–93 season was certainly one to remember. We had made four Wembley appearances, but finished up empty handed. Still, it has to be said that in comparison with some of the seasons we had suffered, these were glory days. The UEFA Cup run did not last long, though. After disposing of Spora Luxembourg 10-2 over two legs we were eliminated by the former German champions of Kaiserslautern. The first leg had been lost 3-1, a result that turned on the dismissal of David Hirst after the Owls had led 1-0. About forty lads went to the game in Germany, and they met up with that international superstar of football hooliganism, Ronald. Ronald was a German lad who liked to join up with British clubs and have a little dance. Martin told me a story of this particular night in

Germany when Ronald was asking who the best mobs in England were. Martin looked at him and replied, 'I don't know who the best mob in England is, but I know who the worst is.'

'Who is it?' asked Ronald, eager for information.

'You're looking at 'em,' replied Martin in his usual deadpan way.

The second leg proved a bridge too far for Wednesday, and we bowed out 5-3 on aggregate. Vans of Germans were attacked that night, and I sat in the Leppings Lane end for the only time. John Gannon of Sheffield United was also in there. He was given plenty of verbal abuse, which he took in good heart.

A 1993–94 season that promised much after the success of the previous seasons showed little. A poor first half to the season left the team playing catch-up throughout the second half, and despite some scintillating football, especially from Chris Waddle, the Owls had left themselves too much to do. The FA Cup run ended with a 3-1 home defeat to Chelsea in the Fourth Round, but the League Cup again gave some hope for silverware. We reached the two-legged semi-final stage again, and were drawn to play Manchester United at Old Trafford in the first leg. I went in a mini-bus from the Freemasons for this one. We had a pretty good mob aboard, including Bentley, Brian and Pea among others. There were also mini-buses going from Doncaster and Stocksbridge, so we knew that we would have a decent presence. A stop was made in Hyde for a few beers on the way, and lots of other Wednesday fans had the same idea. The pubs were heaving with happy Sheffielders looking forward to another prosperous cup day out.

Upon our arrival at the stadium we entered the ground and took our seats. We met up with Iggy and the Stocksbridge lads, and Bainsy, Rick and the lads from Donny. The Owls went a goal down to an incredible Ryan Giggs shot almost from the byline, which proved to be the only goal of the game. What happened for the rest of the match has gone down in Wednesday folklore. The Wednesday fans had recently taken to singing the theme from the *Dambusters*, and this match was no exception; however, the United supporters took exception to it, thinking it was being sung about the Munich air disaster, and they got pretty irate. Admittedly, there were some 'Munich' chants, but these were few and far between. The *Dambusters* chants were being sung in good nature by your average supporter, who really was oblivious to the effect the chants were having on the Mancs.

At the end of the match the gates were opened, and the Wednesday fans streamed out – straight into a huge mob of irate United supporters. The Manchester fans attacked everyone, including women and children. Panicking police closed the gates, leaving a large group of mainly peace-loving Wednesdayites at the mercy of a baying mob. Afterwards, Sash told me of how the Mancs went berserk, and how he saw young children and pensioners being kicked to the ground as the police looked on. We were still inside the ground, and word was filtering in of the carnage outside. The whole Wednesday support surged for the gate trying to get it open. The police and stewards didn't know what to do, and opened the gates. We poured out into the forecourt around the stadium. The scene outside was quite eerie. I walked up the middle of the road with Bainsy, and glasses were smashing all around, but I could see no Mancs.

We reached Warwick Road, and could see the police pushing the United fans up the road. Now that the bulk of our fanbase was out of the ground they suddenly took notice of the police. About forty of us, including most of our bus and the Donny lads, stood firm outside the Warwick Road Hotel. Small groups of Reds came for a skirmish, but were sent packing. I swear they would have had to bring a thousand lads to budge us that day. We were livid at what the Lancashire scum had been doing with innocent fans. There was one funny moment, however, when an Asian-looking kid and his mates came wandering up for a chat.

'Come on, lads,' he said in a cockney accent. 'We're all United, let's stick together.'

I looked at this moron and shook my head.

'We're not fucking United,' I said. 'We're Wednesday.'

I swear to God this kid looked like he had shit a brick. Without another word, or movement, he and his mates ran like the wind. We all stood around laughing at his cowardice. The bulk of the Mancs appeared to have gone, and we were looking at moving on when a big lad, dressed in a Lacoste shell suit, wandered up to Rick and I.

'Easy, lads,' he said. 'Let's get something sorted for the second leg.'

I admired his guts. He was alone, and was showing respect, unlike his Asian comrade. Interestingly enough he also had a northern accent.

'Come to the Freemasons on Hillsborough corner,' I replied.

'We'll be there,' he said and jogged off into the gloomy Manchester night.

We headed for home, proud of the stand we had made, but fuming about the treatment the Mancs had dished out to ordinary supporters. The reverberations would be felt around Sheffield for some time, and the Mancs would be made to pay in the return fixture. After their behaviour at Old Trafford it was open season, and any Manc was fair game.

I was working at a major forging company in Sheffield at the time, and had always worked straight mornings. For the date of the second leg, however, I was working on afternoons. I tried desperately to switch shifts with someone, but no one would have it. I resigned myself to missing the match, but hoped I might get away early to catch any after-match activity. The gods must have been smiling on me, because on the big day it snowed heavily all afternoon and the match was postponed for a week. I was over the moon, and would be back on mornings for the rearranged fixture.

We met in the Freemasons, and there was quite a mob out. There were lads there who I had not seen much of for years. Revenge for the shit dished out at Old Trafford was on the cards. The Mancs never showed on Hillsborough corner, and by 6.30pm Mick had given the order to move out. We exited the pub and made our way along Middlewood Road. There was easily 200 of us out, and that was by far the best mob we had turned out in 2 years. As we reached the top of Leppings Lane Mick turned and told everyone to just walk, but that was easier said than done. As soon as we reached Catch Bar Lane the mob broke into a jog and then a charge. I looked up to see Rick in the middle of the United fans, who just moments earlier had been queuing peacefully. We steamed straight in, and police on horseback had to force us back from the terrified Mancs. Some of their lads were there, and they started mouthing, but made no effort to bring the fight to us. As we moved round the ground pockets of United fans were attacked, and at least one lad was beaten unconscious.

I was among a group who headed up Halifax Road to watch the game on TV in the Travellers. The plan was to meet at the bottom of Herries Road afterwards, and attack the Mancs as they went to board their coaches home. The police had parked the coaches up Halifax Road toward the White Horse. About twenty of us sat in the Travellers and watched the Owls lose 4-1 to end our Wembley dreams. At the final whistle we walked down to the meeting place. There were already a lot of lads waiting, including fans in scarves who had witnessed the scenes of a fortnight earlier, and wanted some payback. One older fellow clad in, a scarf, and with his young son alongside, summed it up perfectly, 'Give it to the bastards, lads. Give them what they gave us.'

The first punch I saw thrown was by a Sheffield United mate of Moores. He ran across the road and dropped the first Manc who appeared.

'They fucking did it to us!' he cried.

There was a huge mob by now, and we began to walk up Halifax Road. Another mob came running out of the Travellers car park, thinking we were Mancs. The numbers were large, and United fans were attacked as they made their way back to their buses. In contrast to the stuff they had dealt out I saw no women and children attacked, although – and I am not proud of this – many fans in scarves were attacked. A number of coaches were wrecked, and pockets of United fans did put up some resistance, but anger was fuelling the Wednesday fans on this evening, and even the police knew it. As we walked back down Halifax Road I overheard the following snippet of conversation between two South Yorkshire officers:

'Look at 'em. These lot are not kids, they're all big lads,' said one.

'Well, a lot of people were angered by what happened in Manchester, and who can blame them?' was his colleague's reply.

In all my years of going to the football this was the only time I ever saw Wednesday fans attack opposing fans en masse. I saw it happen to Wednesday fans on three or four occasions, but we never dished it out, apart from that night. I was involved, and I take no pride in my part, but the fact remains that the Mancs had overstepped the mark in the first leg, and it needed sorting. I don't think they even brought a mob that night, and after what had gone before you have to ask myself why. I have my own theories, but I will keep them to myself.

During the close season before 1994–95 the Wednesday team that had been so successful in the preceding years began to break up. This was the beginning of the end, and the start of the slide down to where we currently find ourselves. Journeyman players such as Peter Atherton came in, but, with no disrespect intended, they simply were not the same class. David Hirst, who had been bracketed in the £4 million range a few years previously, hardly played, and the team began to struggle. I was around at the start of the season, but by the time it ended I had turned my back on the hooligan lifestyle, and even my home town.

In November of 1994 an engineering company in Ontario, Canada approached me. They offered me a job in a new plant that they had opened. It was too good an opportunity to turn down. So, on 18 April 1995, the day after Wednesday had fought out a Hillsborough draw with Everton, I boarded a plane for Toronto, and began a new chapter in my life. Football was no longer to be a part of it. Or so I thought.

I'll let Dougie have the final word in this chapter, with his recollection of a day out in the Big Smoke ...

WGA did Man United in London Town: 1991

Winn Gardens Army (WGA) is a small branch of the OCS, which at its height probably had about 13 members. This is a solid group of lads not to be taken lightly; they have grown up watching each others' backs from childhood.

In Sheffield, every area has its own little firms, each one making up the structure of the OCS. When brought together they are a force to be reckoned with, both in and out of the city. The League Cup final of 1991 was to be a real test for the Gardens Army. Eleven lads in London with time and drink to cope with, and the threat the big city brings. It had been some season, on and off the field, and the weekend with Manchester United in London was going to be no picnic. Some of our lads were young and usually a cause for concern, but at the time I was quietly confident. However, youth and drink don't mix. I know – I've been there, and I'm still learning.

Saturday morning; it's the weekend of the final, and we set off to London early, with all the excitement that any of your best Christmas days can bring. The 11 of us in a van full of mixed emotions, but one thing in mind – drink, and plenty of it. We've got 160 miles to go, and it seems like a lifetime away. Leicester Forest service station is our first stop; a small amount of food and a light watering is the order. Walking back to the van fills me with pride; from a hundred yards I can see the Union Jack trapped in the back doors of the bus, bearing the letters SWFC in white emulsion.

Two hours later we are in London, with all it offers. Driving through it seems like a shithole, and it probably is; bland streets teeming with garbage and miserable-looking people. Eventually, we find a nice little Bed and Breakfast establishment who are prepared to take a bunch of nondescripts from 'Up North'. We drop off our bags and settle into our home for the weekend.

It seems strange. I've been abroad before, but this seemed farther. Northerners in the capital don't seem welcome, but nevertheless we are out. A few lads want to place a bet, so we make our way to the bookies, and all the lads place big bets on the Wednesday to win. With the bets on, and a few chips in our empty stomachs, the lads are drying out. Time to find a boozer and our first port of call is a proper little Irish watering hole full of the obvious. We step inside, and it's all eyes on the strange types; drinking at 11 in the morning when only they are allowed, so it's horse racing and the black stuff all round, but one of ours has got different ideas. He strolls over to the television and switches it from horses to an interview with 'Big' Ron Atkinson (the Owls manager at the time). We have been in our first pub for less than five minutes and I'm thinking, 'This is it. No surrender', with 30 pairs of Irish eyes glaring across the room.

'Oh, oh, no problem,' shouts one of their old boys, probably 82-plus, and the tension recedes.

Twenty games of darts and six pints later we head out, and the mood has changed slightly, from respecting the cockneys on their turf to chants of 'If you hate cockneys clap your hands.' I have a few words with some of the lads, and things calm. The next pub looms, and it's an outside drinking affair. There follows plenty of singing, and the odd remark, aimed at the locals; we are in a busy shopping area close to central London, and at some point, I feel, there will be a firm coming to sort us out. Nothing happens, however, and after a gallon plus of ale we leave. By now we are singing and dancing through the busy streets, seeking to find our way back to the accommodation.

Back at the B&B we shower and change in preparation for our night on the town. First thing is the nearby tube station, and we all purchase saver tickets, giving us freedom of movement around London on bus, tube and train. The first tube arrives and we are on it, not knowing for definite where we will end up. Five minutes later and we are walking through a busy tube station bang in the heart of London. Going up the escalator, and a large chorus of 'Wednesday' comes bellowing through the station: twenty to thirty lads on the piss. It's time for a quick chorus back and we meet, and decide on a swift one or two together. After an hour swilling we decide to part company, and we head for the tube, to get our money's worth of course.

Through the carriage I can see some lads. Who are they? Who cares – at that point we're singing every Wednesday song composed. This triggers a reaction from the set of lads in the next coach, and they decide to make an appearance at the opposite end of our carriage, with a large shout of 'Man U!' and then all the songs they can muster. First thoughts are they seem quite friendly, and are just on the piss – probably not even their lads. After a quick rethink they're not friendly and, yes, they are their lads.

Fifty yards separate us. By this time I'm slowly sobering up to the thought of big trouble on a moving tube. A couple of minutes later, and after plenty of abuse, we've stopped. I'm sure this is it, but we're standing and so are they. At that point some youth walks straight through us. No sweat, he's not with them, but leaving the tube he decides to lob a bottle at us. The bottle in question hits one of our lads in the chest. Luckily it's one of the larger Gardens lads and it makes no impression on his over-generous frame.

The doors shut and we're moving, both sides are now a lot less vocal, and eyes are firmly fixed on each other. I'm not sure, but it seems like equal numbers. The next stop and we're off. There is quite a crowd of passengers moving around, but I can clearly see that the Mancs have also vacated the tube. We are on the platform and walking towards the turnstiles. We're all through and I look back. Man U are coming and they are shouting. Fuck me, they really want it, and one of our lads is caught on the turnstiles and they're dragging him over. That's it, I'm over. First thoughts are 'Kill the bastards!'; next are 'Fuck me, he's a big cunt!' I decide to volley him, which is not successful, and he catches me on the ear, but as he swings round I make a full connection. At this point all the lads are in and bang at it. The fighting goes on, and we're getting topside. Two of their lads are seriously hurt on the deck, but there are still a few bouncing, so come on, lads, let's have it!

I'm sparring with this youth and telling the cunt he's going down, when my younger brother comes running through and makes the sweetest of connections. The Manc youth hits the deck and is well and truly unconscious. His eyes are flickering, and his body's shaking, but he still takes a few volleys from a pair of shiny red Kickers belonging to one of our crazed lads.

I turn round and it's utter carnage, their stunned bodies are all over the floor, covered in blood. Bystanders are in shock and up against the walls. At this point the mist lifts, and reality is setting in, so with a loud but slightly nervous chorus of 'Wednesday!' we leave the tube station. On our way out it becomes obvious that if we get picked up now we're in big trouble. We get in a boozer not far from the incident, and head straight for the bar, which is separated from the rest by a tuppence ha'penny curtain, Fuck me, three minutes or so of full-on battling seems to pass in seconds. No one's hurt, which is a miracle. Even though at the time not one of us would admit it, we were in shock. One or two vessels later we decide to make a move. To cut a long story short, it's Kentucky and feather. We got a result tonight, but the main thing is we got away with it.

Sunlight through the attic window, and I'm rolling out of my adopted bed. I look round at the other five bodies in their slumber. A bit of encouragement and we're up and about. After a hearty breakfast, the bus is packed with our bags, a few cheap ornaments, a fair few bog rolls, and some strong detergent – you never know where and when these essentials may be needed.

Good forward thinking from our lads at the hotel's small expense. Wembley beckons. It's not far, but getting parked is a major problem. After driving round in circles for an hour we decide to leave the bus – who knows where – and we walk the rest of the way. At last, a pub! I know it's early, but luckily it's open, and we're now ready for a proper belly full. We are on the main road to Wembley, within throwing distance of the stadium. We're outside the boozer, and we're drinking with a handful of lads. Slowly but surely our drinking partners increase, and the odd chorus goes up. I am standing talking to one of our lads, when he makes the loudest of cries, with a hint of desperation. Turning and looking at his face I know he's in trouble.

'Fuck me, I've shit myself!'

'Never!' I reply.

Honestly, I wouldn't lie about something so serious, so I ask him to show me, like any friend would. Trousers down and I'm viewing an overweight back valve. Not that I've any experience in this department, but it looks mint. Not a splash or lump in sight. Then he bends slightly to reveal the culprit – a small golf ball-sized lump of shit trapped in his cheeks.

'You dirty bastard.' And the anxious crowd that had developed around him begins to disperse. With his trousers round his ankles he disappears to the rear of the boozer to clean himself, and his attitude, up as this act of behaviour is not encouraged – especially from a high-ranking officer, but it's funny as fuck (especially as it's not you – on this occasion). Two or three minutes later and he returns with evidence on full show. Let me describe: Y-fronts, the pale version, covered in shit. Have you got it? With a large smile on his face he hangs them on the boozer door at head height. This causes some discouragement among the neutrals, but he thinks it's a good advert for the boozer and will attract business.

A large number of coaches appear over the horizon. Fuck me, Wednesday's here! But it isn't – it's Man U, so as they approach we decide to stand in the road and give them a welcoming reception. Four or five coaches later and we're giving it them, which I think is well within the boundaries, but the coppers don't. With a quick lift of the back of my strides I'm off to the sin bin.

Bollocks. I'm going to miss the final. I'm in the van with two coppers, and our lads turn up. With five minutes to kick-off they let me go. What a relief.

'Come on, Wednesday!' We are in the ground, and in the best seats along with some middle-class shitehouses who know all the players' names, and keep telling us to sit down, which is met by the appropriate response: 'Fuck off.' I think they've got the picture. Watching the game the nerves are massive, and it's becoming unbearable. Then the noise of wood and 'Goal!' That's it, we're pogoing and scissor-kicking to our hearts content. Best thing is, the old-type middle classes are jumping all over me, and dragging me down in their excitement. For the rest of the game it's one set of fans. Young, old, rich and skint, it's about being WEDNESDAY.

10

NEVER BEEN RUN ...
NEVER BEEN DONE

Sheffield United. The very name of Sheffield's second club strikes fear and dismay into the hearts of every Sheffield Wednesday supporter. Well, that's what the Sheffield United supporters would have you believe, but I am not buying. To be honest, I really can't say I hate United. I come from a family of Blades, and to say I hate Sheffield United would be to say I hate the members of my family, which is simply not the case. Many families in Sheffield are split along family lines, and there is genuine hatred among both sets of fans, but I have always tried to rise above it – although that has not been easy at times. This chapter will focus on my part in the torrid sibling rivalry that exists between the blue and the red.

Throughout the history of both clubs it has been a case of swings and roundabouts. Rarely, it seems, have both clubs been in the same division for long. Throughout their long histories, the two have traded the title of Sheffield's number one team. There would be few from either side, however, who would deny that throughout the 1980s and 1990s, apart from one brief season, Wednesday held the ascendancy on the field. Equally, it cannot be denied that the 1970s was United's decade on the field. But what about off it?

That little puzzle seems to run in reverse. It would appear that whichever of the two clubs was the more successful on the pitch, their fans would rule the roost in the Steel City off it. During the 1970s United rode high in Division One, while Wednesday floundered down in the Third. The Wednesday mob of that era, the East Bank Republican Army, was far stronger, and bigger, than its United counterpart, the Shoreham Republican Army.

While researching this book I have spoken to many combatants from both sides, and almost to a man they agreed that the Wednesday mob bossed the city throughout the 1970s and into the 1980s. Matches between the two clubs during that era, usually testimonials or County Cup games, would often see Wednesday taking over Bramall Lane, with United's mob totally outgunned.

Again I will hand over to Stevie, as he recalls the days when the Owls held sway over their neighbours:

In the 1970s we were the top dogs in Sheffield. All the town pubs like the Claymore, Crazy Daizy, etc. were full of Owls, and the taking of the Shoreham was a regular occurrence in testimonials and County Cup matches. Even in testimonials for their heroes like Woodward and Badger, we'd go there and take the piss, and if it hadn't been for the OB we'd have humiliated them even more. By the end of the 1970s United had a decent mob, though – known to us as the Barmy Army – and they had some good lads from Heeley and the Manor, etc. But even so we still had the edge.

The Boxing Day Massacre of 1979 passed off peacefully, and it seemed like even though they'd been thrashed they didn't want to know. There were some down Heeley that night, but no sign of any bother. The return on 5 April 1980 was a different matter, though. At kick-off there must have been a good three to four thousand Wednesday on the Shoreham, with me among them, and the line of OB just wasn't sufficient. We were on the left-hand side and all the game kept surging towards United, and to be fair they were having a right go too. There was some brilliant toe to toes, no one really giving an inch. I remember laying into this one bloke and then realising he only lived round the corner from me. People were going down and you'd help them up – getting crushed among that lot wasn't an option. Strangely enough, the trouble seemed to finish after the game, at least I didn't see anything major go off, and town that night was fairly quiet.

The best derby match-off I was involved in was the League Cup second leg game on Tuesday, 12 August 1980. We'd won the first leg the previous Saturday 2-0. We met in the White Lion, Heeley; about half a dozen of us, and strangely enough there were no Blades in there, which, considering the area, was odd. Maybe they were all up in the Shakespeare? Anyhow, we had a few pints and marched off down to the Lane, stopped off for a quick pint in the Earl of Arundel and then on to Shoreham Street. There seemed a distinct shortage of OB that night and we entered the Shoreham through one of the turnstiles just past Cherry Street. After getting in we saw about twenty Owls stood down towards the bottom of the kop and we walked over to them. We talked about going up alongside the Blades at the back of the kop. The general feeling was we'd get battered but we went up anyway, and on getting there we saw another dozen or so Owls already there.

The chant of 'Wednesday' went up and the Blades on the side of the fence where we were scattered, but some better lads came round the back and got behind us. Ugly-looking bastards they were, mullets and scarves tied round their heads. One of them shouted, 'Run, you Wednesday bastards!' and another kept saying they were going to kill us. So we did run – but unfortunately for them, we ran straight at them. Seems their mouths were bigger than their bottles and they were soon getting pasted and were trying desperately to get out.

The fighting spilled out on the walkway at the back of the Shoreham, but by now the OB had seen what was happening and intervened. So we went back inside and tried scaling the fences, but again the police stopped that lark. To be honest, there were a lot of Blades over there, but we were on a bit of a high so didn't really care. All the excitement attracted more Wednesday and by the time things had settled down there were about a thousand of us in there.

The rest of the match was spent hurling insults and coins and all that crap. At the end of the game (1-1) the OB made us leave by the exit at the top end of Shoreham Street, but once out on the street there were no OB in sight, so a thousand of us were left alone to march down Shoreham Street to where the Blades were exiting the ground, and what followed was a classic.

As we ran into the Blades from Shoreham Street the main mob of Wednesday had come out of the ground and was attacking them along John Street, so where they were coming out, the corner of Shoreham Street and John Street, they were caught in a classic pincer movement, and lots were scrambling to get back in the ground. Wednesday were taking the piss, we'd been on their kop (again), which is something they never did at Hillsborough, and done them. We had done them after the match too, and never saw them in town afterwards. It was a top, top night out, one of the best ever.

Then the 1980s Casuals were born and I kind of lost interest; I could never have looked good in the Pringles and Farahs.

Probably the most telling part of Stevie's tale is his comment about United starting to get a decent mob together. Their demise into the basement of the football league in 1981 saw them get a chance to do a bit of 'lower-league bullying'. This stint in the doldrums saw their mob growing, and gelling together, in much the same way as the Wednesday mobs of the 1970s had, but even when I finally started to get involved, around 1985, the older Wednesday lads simply did not rate the United mob at all. Of course, at this time trouble in town was rare, and matches between the two clubs were rarer still. I went to a few matches at Bramall Lane in 1985–86, and saw quite a few Wednesday lads sat in the stands for games against the likes of Leeds and Portsmouth. The animosity, if it really existed then, must have been bubbling below the surface.

Most of the old faces on both sides knew each other, and so did most of the youth. An uneasy peace was the norm but, just like a dam wall, it only needs one crack to start a trickle, and if it goes unchecked, sooner or later that crack will open up, and the trickle will become a deluge. A testimonial game at the end of the 1985–86 season would start to chip away at that crack, and within a matter of months the uneasy peace would be no more, and the seeds of the struggle for dominance, which continues to this day, would be sown.

The occasion was a testimonial game for long-serving United stalwart Tony Kenworthy. The game was to be played at Bramall Lane on a warm May evening in 1986. The United mob had grown significantly over the previous five seasons, and they were starting to make a name for themselves. The general consensus among the Wednesday firm was that they needed to be 'put in their place'. On the day of this game I finished work and headed straight into town. Walking up Fargate I saw Steve Thorn and Bowen, two other Wednesday lads of my age, walking up toward West Street, so I went with them. We arrived at the Hallamshire Hotel to find that we had a good 50–60 already in, despite the fact that it was only 4.30pm. I stood outside yapping for a while with Ash, who was an old mate from school, and then decided to go to Popeye's for a burger.

While I was in there a shout went up and I saw everyone running out of the pub down toward Fitzwilliam Street. I quickly grabbed my burger and raced out to see what the commotion was all about. I got to the corner and saw a mob of Blades, sixty strong, coming up the road. Halesy was at the front of the Wednesday mob waving a stick around and urging the lads in. The 'hoo hoo hoo' went up from our lads and we raced toward them, two sixty-strong gangs charging for each other.

The next thing I heard was a fizzing and I saw a green flare had landed about three feet away from me. It looked like a piece of kryptonite, but if the United chaps thought it would weaken our resolve they were mistaken. A loud roar went up as the two firms collided. No quarter was given from either side and the dancing began. Sadly it was quickly curtailed as the police appeared in numbers. Both firms were split, and *both* marched straight down Fitzwilliam toward London Road.

Sporadic fighting broke out on the walk down, and police on

horseback were forced to make their presence felt on more than one occasion. Our lads were buoyed, though, as it seemed the Blades were definitely on the back foot and trying to reach the safe haven of London Road.

The Blades headed for the sanctuary of the Hermitage, where I expected there would be more waiting. Our mob made an attempt to get to the pub, but a large police presence kept the Blades inside, and we were pushed up toward Ecclesall Road.

The police moved us toward the ground, and I was expecting that they would usher us into the Wednesday end, but to my immense surprise they didn't. We all queued up and gained entrance to the South Stand. There were a few Blades in there, but on the whole it was empty, which was a little surprising.

About halfway through the game we decided that the Blades must have stayed out and were plotting up somewhere, and so we decided to leave. Other Owls fans met us as we passed the Wednesday end – they had seen us leave and decided to join us. The police were keeping a watchful eye, and escorted us back in the direction of town, but then left us to our own devices – or so it seemed.

Our first port of call was the Rutland Arms, a small pub off the beaten track located in the area around the back of the Leadmill. While in there it was decided that we would try and wait near the underground car park beneath the Fiesta nightclub. This was an ideal spot, as we expected the United firm to walk through Pond Street looking for us, and this position offered a clear view of the entire Pond Street area. We made our way up there without too much trouble, and settled in. We had barely been there five minutes when suddenly we heard the beating of truncheons – it was the police, and they were charging toward us.

Panic set in, and everyone was on their toes, running across the car park. As the mob reached the other side a token stand was made, but that's all it was and we piled out the exit. I failed to see a two-foot-high barrier and, along with several others, fell flat on my face with the police in hot pursuit. I picked myself up and headed out the exit, to be greeted by more police officers, one of who aimed a kick at me. They had set us up good and proper, and we were deflated; however, the police back-slapping would allow us the opportunity we needed. Their euphoria at what seemed a job well done allowed us to slip away en masse. The firm, still largely intact, walked up Church Street and on to Surrey Street. The police had let us go, and that error was about to come back to haunt them.

Looking back on events that night, it seems that the police did not realise that a large group of Sheffield United hooligans were simultaneously making their way up the Moor, and were soon to be on a direct collision course with our group. Within minutes two gangs of skilled dancers would be enacting their own 'Ballroom Blitz' in the darkened streets of Sheffield City Centre.

Mark, a good friend of mine, describes the scenes that followed:

At 17 I had been following Sheffield Wednesday for about 4 years and over the previous two had been getting drawn towards the violence that was part of football at that time. As yet I had never participated, but that was about to change.

On this night Wednesday had played Sheffield United in a testimonial for Blades player Tony Kenworthy at Bramall Lane. Whether I even went to the game is something that still escapes me, yet here I was, a green 17-year-old, about to get his first taste of football hooliganism up close.

On leaving the ground Wednesday's mob that night must have made their way into Sheffield town centre, as my first recollection of being there is on Surrey Street, which runs down the side of Sheffield Town Hall.

The following events are still vivid in my mind:

Heading up Surrey Street, Wednesday turned left to approach the Peace Gardens in front of the town hall, and we knew the United mob were likely to be somewhere in the same area. As we turned the corner and the Gardens came into full view we spotted roughly an equal number of United walking the same way along Leopold Street, which runs across the top of the Peace Gardens. They had obviously headed into town by walking up the Moor.

In all honesty I was towards the rear of the Wednesday mob, who were being marshalled at the back by an older, well-respected lad of the day, and the words 'Any fucker who runs will get it off me later' made sure I stood my ground, despite the fact I was both buzzing and shitting myself at the same time.

The two opposing gangs were now about seventy yards apart and approaching a small walkway that linked the street and the concourse we were on.

The mobs spotted each other and immediately the roar went up. Shouts of 'Come on!' and 'They're here!' were hurled from both mobs and the front liners steamed into each other, though Wednesday seemed the keener to confront the opposition. As the two groups clashed and the first punches and kicks were thrown, a young black United lad jumped on a small wall and discharged the first distress flare I had ever seen, which hit a wall high up and fell into the Wednesday lads below. This appeared to give Wednesday an extra incentive and the whole of the mob surged forward to chants of 'Wednesday, Wednesday!'

United were rattled and started to lose it a bit and back off. As many know, once a firm starts to back away it's near impossible to turn the tables back in its favour. Wednesday pushed on and soon had the United mob in full retreat.

Seeing a mob in full flight is great when it's not your own, and Wednesday were now chasing United along Wellington Street at full steam. I passed at least six or seven lads lying on the ground in the foetal position as we charged over them. Chasing another firm doesn't usually last very long – once a firm has been run the damage is done and on that night victory was ours.

Sad to say, though, it would be some time before Wednesday had another victory against United anywhere near the size of the one that night.

The job had been done. The upstart United firm had been put in their place, but although we saw very little of them over the summer, they would be back, and we would need to be ready and able to deal with the threat when it arose.

If the Tony Kenworthy testimonial sowed the seeds, then an incident later that year poured bucket loads of fertiliser on the shoots of discord. Three well-known black Wednesday lads were attacked by Blades while drinking on London Road. One of them suffered severe injuries and was hospitalised. Vengeance was sworn, and plans were made to take a large firm down London Road to exact some justice for this cowardly act. On the night of the meet I turned up at the Royal Standard, and the turnout was extremely disappointing. There were no more than 25 tops, but there were a few of the older lads there, and despite the low numbers it was acknowledged that we 'had enough'. Maybe we would have if we had kept it tight, but we didn't, and once again overeagerness would prove to be our undoing.

We slipped on to London Road virtually unnoticed, and a quick stop at the Lansdowne, which at the time was the main Blade pub, showed nothing untoward. The odd thing was that no Blades seemed to be around. A shout was heard from further up the road, and a few of our lot set off to investigate. Most of us straggled up the road in leisurely pursuit.

'They're here!' went the shout, and lads could be seen exiting the Pheasant pub, some hundred yards or so up the road. Lads could also be seen exiting a pub opposite, and here we were, 25 of us, spread over the best part of a hundred yards – sitting ducks, and heavily outnumbered. Blades came pouring down the road at us. We stood for a few seconds toe to toe, but we had nothing to come, and we had to turn tail and run.

Off London Road we went with the Blunts in pursuit. We made an effort to stand at Moorfoot, and actually backed the first few of them off. Laver shot a firework into their ranks, and this unnerved them, but not for long. More came racing round the corner, and we were off again. We split this time, but one older lad was caught outside a fruit shop. Rumour would later sweep round that he had died, though this was thankfully not the case. Most of our lads headed up Furnival Gate, but about five of us went up the Moor.

Our small group, which included Halesy, was mainly made up of younger lads, but we stood and had a good go with our pursuers. It ended with us being put on our toes again, but not without a fight. I had my new Armani T-shirt torn in the fighting, and although we ended up running again, at least we had put up some sort of resistance.

We all ended up back at the Bell in town, and it was agreed

that we had been far too hasty in our actions, and should have sat tight. The next time would be different, and the Blades would know their place.

The 'next time' was not long in coming; in fact, it was exactly a week later. That night would take a sinister turn, and would end up with three of our lads serving jail time for making petrol bombs. Sash and Ziggy had made a number of crude petrol bombs, and Davy would later be arrested in possession of them. I still don't believe any of the three lads in question intended using the explosives, but that they should have made them in the first place just shows how high feelings were running. Again we met at the Standard. The numbers were higher, probably touching sixty, but we knew the Blunts would be expecting us this time, so stealth was of vital importance. We made our way up to the Sportsman on Denby Street, and set ourselves up. A car load of Blades came for a drive-by, and let a flare loose in our direction. The lads outside the pub cheered as it flew harmlessly by. It was time to sit tight now. We were on their manor, and they knew we were there. All our game pieces were now on the board, and it was time for the Blades to make their move.

It wasn't long in coming. Within minutes they appeared at the top end of Denby Street. Most of the Wednesday mob were still inside the pub, and an almighty scramble ensued as they tried to get out. I was already outside, and braced myself for the coming hostilities. The next thing I knew I was picking myself up from the floor, and looking up to see a policeman with truncheon raised. They seemed to have come straight through the Blades' line, and were going to town on the Owls fans, who were now scrambling to get back inside the pub. I raised my hands, and stepped to one side. Looking up the street I saw the Blades still standing there. I was confused. Why had the police let them alone and attacked us? I looked on as the police then turned their attention to our foes, and chased them off into the night. We split into small groups and headed back into town. To me, and most of the other Owls lads, the night had been a non-event. The police had put paid to our plans, and the game was up. I heard later that the Blades claimed to have 'run' us back into the pub. Maybe that's true, but only if they are counting tooled-up police officers as their firm. A small mob of Owls did make it to the Royal Oak just off London Road. This mob included a couple of the black lads who had been filled in a few weeks previous. A firefight ensued when the Blades tried storming the pub, and a Londoner who ran with the Blades ended up losing an eye.

Things seemed to die down a bit after that night. I think the petrol bomb incident gave both mobs a shake. We still saw little of them in town, but by now the balance of power was shifting. The newly christened Blades Business Crew was growing in numbers, while our numbers were beginning to dwindle.

Apart from that evening we still ran town, but the Blades were developing a reputation outside Sheffield. In the 1986–87 season we had been drawn at home to West Ham. Amazingly, United were home that day to Plymouth, and the police allowed both games to go ahead. As I recounted earlier we had a big firm out waiting for West Ham, but it was our cross-town rivals that filled the thoughts of one of our old campaigners in particular. Everything seemed normal as we drank in the Bell, and most of the talk centred around West Ham. Without warning an old lad, known to all, stood up and declared that we were going to London Road to 'sort the pigs'. No one spoke as he headed for the door, but to a man we followed. We kept off the main routes to avoid arousing the suspicion of the police, but as we walked parallel to the Moor past the Pump public house a lone policeman saw us. He looked extremely confused, and immediately got on his radio.

'We've fucked it now,' exclaimed Ricky

I was inclined to agree, but oddly enough no sudden swoop of police materialised. It was as if they wanted us to do what we were heading off to do.

London Road was quiet when we arrived. No Blades could be found, and so we headed up the street to lie in wait. We found sanctuary in an old pub called the Royal, close to where London Road becomes Abbeydale Road. The plan was to lie low and wait for the Blades to begin filling their pubs on London Road. We would sweep down the street, taking all before us. That was the plan, but it didn't quite come off. A couple of the younger lads went off in search of food, and were confronted by a confused Polak, and a few other BBC lads.

'What the fuck are you lot doing up here? You've fucked it now,' he told them and headed down to warn a number of Blades who had begun to take up residence in the Pheasant. We had to make our move, and so we headed out, not really sure of their strength, but we were confident that nothing could touch us.

About thirty older heads got a bit in front of us, and this group was almost immediately challenged by a mob of around twenty Blades coming from the Pheasant. The bulk of our mob was still out of their view, so the Blades thought the thirty they saw was it. They went straight in, but that was our cue. Someone in the front group blew a whistle and the roar went up. Suddenly the thirty Owls became a hundred-plus and those odds were far too much for the United lads. There seemed to be some confusion initially in their ranks as to whether we were West Ham or Wednesday, but that was quickly dispelled when the chant of

'OOOOOOO-CCCCC-SSSSSSSSSSSSSS!' filled the street. Totally overwhelmed, they had no choice but to run. They headed down to the Lansdowne with us in hot pursuit. When we reached the pub we quickly covered both doors. The old lad who had stood up in the Bell went in through the back door, and emerged from the front a couple of minutes later brushing his sheepskin coat down. The Owls mob was going to town on the pub and the chant of 'Easy, easy, easy!' brought traffic to a halt at the bottom end of London Road.

As we headed back into town, still unmolested by the South Yorkshire police, we passed many Blades who to a man looked stunned to see us. We had shown in force in their backyard when they were at home. Maybe we should have been in town for the cockneys, but that may not have happened, and as it turned out another large Wednesday mob was waiting in the Dove and Rainbow. Little had been seen of West Ham, but more would be seen of the BBC later. They were going to be out for revenge, and we knew it. We expected to be able to meet the challenge head on. I recounted the events at the game that day back in chapter 4, and also described our journey back to town. About forty of us got split from the main mob, and made our way to the Yorkshiremans at the back of Cole Brothers department store. We had not been in too long when a loud crash signalled the arrival of our nemesis. Something had hit the window of the pub, and we were showered with glass. The windows of the pub were made from heavy stained glass, but within minutes they would be nothing more than twisted scrap. A large group of BBC had arrived and they were heaving everything at the pub. Paving slabs from roadworks were crashing through the window; we made an effort to get out, but the sheer volume of missiles forced us back in. The familiar firefight then ensued as they threw things in and we returned the compliment. The sound of police sirens brought about the end of this particular episode and the United mob disappeared into the night air. They had restored a semblance of pride, and we knew it.

Curiously, that was the night I realised just how terrifying an ordeal this type of incident could be to innocent bystanders. Two older ladies emerged from the toilets as the chaos ended. They were visibly shaking, and clearly terrified. What to us had been a 'bit of a laugh' was an extremely frightening experience for these women. Seeing them definitely had an impact on me, and others present.

We left the pub. It looked like a bomb had gone off. The once proud stained-glass windows were smashed to smithereens. The heavy wooden door lay on the ground, torn from its hinges by the ferocious onslaught. This type of scene would become a familiar sight in Sheffield over the next few years. The war for supremacy was now most definitely on.

As the stakes became higher it became clear that the BBC would stop at nothing to try and impose themselves on us. On numerous occasions lone Owls out in town were attacked. My first taste of this odious new tactic came one Saturday night in February 1987. I had gone into town as usual, and met up with about 15 lads in the Golden Ball. After having a couple of pints, Whitley and I decided to take the short walk to the Stonehouse on High Street. We really couldn't have timed it any worse, because as we came up by the side of the cathedral a mob of about forty BBC were coming off Leopold Street.

Whitley was an Owl who had formerly been a Blade, and he was not a favourite of theirs. He saw the Blades walking on to High Street and looked at me.

'Keep your head down,' he whispered.

It was too late. They had spotted us – or more precisely, they had spotted him.

A little dickhead came bouncing over.

'Which one of you is Whitley?' he demanded.

'I am,' replied Whitley.

With that the youth launched himself at him, and the others came bouncing down.

'Run,' Whitley yelled at me, and quite rightly took off. In my naïvety, however, I stood still. They weren't after me, so why should I run?

I didn't have long to ponder as I was suddenly showered with punches and kicks. The most frightening thing was that I realised that they were going to try and throw me through the window of the nearby Halifax Building Society. Before they succeeded the same cockney Blade who had lost an eye at the Royal Oak came running through.

'Fucking leave him!' he yelled.

The mob backed off, and the cockney walked me to a nearby bench by the cathedral.

'You all right, mate?' he asked.

I nodded in the affirmative, and with that the BBC mob drifted off, maybe in search of some other easy prey.

I headed back to the Golden Ball. My eye was badly cut, but the blood made it look worse than it was. The lads in the pub packed me off in a taxi to the hospital, and I had three stitches put in my right eyelid. I returned to West Street in time for last orders. I assumed the BBC must have been about, but no one had seen them. It looked to me like they had simply ghosted in and out of town looking for stragglers to bully, and I had copped for it. On reflection I had got off lucky, but others were not so fortunate.

Over the next couple of years things degenerated. Tit-for-tat attacks became accepted practice for both sides. I do not for one minute condone any of it, but the BBC always seemed to try and take it one step further. On numerous occasions they would go out in car loads looking for certain people. Home visits became a norm with them, and it seemed that any Owl was fair game. The cycle of violence was escalating out of control, and town was becoming a dangerous place to be. Sunday league football pitches became battlegrounds too, as rival Owls and Blades confronted one another while playing football for pub teams.

The tide had turned, however, and the BBC tactics – however brutal – were taking their toll on us. Throughout 1988–90 the BBC would regularly show up mob-handed on West Street, usually when we were thin on the ground. If our numbers were low, Saturday nights became a fight for survival, but we never gave in despite the oppression. Sometimes they would come unstuck, and it would be them being chased, but by and large we were heavily outgunned.

The thing that really bothers me, though, is that they knew when we were only out in small numbers, and yet they still came – not to give us a squeeze, but to kick the fuck out of us. One night there were six of us in the Mailcoach. A Blade walked in, and walked out again. Surely they wouldn't think six of us worth it? About thirty seconds later a mob of about twenty-five were bursting through the door. Gill tried to hold them off, but to no avail, and we ended up having to lock ourselves in the toilets. They tried for a full five minutes to kick the door in, and all the while they were yelling out to me by name: 'Come on out, D! You're going to get it sooner or later!'

I recently read that the writer Irving Welsh has a soft spot for the Blades because they don't bully small groups. Well, Irving my old chum, you obviously never spent any time on West Street in the late 1980s. Many of us felt the sting of the Blade bullies during those times. I will let Linwell share his thoughts on the noble Blunts:

From about the mid-1980s I drifted away from the regular weekly excursions due to the fact that I was trying to build a life, and spending time away from Sheffield. I got back into it from around 1989–92, but then I was off again. During those years we were regularly on the back foot in the city centre due to the sheer numbers that the BBC could muster, and after seeing them up close and personal I can have no respect for them as they were really just bullies. The Limit on West Street was the salvation for us, and the Blunts never took it if we were in. There were some close calls, but they never had the Limit. When the Limit closed it was a big blow for us, as we had no place we could get back to and mob up in.

There are two or three incidents that I remember from that time which sum the BBC up. I am not slagging them here, as they have numbers, and some game lads as well as organisation, but to me they only want it when they are on top.

One Sunday night about thirty of them legged seven of us for well over an hour, managed to capture one of our lads, unbeknown to us, and gave him a shoeing of biblical proportions. For me that proves nothing.

Whenever we had a good little firm out we never saw them and whenever we were low on numbers they were right there, as early as 6.30pm on a Saturday night. Some long nights there, I can tell you, but what are you going to do, go home and leave your mates? Not a fucking chance. At the end of the 1989–90 season we got relegated and they went up on the same day. Did they want it that night? Not a chance, we had to make all the running and they never came off London Road. Anyone who says any different is just bullshitting.

My life is totally different now and the people who know me today would never believe the stuff I got up to. However, the people I ran with in the mid-1980s and for a few years at the end of the decade are priceless. The point I am trying to make here is that at the time I would have gone to war with any of our lads and even numbers put us up against anyone. All it takes now is a look and a wink, and whenever we are in the same company it all comes flooding back. For me it was a rite of passage and a good growing-up period of my life. Never nicked or charged; a very lucky boy.

The incidents outlined here are not just isolated cases. In the late 1980s this type of behaviour was happening every week, and not just in town. One lad I know of had been playing football up at Stocksbridge leisure centre, and had left his colleagues to walk home. He noticed a couple of cars following him, and upon realising it was Blades he was forced to run through back gardens to elude them. The Blades lads in question were well-known faces, and had travelled right over from the other side of Sheffield looking for this one lad. The sad part was that they had no interest in engaging him until he was alone.

On another occasion I had Polak to thank for getting me out of a situation that could have been very nasty. It was the summer of 1989, and I had been to the pictures with a girl I knew. After the show we ventured up West Street. Upon nearing the

Mailcoach I noticed a large number of Blades milling about across the road. I assumed they were paying their usual bully-boy visit and headed towards the pub. Polak was standing at the door, we exchanged cordial greetings and I entered.

Imagine my horror to discover the pub full of Blades. Immediately they started on me. Two of the main mouthpieces were lads who I will call Poet and Tileman. Poet had what he thought was a legitimate reason for kicking off. A few weeks earlier he had been in the Limit on Friday night, and I was there too. A few Wednesday lads had wanted to fill him in, but I had argued against it. Poet left the club untouched, but for some reason he had got it into his head that I had been a major protagonist. I wasn't, and refute the allegation to this day. Of course, he could have taken his concerns up with me the following week when he came on Crookes for a drink, but for some reason he said nothing until he was surrounded by his compatriots.

He obviously liked the odds this night in the Mailcoach, and he found his voice to confront me.

'Remember me?' he said

I looked at him, but never had chance to reply as I came under fire from a flurry of punches that came from all sides. The next thing I saw was Polak rushing in, pulling people away, and yelling for them to leave me alone. Yet again the Blunts had shown their true colours, but Polak had done the decent thing and helped me out. To me the saddest sight was one of their old lads sat at the bar, who turned to me and said, 'Serves you right for being a Wednesday fan.'

Then I saw Aidee from Stocksbridge. They had already given him a kicking as he waited for his girlfriend, who just happened to be the sister of one of the Blades' main lads; truly pathetic. Looking back on that night I can almost understand why Poet acted the way he did. He had felt wronged, and had me down as a major instigator, but nothing was further from the truth. I hold no grudges, and can probably see where he was coming from, but the others just used it as an excuse to bash anything Wednesday. I know now that Blades had their own share of incidents like this, but I can honestly say that I was never a party to it, and those attacks were far less frequent.

After the birth of my son, Cameron, in 1991 I stopped going into town regularly on Saturdays, so I cannot comment on much from after that period, including the two occasions when Wednesday lads were set on fire by the 'honourable' BBC. I was out the night that Martin was hospitalised in the Dickens, but left before that incident took place. Afterwards, he told me how six of our lads had gone in the bar, and had been set on by about thirty Blades. The other five lads escaped, but the bouncers locked Martin in, and he took a severe kicking.

It wasn't just active lads who felt the wrath of the Bully Boy Crew. Steve Baker had stopped taking an active part in the scene by about 1991. He still came in the pub, but he kept out of any trouble. This didn't stop the noble Blades from making him a target, however. Here's Steve's account of an incident in 1996:

Back in 1996, my football hooligan days had been over for around two or three years, but one Saturday evening it came back to haunt me. Mind you I was in piggy land [London Road] to start with!

I had been in town with some non-hooligan friends, having a drink. I decided to call it a night and go and meet my girlfriend Joanne, who was a manager at an Italian restaurant on London Road.

It was around midnight (nice time for the Berties, who

enjoyed sniffing around late at night looking for lone Owls, to be milling around). I walked up London Road without a care in the world and went into the restaurant. As luck would have it, they were not busy. The owner said Joanne could get off, so off we went.

On the next block up from the restaurant there is a Chinese takeaway. We both went in and I went to order our meal. While I was ordering I heard Joanne say, 'Oh my God!' I looked around and saw around ten Berties looking in through the window, shouting and swearing at me. They walked off, but three of them quickly came back and walked in, I jumped over the counter and stood there. There was the usual mouthing at me, calling me this and that, but after a few minutes they walked off. 'Pussies,' I thought to myself.

Once they were all back outside, I heard one of them say, 'Just give it the wanker.' The next thing I knew the same three (I think) came dashing through the doors. One of them ran to the counter and jumped over. As he was coming down, I grabbed him by the neck and started to hit him around the face, not letting go. The other two came round the counter, but I did not notice this, I was too busy giving this wanker a hiding. One of the other fruitcakes picked up the till and landed it smack on my forehead, but I did not go down due to a huge fridge at the side of me, which held me up. I did not let go of the Bertie I had hold of either.

While all this was going on Joanne had gone outside and phoned the police from the phone box across the road.

Back inside, once the till had bounced off my head, they backed off and went back outside. I let the Bertie go and he ran outside. By this time, blood was pouring down my face and on to the floor.

The shop was a total mess, bottles of pop lying around, the till in pieces, and blood everywhere. I bent down, picked up some of the bottles, said sorry to the owners and left.

Walking up the road were the Berties, all laughing and shouting. I shouted up after them, 'You are all nothing but wankers, and three of you cannot even do one Owl, tossers!' Joanne started waving a taxi down and told me to shut it, as they had started to walk back down to me.

The taxi came and off we went.

My view on this period is that United went too far. I would go so far as to say that there are a number of their main faces who are nothing more than cheap thugs. They use the football as an excuse to throw their weight around. That's not true of all of them, however: there are a number of lads in the Beeb that I respect greatly, and they are good and fair lads, but no one ever took the nastier elements to one side and had a word. Why? I believe that they are scared of them, for whatever reason. I don't presume to know enough about each one of them personally, but I do know that some of the 'nasty' boys had contacts with criminal figures. Maybe the decent lads felt it wise to not rock the boat.

The bully-boys didn't just look to bully Owls. Even within their firm they laid out a policy of 'taxing' younger members. Right back in to the mid-1980s certain top boys would take money or clothes from young lads who wanted to get involved. I even hear stories that this policy persists today, and that it is the same people perpetrating it. Twenty years of vicious bullying from the same individuals and the good lads turn a blind eye, and even excuse it in some cases. This kind of behaviour is what set us apart from them. They had a big, strong mob, and didn't need to indulge in some of the shit they pulled. The firm they could put out demanded respect, but the bully-boy antics soured it, and for that they get no respect.

In my time there were many clashes between Owls and Blades, but I would have to say that the vast majority were small-scale skirmishes. Of course, the publicans who saw their pubs wrecked in these disturbances might not see it that way, but it was rarely both mobs at full strength going at it. Most of these incidents would tend to go the Blades' way, but by no means all. Of course, they never admit to getting done, and if they do there is always a long list of excuses, or flat-out denial.

If I gave an account of every single incident involving the two factions I could write for the next twenty years, and so I intend to focus on a couple of major flashpoints. I have already focused on the Kenworthy testimonial. The next major heavyweight clash did not occur for another three years. The Blunts may point to the Mark Smith testimonial at Hillsborough late in May of 1987, but really that was a nothing night. They didn't show at Hillsborough, despite repeated threats to the contrary. After the match we headed to town, and found them at the bottom of Fargate. Police and dogs split our mob. Most of us were forced into the Blue Bell; I myself suffered dog bites to my legs. The few that escaped got run by a much bigger mob of petrol bomb-wielding Blades. Of course, to them that is a major result, but to me it was nothing.

A little over three years after the Kenworthy testimonial, in August 1989, a pre-season friendly was arranged at Bramall Lane; I think it was a testimonial for one of their players, but I cannot be certain. During those three years the balance of power had shifted dramatically to the Blades, and so a big show was going to be needed to put them back in their place. I was living on Crookes at the time, and a lot of the Blades there admitted that if all the Owls lads who said they were going to turn out did so, then the BBC would have a big job on their hands.

The meet had been set for the Arbourthorne, and on the morning of the match I headed up with Dob and Gill. I was full of confidence, as were we all. All our big lads would be out, and it was time for some payback. We entered the pub to find exactly what we expected: lots of big, nasty-looking lads, many of whom I had never seen before, or not seen for some time. I remember thinking to myself that the Berties were going to suffer some pain that day, and they would fucking well deserve it.

By the time we came to leave there were only about seventy lads in total, but they were all heavyweights. I could honestly say that looking round the room we had the cream there that day. There were about a dozen black lads who rarely turned out, but who, on this day, wanted a piece of the BBC. Many worked as doormen, and had suffered during run-ins with the Bully-Boy Crew. As we headed in taxis down to the Earl of Arundel, close to the ground, few of us had any doubt that this would be our day.

The Earl of Arundel and Surrey pub sat at the bottom of a hill that led up to the top end of Bramall Lane. The plan was to get in, and march en masse to the ground, scattering any resistance; once again, though, overeagerness would prove to be our undoing. Upon our arrival Steve Bowen and a couple of others decided to go for a scout. They came back with disturbing news. A large force of Blades was already positioned in the Wheatsheaf pub about a hundred yards up the hill. Mick and many of the other main lads wanted to wait, and stick to the original plan. Our position was not strategically a good one to go looking for them. They would have the advantage of coming down the hill into us. There was no major concern, and the mood remained relaxed and confident. Unbeknown to the majority, however, a small group had gone to the Wheatsheaf. Within minutes they were heading back down the road, and a huge mob of Blades appeared behind them. I swear to God that as I came out the doors of the pub it looked like the start of the London marathon at the top of the hill. It now became of the utmost urgency to get everyone outside in double-quick time. That was not going to happen, though – and even if it did we had no time to adjust to the numbers heading our way. Those of us outside ran up the road, but we became engulfed, and quickly turned tail in the face of overwhelming numbers. I am not using the numbers as an excuse – although they had a numerical superiority I do believe we had the quality – but we never had time to organise ourselves. That's the price you pay, though, and you have to be ready because Queensbury rules do not apply in the theatre of the football firm.

We were pushed back past the pub, and split. First blood had gone to the BBC, and many of the old boys were livid at our amateurish organisation. The majority of the lads went to the match, but I was in a group that slunk back into town totally demoralised. None of us had expected to face the numbers that we did, and to be honest we were in shock. To this day, I honestly feel we could have turned them over, but we didn't keep tight and we suffered for it.

Most of the time the match was on is a blur to me now. I remember being at the Pump with a few others, and walking down to St Mary's Gate where we saw Black Kenny driving about in his car. He had been scouting around, and he told us the BBC had a massive mob. He hadn't been with us at the Earl, and so he hadn't seen them up close like we had. The next thing I recall is that the match was over, and we watched as the bulk of the BBC mob marched up the Moor. Joe from Crookes was at their head, and I have to say they looked impressive. The remnants of our mob were meeting on Trippet Lane at the bottom of West Street. When I walked in we looked bedraggled, and down to about fifty or sixty tops. The mob of Blunts I had seen were easily 150 strong, and my view was that we were in for a long night. Mick was having none of it, though.

'It's my fucking thirtieth today, and I'm not getting turned over!' he yelled at the assembled mob.

The BBC had headed for Silks on Bank Street. It was about 400 yards away from where we were; a brisk walk on Campo Lane and we would be there. Mick's words had the lads fired up, and off we went on a Blade hunt. The odds were against us, but if we hit them right we could do it. Along Campo Lane were some roadworks, and Mick pulled a metal pole out from the ground. Waving it over his head he urged the lads on.

'Come on, Wednesday ... kill, kill, kill, kill!' he screamed

To a man we joined in. The cries of 'Kill!' echoed out down the street. The brisk walk became a jog, and then the jog turned into a sprint.

The running mob of screaming Owls turned down from Campo Lane on to Bank Street. I was close to the front, and as we turned the corner we came across a large group of Blades standing outside Silks. There was no hesitation on our part as we tore into them. The startled Blades ran for their lives. A couple were caught, and kicked into oblivion. As I looked down Bank Street I could see Blades vaulting the railings on Snig Hill. More of them tried to get out from inside the pub, but they were forced back in. A black lad of theirs came to the door with his Rottweiler. I have heard stories that he dropped some of our lads, but if he did I never saw it. He was there for about thirty seconds before disappearing back into the pub under a hail of bottles and bricks. Another tale I have heard is that we put the windows in and ran off. Not true at all. The only windows that went in were in the doorway. The big glass panes would not go through, and I remember clearly watching them wobble as metal poles bounced off them. The sound of police sirens told us it was time to vacate, and off we went. Some went back to Trippet Lane, but I was in a group that headed up to High Street and into the Blue Bell. The funniest sight was seeing well-known BBC faces standing in bus shelters trying to act nonchalant. We had executed our plan to perfection, and saved some face. Tileman came into the Bell, and after looking round said to Dickie, 'Looks like it was a 1-1 draw, then.'

We enjoyed a night of celebration on West Street that night while the BBC slunk off to London Road. The upstart Blades had drawn first blood, and probably shaded the day overall, but we had come back well and had something to sing about. Oddly enough, one of our casualties on the day had suffered a stab wound to his back. Surely that couldn't have been the case, though, because – as everyone knows – the BBC don't carry weapons ... When I finish laughing I will move on.

The 1991–92 season saw both Sheffield sides back in the top flight for the first time in over twenty years. They would also meet in a league game for the first time since Easter 1980, and so the fixture list was eagerly awaited. The first meeting of the sides came on a sunny Sunday in November, and saw United win 2-0 at Bramall Lane. For some reason I was not out that day, but Wednesday turned out a decent firm by all accounts, and quite a few infiltrated United's South Stand. There really was little doubt that the balance of power had shifted in the city since the last time Wednesday had played a league match in S2, but Wednesday held their own that day.

The return match at Hillsborough stokes up quite a memory bank for me. The stories that I have heard from Blades about this match do not fit with anything any Wednesday fan I know says, or my own memories. The game was due to be played on a Wednesday night in March, and the word was that the BBC would be marching down Penistone Road in force. We decided to meet in the Spot On Snooker centre on Langsett Road. This club offered an excellent overview of Penistone Road, and would serve us well the next year against Sunderland. The turnout was good for a Wednesday afternoon, and by 4pm we were about seventy strong. It was felt that United would have large numbers, but our advantage would be the higher ground, as had served the Beeb so well at the Earl of Arundel.

By 5pm nothing had been seen of our fearful opponents and the Masons was due to open at 5.30, so we headed out into the sunlight, and made our way to Hillsborough Corner. More lads were waiting when we arrived, and by 6pm the pub was absolutely packed. Maybe not everyone in that night was a lad, but the majority were, and it was largely old hands. If the BBC showed we would be ready and waiting. Word kept coming through of the Beeb's impending arrival, and a couple of shouts had gone up, but still we had seen nothing. The anticipation was building. The United 'superfirm' had to put on a show at Hillsborough. Whatever they had done in friendlies, while impressive, needed to be repeated in our 'backyard'. More and more rumours circulated, and by 6.45 everyone was buzzing. And that is when something finally happened.

Just up the road from the Masons is a small gennel that lead round the side of the old Hillsborough baths on to Langsett Road. Without warning a number of familiar faces appeared at the end of the gennel. The roar went up, and the pub emptied into the street, filling the bottom of Walkley Lane.

'They're coming over Morrisons now!' came the shout.

The first few scouts had vanished back down the gennel, and now the hunt was on. The mass ranks of Owls headed off in pursuit. Like champagne bursting from a bottle we emerged from the gennel on to Langsett Road. A number of main Blade faces were just emerging from Morrisons car park. They bounced around for a few seconds, but on seeing the numbers we had they turned tail and fled back from whence they had come.

We knew that if they were going to the match they would still have to walk on Penistone Road, and as one we headed down Bradfield Road to try and cut them off. I have to say we looked pretty impressive that night, for the first time in a while. The whole road was filled with lads, bringing the traffic to a halt. The only police presence was a single Maria.

We emerged on to Penistone Road to see the BBC lads on the other side of the dual carriageway. Here the police presence was much stronger. I remember watching the Blades continue to walk down toward the ground. There were only about thirty of them, but it was some of their main actors. Tileman was there swinging a pair of crutches, so was Polak and a number other well-known characters.

We had large numbers, but our efforts to cross the road were continually thwarted by the police. If I am honest I will admit we really didn't make as much effort as we could have, but having said that the BBC lads made no effort at all.

The stand-off continued all the way to the ground, and quite a few of ours were arrested in doomed forays. As we entered the ground the small band of Blades could be seen under escort heading toward Herries Road.

About thirty of us had tickets for the North Stand, and we took our seats toward the Leppings Lane end near the front. About ten minutes into the game we saw the police move into the kop and bring out the same BBC lads who had marched down Penistone Road. Now, I have read somewhere that United had 400 on our kop that night. Well, it must have been an invisible 400, or the source needs to have his eyes checked. This motley group of 30 was the limit to their numbers on the East Bank; good game, lads, but hardly 400 strong.

The South Yorkshire police are as savvy as they come, but once again they dropped a major clanger this night. They put the thirty Blades into the North Stand right in front of us.

At half-time every lad in the stand was down waiting for them, and to their credit some of them came out the back for a word. The lad Tileman was game as fuck, and would not back down. A few scuffles broke out, and again Wednesday lads were arrested, but still Tileman, and a black lad who I didn't know, refused to be intimidated. Whatever my personal feelings were to Tileman, I took my hat off to him that evening. At the end we left the ground and headed back to Hillsborough Corner. Some years later I heard the Blades claiming to have run us in the North Stand. I don't know who they ran, but it certainly was not our firm. I didn't see another Blunt all night, despite the fact that they had told us in the ground that their entire firm was getting together to come on the Corner. They never did show, although I heard a few of ours got turned over late on in town. I am still wondering what happened to the bulk of their firm that night. I don't, for one moment, think that thirty was the extent of their turnout, but something must have split them up because that was all we saw. That was about the best I ever saw of them at Hillsborough, though. In the next couple of seasons they didn't show, or came in escort. In the last couple of years they have made a habit of meeting in Crookes and coming down in escort. They then claim to have marched through 'unopposed'. That's the thing with our dear Bertie brothers: when they are in escort they have been 'rounded up', but when we are in escort we are 'hiding behind the police'.

The accusation of hiding behind the police was levelled at us for the game at Bramall Lane the following season. Again we met down Ecclesall Road, and Aidee and I were quick to spot an early spy having a sniff. He came in the pub, had a peek, and left. We followed him out, but he had vanished; just as we were about to go back in, he reappeared out of a shop doorway.

'You a Blade?' I asked.

'Yes,' he replied, looking nervously around.

I gave him a quick kick up the arse and told him to vacate the area, which he did. Our numbers started to swell, and by 1.30pm the pub was full, but this game would be the first where I began to notice the police using video cameras in the street. Every time a few of us went outside we would be pushed back in by police, and they had cameras mounted all around the pub.

By 2.30pm the boys in blue decided we could leave, and came inside the pub, throwing their weight about. We made our way, in escort, toward London Road. The numbers looked good, around 100–150, but it would be tough slipping the police. We appeared on London Road around 2.45pm; there were a number of BBC hanging around. A few came to the back door of the Hermitage, or whatever it was called by then, and shouted a few niceties. Down toward the ground we marched, and just before reaching Bramall Lane the police tried to split us, but we outwitted them and quickly shot down a back street, coming back together near the ground.

As we approached the Cricketers a number of Blades came out. The police were quickly on the scene, but not before one of our lot fired a flare straight through the nearby petrol station. (I never said we were all intelligent as well as handsome.) The police pushed us back down Bramall Lane, away from the ground. Our plan was to meet afterwards at a pub up on the Netherthorpe estate. I was with Bentley, Evan and a few of the Kiveton lads, so we headed up now to escape the attentions of the police.

That really was it for the day, though. About sixty of us met up after, and headed to town, but there was nothing happening. At the Forresters pub later on another Blade scout was caught and given a clip round the ear. The problem was that the police were on us, and kept marching in the pub with cameras. I had had enough and headed back to Hillsborough.

This was the beginning of the end of my trips into town. My civil liberties and freedom of movement were under attack by then, and I knew it would not get any better. That was also my last trip to Bramall Lane, although I didn't know it at the time. Over the next couple of years my life would begin to take a radically different path.

I can't really write a chapter about Sheffield rivalry without a quick look at what was probably the biggest Steel City derby ever played: the 1993 FA Cup semi-final. It was the first semi for us since the 1986 game against Everton, and I expected a good show from us. What we got was a pale shadow of the turnout we had had seven years previously. About sixty of us met to travel down on the early train. It was all good lads, but we knew that we would have our hands full. A small band of Chelsea lads met us on our arrival in the capital, and the rest of the day was spent having a few pints. There was no sign of our neighbours.

As we headed up Wembley Way our numbers had swelled to about eighty or so, and as we reached the top we found out why we had seen nothing of the BBC. About two hundred of them came into view. It seems they had been walking round the stadium, intimidating the Wednesday scarfers. A scuffle broke out, with young Winny steaming straight into them. Winny was the younger of two brothers; his older brother had been a stalwart of the Wednesday mob in the early 1980s, and still put in an appearance now and again. Both brothers were game as fuck, and were well respected in the Blade ranks. The police were quickly on the scene, though, and the handbags were withdrawn. The United firm was moved toward their own section of the ground. I didn't have a ticket, and headed away to find a pub in which to watch the game. Evan, Donny and a few Chelsea lads accompanied me. On our way we bumped into Simon, one of the Blades' main faces. He was with a Millwall lad who lived in Sheffield, and oddly enough we all headed to the pub together. Anyone there that afternoon would have seen lads from both of the Sheffield clubs, Chelsea and Millwall all sat in the same pub together enjoying a pint and some largely friendly banter. Wednesday won the match 2-1, and even though Simon was gutted we all shook hands. Simon and Millwall told us if we got collared later that they would stick up for us. I have to admit they were good company, and we had a laugh together.

Heading back toward the ground I bumped into Link, an older Wednesday lad who worked in London a lot. I hadn't seen him in a few years, but he was still the same sharp-dressed man of old. We chatted for a while and headed toward the stadium. Our firm was on one side of Wembley Way, with Erroll at the front, and the Blades were on the other. It was no contest really, and to be honest it was embarrassing. On our side was a massive firm of around 50 straining at the leash, and the Blades, who were visibly quaking, could only muster around 400. Mismatch really, and a good job the police kept us from them! Seriously though, it truly emphasised the difference between the mobs at the time, and showed how far we had fallen. They were herded away, and Dickie and I somehow got separated, along with another young lad. We jumped on a train, and for one brief moment thought we were on the same train that the Blades would be put on to. Thankfully that was not the case, and we made it back to King's Cross in one piece. I mentioned earlier about what happened with the unidentified mob at King's Cross, so I won't revisit it. The late Tony Pritchett (*Sheffield Star* writer for United) and Dennis Skinner MP, the 'Beast of Bolsover' as he was known in the media, were on our train, and we had a good time ribbing Mr P about the result. He was a top bloke, Tony Pritchett, and gave as good as he got. It was a major loss to sports journalism in Sheffield when he passed away.

A United supporter with a heart condition died at the match after a fight with some Wednesday lads. A Wednesday lad, and one of our top boys for many years, delivered the fatal blow and went to jail for it. It was a tragic accident, and both firms knew it. A sad end to an uneventful day. We had won the match on the field, but off it we were seriously outclassed.

My last clash with the Blades came in April 1995, just before I left for Canada. We had been narrowly beaten at home by Nottingham Forest, to the tune of 7-1. About forty of us had made our way to the Frog and Parrot on Division Street by 9.30pm. We had scuffled with a group of rugby players, and most of our group had headed up West Street to meet the Diggers' mob, who were out celebrating a birthday. About ten of us remained, Bentley, Young Linwell, Martin Hayes and Sash among them. I didn't notice anything untoward until Bentley turned to me and said, 'They're here.'

I looked at him, bemused. 'Who is?' I replied.

'Sheffield United.'

With that a fist landed on Bentley's jaw. They most certainly were here, but if they expected an easy ride they would be mistaken. Bentley grabbed for his assailant, but he had run back out. There were about thirty or so BBC pushing to get to the door and we had no choice but to pick up whatever was at hand and fight a rearguard action. We managed to force them away from the door, with Bentley leading the way. I still remember him with beer glasses in both hands yelling for the Blades to 'Come on!' Once again a fierce firefight ensued, although this one was far less intense than some I could recall, such as the one at the Yorkshireman's in 1987. This time the police arrived very quickly, and it was soon over. We had held our own, and I was proud. It hadn't always been that way, but on this night, my last night out in Sheffield before I left for pastures new, we had done well. We headed up West Street buoyant.

In the years since that night things have changed drastically. CCTV and riot police now control the streets. Confrontations like the ones I have described are few and far between nowadays, and the penalties are much harsher, but the battle for supremacy goes on. The Wednesday mob has grown, but the BBC still hold sway. Results have gone both ways in recent times, but the Wednesday mob is mainly youth today, whereas the BBC front line is largely unchanged from what you would have seen in late 1987. As both mobs grow older things may change. Our 20–25-year-olds will get better, and their 35–40-year-olds cannot continue forever. The tables can turn again, but it will not be easy, and the BBC will not relinquish their position without a fight. When you throw in legal considerations as well, it is clear that the struggle is going to be harder than it has ever been.

I will hand over the next tale of Owls–Blades conflict to a young head. Service is one of the new breed, but what makes this young lad a little different is that he is a Wednesday fan from Leeds, of all places. The story he will relate occurred in early 2003.

We played Wolves that day and had a pretty good mob of around 150 out, but as was generally the case the day was a lot of walking and not much else. We decided to call it a day and the consensus was to get rat arsed (pardon my French!) in town. So we were having a few drinks when some lads decided to do their rendition of the OCS chant outside, and what do you know, within ten minutes riot police had surrounded us. A load of ours scarpered into the bus station and about fifty of us remained until the Old Bill made us move out, so we all split up. A rumour had circulated that the Berties [BBC] were in a place called TP Woods, so about fifty of us made our way to a pub farther into town. Within ten minutes the coppers were here again:

'If tha don't go t' 'Boro now, yer all nicked.'

So they eventually got their way and I was royally pissed off and decided I was going to do one when we got to the next tram stop, but as the OB directed us out we were well aware that the direction we were going was towards TP's. Six of our main lads went ahead to have a look and suddenly the roar went up and everyone started running – at our own lads! False alarm, but within twenty seconds the roar went up again. No false alarm this time. I sprinted like mad till I got to the entrance of TP's, I pulled some guy, in his twenties, off one of our lads and elbowed him across the side of the head, knocking him into the doors to the pub. Then a young lad of ours came across me, sparked out. I saw him getting carried away; he didn't look too good. The pigs [BBC] were clambering over each other trying to get back into the safety of the pub. I then thought of the cameras and the Old Bill and took a step back, to see M lamp some kid and as he went down J volleyed him in the air. Humorous, to say the least!

At this point the number of people had decreased; most of theirs were inside again or had done a runner. All of their main faces could be seen through the windows, **, **, **, ** etc. (despite their claims to have gone to Millwall, and other various bullshit stories). Glasses and bottles were being thrown out from the pub, missing everyone. One clown tried throwing a jug and it smashed on the arch of the doorway, showering his own in glass. There's always one, eh?

During all this time ... no coppers? Now, this is about as rare in Sheffield as the excrement of a rocking horse. On cue the sirens sounded and everyone ran off and split up. About twenty of us met up at the Harley for a celebratory drink and sing. I remember the barmaid asking: 'You just got beat 4-0, didn't you?' I just laughed and walked off. I don't think she would have understood!

Rumours began circulating that the young lad had died, that we'd been set up, all of which were later dismissed.

I'll never forget the buzz after; there is no way of describing it, better than any drug available. I was on one all that night, and got back to Leeds with a permanent grin, which I wore for a good week or so.

H, one of the young Wednesday lads from Doncaster, was also out that night, but he was in a different group. Here is his recollection of the evening in question, and of another smaller-scale skirmish with our beloved brethren from Sheffield 2:

We decided to try to mix it up a little and meet away from the usual Hillsborough Corner haunts, so by about midday there was about a hundred of us in a pub on Langsett Road, hoping that Wolves would get that far as there was, for once, no OB presence.

However, despite the usual rumours about a visiting superfirm, nothing materialised at all and we didn't even sniff Wolves all day, so as usual we thought we would mob up and go to town. About a hundred of us attracted OB presence in various pubs around the bus station, culminating in most of us getting locked in the Brown Bear, while a few of us (about ten to fifteen) backed off and thought we'd stop in the Surrey and Fringe around the corner and enjoy a pint without the boys in blue for company. How I regret that decision now ...

The few of us in the Surrey got the call that the main mob had been let out and were heading up West Street, so we agreed to finish the drinks and make our way in a few minutes. When the time came, we heard a huge roar from the top of Fargate, followed by the usual 'Ooo-ooo-ooo!' chants. At this point we knew we had encountered the Blades, and clearly saw them off. I could go into all the tales from trusted people about the exact 'happenings', but I make a point of not recounting events I didn't actually see – I am sure that elsewhere in this book the truth will out. What I am sure of is that the Blades went very quiet in the aftermath of this, save for atrocious excuses such as 'We were all in London visiting Millwall' – strange that, as Millwall commented on being disappointed by a Blades no-show!

Anyway, in a victorious mood we larged it round town for the remainder of the evening, with numbers dwindling throughout, and admittedly a bit of Blades-style bullying in our overexuberance! Finally about five of us headed for a taxi from Fitzallan Square, only to find almost equal numbers of Blades there for the same purpose, and understandably not in great moods (must have hurried back from Millwall!). The group I was in was youth without exception, whereas this mob had at least two older heads present, one of whom told us we were not getting a taxi from there if we were Wednesday. At this we strolled back around the corner to get ourselves together, knowing full well we were not going to stand and get told where we could and could not get a taxi from without a fight.

As we were temporarily retreating we did bump into one slightly older Wednesday lad, who led our charge back around the corner, bouncing up and down and leading a very successful pop at them. Their older lads tried their best but were on the back foot straight away, while the youth absolutely shit it. And claimed to not like football – very different to what had been said two minutes previously.

As per usual South Yorkshire Old Bill was there in a flash, and we split. I ran down a flight of stairs towards the bus station, only to hear footsteps behind me. At first I thought it would be the cops, until I heard the cry 'Come on then, you Wednesday bastard!', and lo and behold it was the fat old tosser who had wanted to dictate where we could get a cab from! Now, I am happy to go one on one in situations *where I would not particularly back myself and instead of legging it (trust me, I think I could have outpaced this lump of lard!), I decided to get to the bottom of the stairs, turn and swing. But as soon as I hatched this plan, fat boy appears in a blur to the side of me – rolling down the stairs! Despite being doubled up with laughter at the time I gave him a volley or two to help him on his way, leaving him an absolute state (largely through his fall, I may add) at the bottom of the stairs! I briefly thought about finishing the job off as he lay in agony (I guarantee he would have – and he would probably have robbed me too), but knowing the coppers would still be about I thought better of it, deciding instead to walk back to the place I was stopping at, feeling better that at least I compensated to a degree for missing the bigger off earlier on.*

To me this sort of day sums up the situation in Sheffield – even when the visiting mob bring nothing or cannot be got at, there is always some sort of fun between Wednesday and Blades. Usually it is not on the scale that happened outside TP Woods, but there is always the likelihood that small mobs will meet and greet each other in the way we did at the taxi rank.

On the night of Wednesday's last match of the 2002–03 relegation season the two mobs clashed again at Aunt Sally's on Glossop Road; this time a large Wednesday mob was split by the police, and the Blades turned the tables putting the new-look Owls mob to flight. A season of improvement – off the field – had ended in setback, but it should be looked on as a learning experience. Nothing comes easy.

In the years since I left Sheffield I have made peace with a number of my old adversaries in the BBC. We can laugh about things that went on now, and I have developed a healthy respect for many of their lads. On their day the BBC could be a top mob, but too often certain members of their fraternity let them down with over-the-top bullying, and taxing. I still feel that man for man we had a better mob, but we were vastly outgunned, and too often on the back foot before we knew where we were. It was painful at the time, but looking back now I doubt it would have been too different if we had been in the ascendancy.

Sheffield people are a stubborn bunch, and whether red or blue neither will ever give up the ghost, even if it looks hopeless. The Wednesday mob of 2004 is bigger and stronger than it has been for almost twenty years, but the task is doubly difficult today. Twenty years ago there were no riot police or cameras. The Blunts will still take some shifting, but that's how it should be. If the tables do turn then I would hope that the Beeb would be able to hold their hands up and admit it, as we have done, but I doubt it because to hear some Bladesmen talk *they have never been run, and never been done.* As the famous news reporter is fond of telling us, 'Respect to those that deserve it.'

To round off this chapter, here's a tale of Owls–Blades conflict from Dougie:

Treat them all the same: the Blades

Sheffield United, Grimsby, Oldham – personally it never made any difference to me. Growing up in Sheffield 6 in the 1970s and 1980s left the majority of our age group no option other than to support the blue side. Having said that, you did get the odd Blade bouncing off the wall at the school disco to the sound of 'Hi Ho Silver Lining'. This got more serious the older you got. In Sheffield you're either red or blue, as I found out as a 17-year-old out on the town in Sheffield at a nightspot called Steelys.

The night was going swingingly, until the almost famous – in Sheffield anyway – hit the turntables: 'Hi Ho Sheffield Wednesday'. I was sporting my new tank jacket, a proper one with the metal zip, from the army stores near the town hall; a full week's wages at the time. With one side of the dance floor taken over by the Blades, and the other by us, the music began. I can't explain to the neutral reader, but this spelt danger, and after a few choruses the floor parted; with that the battling began. In those days 'dancing' on the dance floor meant full-on battling, and that's what happened, from end to end.

I can remember the ageing bouncers splitting us up, but on the edges you could still get a result, as they were outnumbered. The fighting was out of this world looking back now – it was the survival of the fittest, or the fucking best swinger.

I managed to escape being thrown out, which was a massive result as this was Blades territory, and a large number of their boys were out on their ears. As the night came to an end the bouncers started rounding the Wednesday lads up. My old mate and me were the first two out of the doors, with no sympathy from the old bastards that lobbed us out. The doors shut and I looked down the stairs. There was a firm of Blades ready to kill, sheepskins and all, we had no option other than to fly straight into the cunts. A fucking slimy bastard ran up the stairs and whacked my mucker full on, which he took like a trooper; I can still hear the noise, and it still makes me feel sick.

All hell broke loose, with twenty of them on to us two. I'm not bragging, but I never went down – something I put down to overcrowding. I managed to escape with a few bruises and my jacket ripped off my back. That was an early incident with the red side, and later in life there were to be more, but I didn't get involved in too many other toe to toes, apart from at Silks and the like.

People in this industry talk about respect, and I felt no finer respect than on one winter's night in Sheffield when the red side took over the North Stand. You can dress it up all you like, but they came and on the night they got the result. God knows how many, but they certainly looked the part. A small firm of us tried to prevent the onslaught, but it was to no avail. On the night we won 2-1 on the field, which meant so much to the majority, but I couldn't get my head around the fact that there were so many on our stand. It was only a few years previous we were running these lads all over Morrisons car park after a quality turnout. Where had we all gone?

I think it's a miracle that any Sheffielder, blue or red, can remember in depth any stories, as drink is – and will always play – a major part in the day's events. With that in mind I have to give respect to a few firms that I remember personally:

Preston, you set of bastards, we had a pop at your cunts in the early 1990s. You did two of our lads, and when we came at you after we grouped up you hid behind the coppers, and six of my mates got locked up. The coppers knew your names, and looked after you. It's a rough old place, Preston, but when the numbers were even the bottle went. I must thank Man City for shoving half a house brick in my mate's face at theirs. Derby were always game, and proved themselves on many occasions. Leicester were also quality. I can remember going to Bristol Rovers when they played at Bath and saw nothing. Personally this meant nothing, though, as I knew they had some game lads. We took it to Man United at Hillsborough one night, but had to run – totally outnumbered.

My utmost respect goes out to Chelsea. We had a pop with some of theirs on the South Stand in the semi back in 1991, but the sight of their lads outside the Britannia in the first leg was just unreal; without a swing or a punch I knew that these were the top firm in England.

11

I TRAVELLED AMONG UNKNOWN MEN

On 2 November 1994 I returned home from work. Little did I realise that within the next hour or so I would receive a telephone call that would change my world. The call was from a forging company in the small town of Brantford in Ontario, Canada. They had opened a new ring-rolling plant and they wanted me to come and work for them. It would be a massive wrench for me to leave my friends and family behind, but I had to take it. I really would not have been able to live with the thought of 'what if?' should I turn the opportunity down. I filed my application to emigrate within the week, and sat back to await my fate.

By law Canadian companies have to advertise any jobs nationally before they can offer them overseas. The company assured me that they knew no one else would be able to apply for the job, and that it was just a question of time before they could officially offer it to me.

Early in 1995 I received the news that the job was mine, and all we were now waiting on was the Canadian High Commission in London granting me a work permit. I have to say, my mind was a whirl of mixed emotion at the time. I had only just started a new job, within a ten-minute walk of my home, and I was enjoying it. There was plenty of overtime, and my work colleagues were a pleasure to be with. Over the next few months I would often make up my mind to stay put – usually after coming in from the pub – but the wind of change was everywhere, and it was blowing me across the sea.

On 18 April 1995, I boarded a plane for Toronto and a new life. A life well away from football, well away from the eternal struggle of the OCS and BBC, well away from everything I held dear. It was a hugely emotional day for me, and to be honest the enormity of what I was doing had not hit me until the day before.

Wednesday were playing Everton at Hillsborough. I travelled around saying goodbye to my family during the morning. It felt particularly poignant when I said goodbye to my grandfather. I did not know it then, but I would never see him again. He died just seven months later, and he had said to my mother on the day I left that he would never see me again.

I spent the day drinking with Gill, Cowley and Phil. An old Wednesday lad named Chap, from Donny, joined us. Chap had switched allegiances from Wednesday to Everton a few years before. We drank all day around Hillsborough and Wadsley Bridge, and it wasn't until I headed for home at the end of the night that it finally hit me. As I headed for my front door I realised that this was the last time I would enjoy a night like this. A tidal wave of emotion crashed into me. How could I leave behind all this?

Leave it behind I did, though, and I headed off to Toronto the next day to start a new life. I found it difficult to adjust at first, and was terribly homesick. On many occasions I felt like packing it all in and heading home, but I was no quitter. The only access

I had to England, at that time, was via the telephone, and my first few months in Canada saw me running up hefty phone bills. There was a Saturday soccer show on one of the cable channels every Saturday which showed highlights of Premier League games, but it largely concentrated on the big clubs, and so I knew very little of what was going on with my beloved Sheffield Wednesday. I also found the weather difficult to bear. The summers were blindingly hot and humid, whereas the winters could drop to a bone-chilling -20?C. I also found the Canadian people difficult to judge. Their lives seemed very simple in comparison to the life that I had left behind, and they had no interest in soccer. Ice hockey was the be-all and end-all for your average Canadian. It was hard but I persevered, and began to win over many of my workmates with my attitude. They loved the way I took no shit from them, and I became a popular figure at work.

In the summer of 1996 I bought a house in Brantford, and started to frequent bars for ex-pat Brits. I met many English and Scottish people who became my friends, and my past life began to seem very distant. At this time the Internet was also starting to become popular, and I became connected to the World Wide Web early in 1997. I now had a home, a good job, and most important of all I could keep in touch with all the latest footballing developments from Hillsborough. But it seemed that my association with football hooliganism was to remain dead and buried.

On 25 March 1998, a day after my thirtieth birthday, I went to work expecting a day like any other. I couldn't have known that a very difficult, and painful, phase of my life was about to begin. I was a forger by trade, and a very good one. There seemed nothing untoward as my hammer crew and I set about a day of making alloy steel rings on the 6,000lb hydraulic hammer. Everything was proceeding to plan until around 11.10 that morning, when one of the punches, which we were using to put a hole in some steel blanks, broke. A small piece about the size of an orange segment flew my way and embedded itself in the left side of my neck. I realised immediately that something was wrong, but didn't know what. I could not move my arm, and the world seemed to be moving in slow motion. I looked down and saw my blue work uniform turn black. I watched in total horror as my clothes became saturated in blood; my own blood. I had a gaping two-inch wound in my neck, and the blood was gushing out. I honestly believed I was going to die that day.

I remember looking round, as my workmates led me to a nearby office, and thinking, 'This is not how it is supposed to be.' For the next ten minutes my workmates fought to keep me alive as we waited for an ambulance to arrive. They took it in turns to apply pressure to my neck in an effort to stem the bleeding. My life was literally ebbing away in front of me, but all I cared about was that my back was aching. Although I was conscious throughout, the rest of my day is a haze. The ambulance came and rushed me to Brantford General Hospital, where I underwent emergency surgery. I was then sent twenty miles to the Hamilton General Hospital where I spent the next three days in the Intensive Care Unit. I was extremely sick, and in bad way during that time, but by day four I was able to move on to a regular ward. A few days later I underwent more surgery to repair nerve damage to my left arm and shoulder.

Nothing I had ever faced in football can compare to what I underwent during this time. I was lucky to be alive. The doctors told me that if the shard had gone an eighth of an inch further to the right my jugular would have been completely severed. As it was I had just nicked it, but I had also severed my carotid artery and brachial plexus. The brachial plexus controls the muscles to the arm. I had lost the use of my left arm, and would undergo three years of difficult physiotherapy in an effort to get it back. The upside was that I never had to return to factory work again, and now enjoy a rewarding career in the world of Health and Safety.

How did this event bring me back to the world of the hooligan? Quite simply, I had a lot of spare time on my hands between hospital visits, and I amused myself by patrolling the Internet. At the time there were very few of my old friends online, and I never even thought to look at Internet sites about the Casual culture until I got chatting online to an old Wednesday lad from Rotherham. He directed me to the Paul Dodd website; Paul Dodd was a well known lad from Carlisle who found 'fame' by the bucketload during various trips abroad following England. This was the first hooligan-focused website I had ever seen, and it felt weird reading posts from lads all over the UK. describing various 'offs' that had been occurring. I had kept in touch with Gill and various other old lads, but they were all off the scene, and didn't really pay much heed to a lot of the comings and goings on the Sheffield hooligan front. These were actually the halcyon days of the Internet football hooligan. It was obvious by the postings that the vast majority of posters on this site, and others such as ITK, were the real deal.

Within a couple of years the availability of PCs to the masses gave rise to the 'cyber-hoolie'. Often youngsters, the cyber-hoolies liked to tag on to the firms, but never really have any proper connection. After every game they would appear rubbishing their opponents and bigging themselves up even if nothing at all had happened. It is sad to say but Wednesday had many of these types, and some posts made in the name of the OCS made me cringe. The cyber-hoolies nowadays account for most of the posters on these message boards, and virtually every club in Britain has at least one message board; every weekend the cyber-hoolies go to war and emerge with tales of no-shows and police escorts. Laughable really, and anyone reading these boards does need to take what is said with a hefty pinch of salt.

Slowly but surely, though, among all the bullshit merchants I started to bump into old friends, and foes. I made contact with old acquaintances who had now got on to the information superhighway, some of whom I had not seen for almost ten years, such as Steve Bowen. I made new friends among some of the good young lads coming through the Wednesday ranks, and I got to know old enemies such as 'Author Askie'. When I came over to England for Christmas 2001 I met many new faces, and also sat down and drank with former rivals. My active days were well and truly over, my injuries had seen to that, but it was still good to hear tales of lads still trying to keep the traditions alive. I fear, though, that they are fighting a losing cause. Draconian police powers, which would have been roundly condemned by our government if the Cold-War Soviets had used them, are now used without mercy against ordinary lads looking for a tear-up. Fans nowadays that have been found guilty of no crime can be banned from watching their favourite team. Police brutality against fans would appear to have become the norm. Riot police hiding their identities behind face shields has replaced the everyday match police. It is not just lads from the firms who feel the wrath of these bullies in blue. The weekly message boards of the everyday fan often tell of women and children trampled by wild charges from these legalised thugs. I attended the Sheffield

Wednesday–Chesterfield match over Christmas of 2003, and watched in astonishment as a squad of *12* officers in riot gear went into the crowd to apprehend a young boy who had apparently been shouting obscenities. It was unbelievable, as was my walk back to Hillsborough that night after the match. Every few yards there were snatch squads of riot police, dogs, horses and even a helicopter. Crowd trouble is a fraction of what it was in the 1970s and early 1980s, yet the police presence is growing.

Who the hell is paying for this shit? The police forces around the country must be laughing their bollocks off. More and more money is being demanded to fight the 'hooligan menace', yet if anyone actually took time to examine the situation they would see that the 'hooligan menace' poses a very limited threat. Britain appears to have become a police state almost overnight, but it is only the football fan that needs to live in fear. Real criminals, such as paedophiles, drug dealers, and the scum who mug our old folk, need not worry. It may sound odd, but most football lads do believe in the cause of law and order and, outside of the heat of battle, most lead completely law-abiding lives. The sentences for 'football thugs' are out of all sense of reality now. An example: in August of 2003 the police in Sheffield clashed with Sheffield United fans at a pub near Bramall Lane. A number of known BBC faces were in the pub and they were seeking to raise other lads to head for a meet with a nearby gang of OCS. There may have been BBC in the pub, but there were also ordinary fans, and families enjoying a warm Sunday evening. Many people were injured and a number of people were arrested, and would subsequently be jailed. None of the arrested were core BBC, and allegations of heavy-handed police tactics during the incident persist to this day. I laughed heartily recently reading police spin on a Sheffield United–Cardiff match at Bramall Lane. 'Worst violence in thirty years' screamed the police publicity machine. Read on and you find a total of *six* arrests were made. Either the police are not doing a very good job, or they are overstating trouble for their own political ends. It will only get worse I am afraid, and that is why I am so very glad to be well and truly out of it. When I started the police tried to outwit you, and they were worthy opponents. All the lads had a healthy respect for the boys in blue, but their Gestapo tactics today make them a target of hatred. Good luck to all lads from around the country – you will need it.

So what of Sheffield Wednesday since I departed England's shores? They had been in the Premiership when I left, but relegation in the 1999–2000 season has seen them go into rapid decline. Three seasons of struggle ensued in the First Division before relegation to the Second. Hopes of a quick promotion soon faded, when, after a bright first month, the Owls once more went into struggle mode; we only avoided relegation to the bottom tier of English soccer for the first time by a mere three points. A cloud of doom and gloom hangs over Hillsborough. A debt of around £26 million, combined with arguably the worst on-field presentation for thirty years, makes being a Wednesday fan tough at the present time.

As I said at the beginning of the book, it often happens that when a club goes into freefall through the leagues the fans begin to play up. In the past three or four years the once small Wednesday firm has grown to large numbers. Many old faces returned to add to the new ones that had finally come through after years of stunted growth. The 2002–03 season saw large mobs of Wednesday boys travelling the country regularly. Trips to former tough hunting grounds such as Derby and Leicester saw the OCS taking liberties that they could never have dreamed of ten years previously. Dougie will talk about the trips to Leicester and Burnley later, but first I want to give Jambo an opportunity to recall the home game with Leicester. The Leicester Baby Squad laughingly denied the following account at the time. Every excuse under the sun was trotted out before they finally admitted to being well and truly done: 'It wasn't us'; 'It was just some young 'uns'; 'We had already gone'; 'We were in a different pub.'

Take it away, Jambo!

After numerous threats and counter-threats it was decided we would fuck the game off and head into town at half-time and look for the Baby Squad.

After a quick check that G (the local NCIS copper) and his cronies had disappeared, thirty of us boarded the first tram into town.

We got off the tram at the Bankers Draft and headed to (some help needed on the name of the pub!).

Before we even had enough time to finish our drinks, the word came back saying Leicester were in the Queens Head. We all piled out and walked down a quiet back street that leads to the boozer. As we turned the corner around 45 Leicester came pouring out of the pub. They threw their glasses into us, but that was it – their bottle went. The shout went up and Leicester were chased all over with three of their lads standing on their own, only to get a kicking. They would have managed to get away if their mates who ran off hadn't locked them out of the pub they had run back into! The best sight, though, was two of our lads arguing with each other about who was going to throw the huge sandwich board sign!

The sound of sirens told us it was time to scarper and around ten of us headed up towards the Surrey, where we bumped into the same number of Berties. They came out

with the worst line ever: 'It's all right, lads, we're Blades.'
They thought we were Berties as well! They were chased off.

We knew they had come from the Stonehouse, so we
headed there. One lad went in and told them to come
outside. They came to the doors, had a look, then locked
themselves inside! A few chairs were thrown from the pub
opposite, but with South Yorkshire's Old Bill if you start
acting up they will be on your case straight away, so we
made a swift exit.

The 2002–03 season had ended on a sour note for the OCS after
the setback to the BBC at Aunt Sally's, but the coming season in
Division Two showed promise. By now the OCS had a youth
wing, the aptly named ITI. ITI stood for 'Is That It?' – a few
older lads had thought up the name one night as a joke. The
Blades had chided us for years about our numbers: 'Is that all
you've got, Wednesday?' they would mock. The formation of the
ITI showed that we Wednesday lads could even laugh at
ourselves, and it was quickly taken up by the new youth.

Bristol City's CSF was the stand-out mob in the division. They
had been up there for years as a top firm, but when the OCS/ITI
headed for the West Country in October they matched them stride
for stride on their patch. Another huge show at QPR a few weeks
later confirmed Wednesday as the mob to watch in Division Two,
but a time bomb planted back in the summer was ticking, and it
was about to blow the new 'superfirm' out of the water.

On 15 July, a number of Wednesday lads headed to Doncaster
for a pre-season friendly. It was a warm summer's night, and the
lads were looking forward to a few pints and an opportunity to
watch a new-look Wednesday side in action. No aggro was
expected, but trouble did flare in the town centre. In the old days

it would have been looked on as minor scuffling, but these are not the old days.

Over the next six months numerous Wednesday lads were arrested over the incident, many simply for being in the vicinity at the time. Others not connected to the incident found themselves in civil court facing banning orders. Over thirty Wednesday lads appeared in Crown Court in connection with the incident. Five lads were jailed and the local press made the story front page news. Oddly enough they failed to mention those lads who were found NOT GUILTY. I saw much worse violence during the 1980s than was seen that night, but times have changed. The Blades lads I referred to earlier can attest to that. The 'Donnygate' incident knocked the stuffing out of the fledgling Owls mob. Many lads kept a low profile for much of the season, and the away days dried up. A fractured Wednesday mob faced up to Bristol City on the outskirts of the city for the return, but the confidence of October was gone, and the CSF eventually proved too strong. The momentum will return, but it's going to be a long process, and the environment will grow increasingly hostile. The coming seasons will be make or break.

As for me, well I am happy to sit back and reflect these days. I wasn't part of the ICF, the Headhunters, or the Red Army. I was part of a much-maligned firm of Sheffield Wednesday supporters, and I wouldn't have it any other way. We were a family together. We argued and fought each other much too often, but we always shared something the Blades never could. We were all fans of the team. We didn't have gangsters in our ranks looking to pull strokes. We had Sheffield Wednesday supporters. Sometimes our efforts were piss poor, but I'll take that because on our day we could live with almost anyone. Those days may have been few and far between at times, but it's what we all lived for.

I'm a million miles from any trouble these days, but I get a warm glow remembering the times we had, remembering the friends I made who endure to this day. People of the stature of Erroll, Martin, Trev, Chappell, Mick, Gill, Iggy, Cowley, Bentley and the Glazier brothers are top boys in my eyes, and they always will be. They made my involvement easy by being the characters they were, and continue to be. I wish I could have named all of the people I stood alongside, but space would not allow. Rest assured, I am proud of you all. There really is no other life like it, and I feel for those who don't understand the pride that you get from standing up for your club – especially a club like the one in Sheffield 6.

To be honest, the scene has changed today from what I remember. The price to pay is much too high, and I would never, ever encourage anybody to put their neck on the line. It's really not worth it, but all around the country young lads still feel the need, so it's fitting that the final words should be written by one such lad – 'Service' – who was not even a twinkle in his mother's eye when I witnessed my first taste of crowd exuberance:

I was a hundred per cent normal kid, never hit anyone, and didn't really have a violent thought in my head. I loved football and Wednesday were my life; I cried my eyes out when we lost the two cup finals, even though I was only nine! I remember watching the Republic of Ireland v. England at Lansdowne Road wondering why these men were ruining the game, throwing chairs and hitting people. When England played away I would hope that our 'fans' wouldn't ruin it in case they cancelled the game ... the thoughts of an innocent young lad and probably most of the population, but however innocent I was, I had my mean streak – a streak I released on the football pitch. I never claimed to be hard or acted like a hard case, if anything probably the opposite, but once I was on the field I would become ten men, mouthing off, sly kicks, elbows. Playing football was my way of releasing any anger, annoyance or any other tribulations which may have been occurring at that time. Ironically, this style of playing is probably what got me where I am today.

On 10 October 2001 I was playing for college in Scunthorpe and this fat bastard, who couldn't play football for love nor money, couldn't handle being laughed at, and the verbals he was getting. He decided to tackle me from behind a couple of light years late, leaving me looking down at my shin sticking out in areas it shouldn't have been. I was in plaster for 22 weeks and on crutches for almost 9 months and still can't play football to this day. Looking back, being stuck in, sat in the same position all day, the fracture clinic being the only time I got out, was enough to send anyone a bit mad, but on top of that the anger and hatred towards the kid who did this to me was, and still is, immense.

When it came to the point I could get out and about again, I'd be out in pubs and clubs and found myself scrapping in one way or another what seemed like every other week – if someone looked at the girl I was seeing, or knocked a drink, brushed my leg, anything, I'd lose it. I didn't know what was up with me, but I was an angry little fellow.

Around that time I had a mate here in Leeds who was a Leeds Youth, and I also knew most of his mates too. I never showed any interest but knew he was well respected by all ages of the Leeds United 'Service Crew'. One day we were having a discussion about how much they hated Man United and how he thought it was a greater hatred than ours for Sheffield United. Obviously I disagreed, but in his attempt to prove it he asked me to come to Leeds v. Man U at Elland Road. I agreed and went down with him and some of his other mates.

After drinking in various pubs I realised I'd underestimated them. It seemed like everyone knew who they were. We arrived at the final meet and started to walk down towards Elland Road. I looked in front of me and behind me and there were at least 500 lads marching down the road. It was quite a sight.

As we got nearer the ground a few buses with Man United fans on them came past and got smashed to pieces – people dragged out of emergency exits, it was mayhem. I stood back and watched, thinking to myself, 'Fuck me.' I went home thinking hard about what I had witnessed.

It wasn't long before my mate rang to get my impressions. 'So ... did you get a taste for it?' he said, very matter-of-factly.

'No, not really,' was my reply, but during the journey home I had this feeling inside that I wanted to fight. It was weird. I thought about how if that was Wednesday it'd be different because I'd feel something. So, on to the Net I went. I knew enough about the Casual world from my mates yapping on about it, and how shit Wednesday's firm was. So I posted valid points on how many fans we have around Hillsborough, and how we have the numbers, etc. but needed better organisation.

During the 2002–03 season we grew massively. We had more organisation than most days such as 200-plus at Leicester, marching through town, after coming down on 12 *mini-buses and 2 coaches. Turning up in a country pub in Derby, with the police on both occasions having no idea how we'd got there. We're on the up and the tide is turning, and them down the Lane are being found out by just about every firm they come up against for being pure reputation.*

Three more stories from Dougie to round off this final chapter, this time from the more recent past:

Leicester too little too late: 2003

Aye aye aye, marching on to Leicester, and it's getting very interesting now. This is an extremely large movement of lads, well organised and certainly game for anything that Leicester that may have to throw at them. This season's had a noticeable swing from the kop band to the South Stand, and the youth from the premier years onwards have matured into a solid set of lads, fitting in well with the older end, and still getting results on their own. It's these boys that will eventually put us back on the map and hopefully turn Hillsborough into a bit of a fortress, and not just an easy pushover. The shirts have gone now, and the Stone Island badge seems to be everywhere, but I know deep down their hearts go out to the club they love.

After the Derby game we decided to meet at several different venues and, eventually by phone contact, get together in a boozer on the outskirts of Leicester. This turned out to be successful, and we settle in a little boozer somewhere in Loughborough. I'm not very good at judging numbers, but I know for a fact that I've never seen as many lads before in one boozer, and the vans outside were the proof of the pudding. There had to be 200-plus, all boys, from the youth to the set of old bastards that drag themselves out expecting a pop at a top firm. The bar is solid and the staff can't believe the velocity of the swill going down.

After an hour we've got some contact from Leicester, so we vacate the dram shop, with some protest as per usual. Eventually we're in the vans and on our final bit of the journey, and the stomach's going a bit. I know that Leicester are top notch, and even though we've got the numbers today, they will be no pushover. We're heading for a meet in a well-known DIY car park out of the way of the law and cameras, and on our approach we've split into two groups. To this day I don't know if it was intentional or not. The van's still moving as we jump out, and it's the same for the others. By now we're running up the road expecting a large firm of Leicester to greet us. We turn the corner to the car park, and it's empty. You cannot imagine the disappointment throughout the firm, so we make our way down the side street; heading for the park area to meet up with the rest of the lads, where our friend from Derby appears. He looks excited and joins in with the crowd. After walking what seems like fucking miles we all meet up, and Leicester are asking us now to take to the streets, and make a show at their boozer.

We group up in the underground and quietly make our way up to the town, where the full force of the OCS walk straight to their boozer doors – from which, two minutes earlier, we had seen them leg it. We keep moving, only by now we've got the OB with us in small numbers, and man are they nervous. This is Saturday afternoon in the busy town centre of Leicester. We know we're not going to get a result, so the singing begins and the sound of 'OCS!' rings round the market place. God knows why, but the OB start chasing us, so we leg it in and out of shop and boozer doorways; fucking hilarious, as the onlookers stand with their gobs wide open, and the whole marketplace comes to a standstill. Some lad's down with his arms up his back, so the OB get manhandled out of the way, and the youth breaks free. After five or ten minutes of bedlam the OB restore the order, and march us up to the top end of town, where we eventually get another vessel; only these are free. The bar is empty, and there's full pints all over the place, so we help ourselves; don't ask me why. It's a nice boozer full of Leicester memorabilia. I manage to neck a couple of free vessels, and the OB's got us on the march again; fucking miles to the stadium. Approaching the ground our young 'un's detained against the wall, and I'm convinced they are taking him, but after a long debate they let him go. The game wasn't the best, and due to a goalkeeping error we drew. On the day, personally, I thought we were lucky to get the point, and their midfield dynamo Izzet was the man of the match.

Two minutes before the end we group up and make our way out to find the car park full of your average supporter making their way home. We are grouped on the corner near the burger stall, and I walk across the road away from our lads with Mr B, a good old boy. We are standing outside the stall and a group of only four or five are standing with us. These are Leicester's firm and they want a pop, so I make my way back towards our lads. In the confusion they think I am Leicester, but order is restored as the Leicester lads move in with all the bottle in the world. I take my hat off to the few that came across the road that day, only it was never going to happen, and the skinhead type and his mates get a few knocks.

The crowd splits, and the OB move in; it's over. One thing, though: where is our bus? He's in the line with the rest. He approaches the scene, and we climb aboard the comfort of our little battle bus. On the down side, that evening one of ours got turned over in a big way after the game in their town centre. He came round after the rumours had it that he would die, thank fuck. Respect ...

Burnley: 2003

The ITI is marching on to Burnley; the ship's fucking sunk, but the lads off the field are rowing to shore with hope in our hearts and the thoughts of promotion next year. In the way today is a firm that, with its full attendance, could run with best in the north, but banning orders and the long arm of the law could keep the numbers, and the enthusiasm, down. We don't give a fuck and the plans begin: buses again and this time different meeting points, as the law could be on to us – this isn't the first time a convoy has left Sheff with one thing on its mind.

On this occasion Blackpool is in the frame for a good percentage of us, and could throw up a few surprises. Bradford's out with a few and are trying to arrange a meet, but there are a hundred-plus OCS on the march to the lights and all it offers. No disrespect, but I don't think Bradford could match the numbers. We know they're no mugs, as we found out one afternoon last season in a quiet little boozer in the heart of Bradford's manor. I'm going off the subject here slightly, though, so back to Burnley.

Early start again, and I'm out with the same little firm that I like to frequent the odd game or two with. I know for a fact today there's going to be a big firm out, and as we meet I can see the full potential of what's going to be a force again, and – with the help of a good few faces – will stand toe to toe with the red side of our fair city, and any other fucker on the Casual-scene side of football. We leave Sheffield with a solid set of OCS mini-buses; some with the comfort of seats, and others without. As per usual the buses get split – and I mean split. One hour later and we're almost shagging sheep on Saddleworth Moor, totally fucking lost. This wouldn't be too much of a problem, only it's an early kick-off and the chance of getting a decent drink is becoming slimmer.

After stopping three or four times to ask directions, I think we're back on track. The phone's not stopped ringing. We finally meet, and it looks like were getting a gargle. Thank fuck. I get off the bus and see the full force of the OCS. Fuck me, it's going to take something special to rattle this crew today. The landlord of the Morris Dancers has been informed by the law not to let any Yorkshire bastards in, and turns us away, so it's all aboard, but some silly cunt's gone to find a sandwich shop and about three buses have already set off.

Fuck me, a bit of organisation wouldn't go amiss here – we're all split up again. We're heading in to Burnley and we're running about like fucking loonies looking for each other. By now the lads on our little adventure are hanging out and if we don't get a drink soon we are all going to die, but with the help of the old blower we're on track for a meet with the rest of the lads in one particular boozer, which is known to the odd one or two on our bus. We're in the traffic bang in the middle of the town centre without any sign of Burnley, but then some little Stone Island type walks past us and makes the odd gesture. Most of us laugh this off, as he is a fat youth and poses no threat, but one of ours jumps off the bus and is about to kill the cunt. Not a good idea, as this will blow our cover, so we stop the onslaught.

Half a mile later, and we're meeting up. We drop off in the car park across from the dram shop. There are no OB in site as thirty lads from two buses walk across the road and enter the boozer. Inside there are a good few already, but we've got a problem: the OB have found us, and within minutes they're outside doing the Robocop bit. At first it pisses me off slightly, but this type of policing is becoming the norm, and because time's cracking on, drinking becomes the order, and they go unnoticed. By the way, the drink's like shite, and, at £2.50 for a tin of warm Red Stripe, I think these Lancs twats are taking the piss, but at least it's flowing.

We're running out of time, and the OB want us out, so we've got no choice if we want to see the kick-off. Yet again it's another impressive police escort. We've been walking twenty minutes now and there's no sight of the ground. We've missed the start, but we're not that worried as goals this season have been few and far between. Five minutes later, and one of ours gets a call from the ground: believe it or not we're already 2-0 up, which is just typical.

Eventually we reach the ground, and I'm in full conversation with one of the law, who makes a comment about our impressive turnout today. He says he's not seen anything like it for years, and adds that the last firm to bring these kinds of numbers was Manchester United years ago. I'm not at all surprised, as this is some following. After a good frisking I'm in, but some lads outside have had their van keys confiscated, for obvious reasons. By now we're 3-0 up, and the atmosphere as four or five thousand sing their hearts out for the lads as the goals go rattling in is impressive, to say the least.

There is disappointment too, though, as the Burnley lads are nowhere to be seen. We know they're out and about in small numbers because they were spotted earlier. I think they're keeping a low profile, but we've got phone contact now, and they're not making any promises. It's half-time, and we head for the shitty little bar backstage. The numbers are getting out of hand. There is talk of hundreds being out today and this doesn't surprise me, but don't be fooled: a solid 70 is better than 200 who aren't quite sure. I head back to the stand to watch goal after goal go in, and celebrations like it was a cup final; it's all a bit confusing really. The Burnley faithful don't like it and respond by tearing up their season tickets and throwing them on the pitch.

It's nearly over and there are a few young 'uns winding one or two of ours up, and as the whistle blows the Burnley youth take to the pitch. The chorus of 'OCS!' goes up and there is a surge to the front, with quite a few spilling on the pitch, but with the police presence it's not worth the bother as these aren't their boys. We vacate the stands hoping to get a pop at the fuckers outside. I'm out and the coaches are miles long – only, in between them is the Old Bill and this is a bit of a shield against the odd loud-mouthed Burnley type. I'm a hundred per cent, but one of our buses isn't outside and we're getting reports that the lads that have gone looking for it are battling with Burnley and they have stood their ground. This makes us more and more keen for a go, but there's no one in sight.

Some twenty minutes later, the crowds are dwindling and the OB want us on our bus. There is an offy just up the road and one of ours, armed with a small order, heads for the oasis. The only problem is that we are moving now, and the cunt's not back. A few of us get off and refuse to leave until he returns. The police respect our wishes, and I set off legging it. I'm shouting down the street and he responds just in time, as the driver of our bus is becoming impatient. Finally the bus is rolling. We're all on, but the convoy's gone, and we're behind with no OB in sight. We're driving through the town and I can see a few of their lads milling about. The odd shout out the window comes to nothing; it's over.

We're just pulling on the dual carriageway outside the bus station, and we spot one of their boys, so I shout at the cunt and he replies with an open invitation. In a split second there's now about six or so behind him, so we politely ask the driver to stop. At this point I'm out running up the middle of the road with a mini-bus of lads round me. They couldn't have picked a better bus. They are coming forward, but the railings are in the middle of the road, and 200 yards keep us apart. Three or four leap over and are running towards me. By now I'm running full on, slightly in front of the rest of ours, and I'm straight into the cunts. I'm down and getting volleyed, but the rest of the bus are here and are battling with the developing numbers. Bollocks – my favourite hat's gone.

We're toe to toe now with a game set of Burnley lads. I've got this Burberry type, and he's receiving a large velocity of punches to the head and body. Then one of ours volleys the cunt up the arse, and I feel him leave the floor. We're now faced with a small firm and their numbers are growing. I think to myself that we've been ambushed, but the battling goes on. One lad in particular sticks out in my mind. He's got the frame of a giant, and the face of a baby; he takes so much punishment but totally refuses to go down. This youth looks like one for the future Burnley, and even England.

By now we're outnumbered and our van's on the move without us. The lads are in the street battling like fuck. I make the shout that our bus is leaving the scene, or somat like that, and with that we begin our retreat chasing up the hill towards our bus. But one of our lads has been left behind and is getting volleyed all over the tarmac. A few run back and the bus is stopped. Finally we're all back at the van and another mini-bus of ours turns up and the back doors open. The lads pour out – just as well, because by now Burnley are everywhere. We're half in and half out of our moving bus, and it's leaving again, with a very nervous neutral driver, and the back doors swinging. We're chasing it, and the Burnley are chasing us, and, by now the OB are chasing them. Benny Hill springs to mind. We make the bus and we're off. Fuck me, this was a last-minute result and we made the most of it.

Bristol home and away: 2003–04

Just when you think you're getting things sorted and the firm is making a natural progression – gaining respect for all the right reasons – something comes along and kicks you in the bollocks, as we found out one summer's night in a pre-season friendly. I'm not prepared to go into detail, but the firm – or should I say part-time fucking nondescripts – led us up the garden path. In this case straight into the arms of the law. Some say we let ourselves down, but you had to be there to realise the passion and the seriousness of the situation. The aftermath caused a bit of a stir through the ranks. Faces and well-respected members kept their heads low. I'm not making excuses here, just putting you in the picture. It's a fact that the majority of active firms in the British Isles are going through the same procedure, with lads getting their collars felt, banned, or in the worse cases, sent to prison. 'Fucking long story ...'

Bristol is a fixture that to your average supporter means just a day out down south on the cider, but to us this meant the biggest fixture of the season. Bristol are a well-respected firm and carry a lot of weight in the Second Division. Personally I don't think they show us the same respect. They later found out that we were no lightweights, and that to underestimate us could make them look like amateurs on their own turf.

We needed to get our heads together for this event, and to get Bristol on the back foot was the only way, so a bang-early start was the first move. We left Sheffield in the early hours after a hearty breakfast. Not for me, though: bacon and lager don't mix at 5am, so I stuck to the obvious! Yet again, we had got a solid set of lads. Some needed rounding up, but they were the ones that were worth it.

Four mini-buses leave Sheffield that morning heading for the cider country to meet up with others that had spent the night in Bristol. After a few piss stops, and the odd hundred miles or so, the chief makes contact with one of the so-called Bristol top boys. He's just got out of feather, and he thinks we're just setting off, but we're nearly on his manor, and the silly cunt hasn't got a clue. He's pointing us to a place just on the outskirts of Bristol where he reckons his lads will be waiting for us. We let the overnight boys know the destination, and they make their way across the city.

We've got about twenty minutes to go now, and the Friday boys are already in place. After a bit of a runaround we land at the dram shop to meet up. We've got sixty lads or so, and there are twenty already on the piss to greet us. The only problem is that the OB are getting involved, with a small presence, so we decide to split and find a dram shop farther up the road. We eventually end up in a proper posh-type hotel bar, big enough to accommodate us all. The only problem was Bristol had chosen the same venue, and they had got a few lads milling about in the beer garden. It's only twelve bells and a drink is the order, so the four or five Bristol are of no concern, but the OB have different thoughts, and begin to eject the lads. Some of ours try to prevent this, but they are wasting their time. It calms down slightly, and the drinking commences until two Stone Island types take to the room and begin asking questions. These lads had some real bottle fronting us, but it didn't last – one got a drink over his head and the other a glass lobbed at him by one of our youth. When I say drink I mean coffee, not ale – strange that. This causes the worst problems: standing in the streets once more with fucking cameras shoved in your face, and OB everywhere.

They're getting the picture now. We're here in numbers, and eventually they march us to a new venue down by the canal where we meet up with the rest of the boys, probably 200-plus. The bar's solid, which nearly kills you when you're busting for a vessel, but with patience we get our reward, and it's solid Wednesday inside, and out, and at least 90 per cent are boys. The chief still had contact with Bristol, and – fuck knows how – is guiding them in towards us down some back alley. We've got the OB with us, but they think they've got it sown up and don't pay much attention to the left flank of the boozer where eventually the Bristol boys turn up in all their glory.

There are a good few lads, and at first they look pretty keen, and certainly the part, bouncing like fuck and throwing the odd bottle from a distance. We oblige, as you would, and chase the fuckers off. Only problem is, we've got the OB to the rear of us, and they spoil the party. A half-hearted attack, which was a bit laughable really, but it got the ticker going a bit, so who fucking cares? Back to the ale, and then the march to the ground. It seemed like miles again. Approaching the ground we spot some of their boys outside a boozer, and make an attempt to get to them, but yet again the OB are on top and prevent us.

After the game we all meet and make our way to the level crossing, but Bristol don't show. There is the odd report that it's kicking off in the park up the road, but sorry, Bristol, you underestimated us and you never had the numbers or quality to deal with it. We had a lot of good lads out that day. Like I said, I'm not claiming a result, but it was just nice to see the boys back together again; a bit of a morale booster, if you know what I mean. Bristol returned the favour at ours, only they got their points off the field that day with a quality show of lads on the outskirts of Sheffield. Not trying to take anything away from Bristol, but on the day our organisation was all over the place, and this cost us.

The lads met early in a neutral boozer with plenty of firepower to take to the Bristol firm. We had got a solid hundred, and we were very confident of giving Bristol a proper toe to toe, only we needed to get to them, and that's where it all went wrong. After leaving the boozer and heading up towards the Bristol boys, the lads got split up into several groups. The first set of lads to get to Bristol were definitely our proper boys, but we were outnumbered. As it was kicking off on the front line our boys were still turning up in cars. Less than half the firm got near Bristol that day, and we made the fatal mistake of being overkeen and underestimating the enemy.

* * * * *

A final thank-you to all the lads who have contributed to this book – not just in stories, but in support too, especially Stevie Steve who gave me so much support as I wrote. It is truly sad that Stevie would be taken from us before he had the chance to read the finished article. As I said at the beginning, everything you have read is recounted as it was seen by the person telling the story. There is no need for bullshit or gross exaggeration. We are Sheffield Wednesday, and whether you like us or not, rate us or not, we're a cut above.

Up the Owls.